TABLE OF CONTENTS

FOREWORD

The process of selecting repertoire for our ensembles might well be the most critical responsibility that we shoulder as dedicated and passionate music educators. Joseph Kreines' life-long love and dedication to the wind band and its repertoire and his unyielding pursuit of musical excellence has resulted in this carefully considered compilation of selected and graded literature for band by Mr. Kreines and Professor Hansbrough.

Music for Concert Band is an invaluable resource that should reside on the bookshelf of every first year teacher as well as the most seasoned and experienced wind band conductor. It is a resource that I am pleased to endorse with confidence as a significant contribution to the wind band profession.

Craig Kirchhoff, Professor of Music, Director of Bands, University of Minnesota

SECOND EDITION

MUSIC FOR CONCERT BAND

A Selective Annotated Guide to Band Literature

JOSEPH KREINES
ROBERT HANSBROUGH

Published by
Meredith Music Publications
a division of G.W. Music, Inc.
1584 Estuary Trail, Delray Beach, Florida 33483
http://www.meredithmusic.com

MEREDITH MUSIC PUBLICATIONS and its stylized double M logo are trademarks of
MEREDITH MUSIC PUBLICATIONS, a division of G.W. Music, Inc.

International Standard Book Number: 978-1-57463-398-6
Cataloging-in-Publication Data is on file with the Library of Congress.
Library of Congress Control Number: 2014930053
Printed and bound in U.S.A.

INTRODUCTION

This book is an outgrowth of an earlier one written in 1971, entitled *Band Music Handbook*. For a number of years since its appearance, I have been besieged by band directors to update it, but I had come to realize that a new approach was needed should a new book become possible. It became increasingly clear that directors have become less aware of the substantial body of quality literature that exists, in many cases because it is no longer available. So I decided to examine as much literature as I could – including old and new, current publications and out-of-print ones – in the hope of identifying at least some of the better literature, and providing a descriptive paragraph for each entry in order to enable interested directors to make some of the same discoveries I have. Here is the result of my efforts; I hope it will prove to be valuable. Most important, I hope to hear from many directors and other interested people who may have suggestions, criticism and comments, in order to make corrections, improvements and additions for future editions.

Introduction to The Second Edition

In response to many requests from directors and colleagues worldwide, we decided to prepare this new edition, which features many publications that have appeared in the interim. It is hoped that this new effort will be of use to the profession.

Joseph Kreines
Robert Hansbrough

This book is dedicated to the memory Dr. James Croft, Director of Bands and Professor Emeritus at The Florida State University.

The book is organized into two main categories – concert music and concert program materials. For the concert music lists (and their supplements), information for each entry includes the composer and/or arranger, title, publisher and approximate duration. The entries are listed in alphabetical order by composer according to levels of difficulty as follows:

EASY — (Roughly equivalent to Grades 1 and 2) – Basic rhythms, technically limited with simple textures, effective doublings for ensemble security, limited solos.

MEDIUM EASY — (Grade 3) – More elaborate rhythms, increasing technical facility, expanded ranges, greater technical independence, more solo and small-choir scoring.

MEDIUM — (Grade 4) – Varied rhythms, expanded technical demands, more complex harmonic and contrapuntal content, metric variety, greater range of keys, more musical and scoring subtleties.

MEDIUM ADVANCED — (Grade 5) – More substantial musical and technical requirements, maturity of tonal, rhythmic and stylistic concepts, soloistic capabilities.

ADVANCED — (Grade 6) – Fully developed musical and technical ranges, including complex rhythms and meters, intricacies of articulations, full dynamic spectrum, full solo and section capability.

Grading is always problematic, particularly when there is a definite disparity between musical and technical difficulties. In general, the criteria are weighted toward the playing demands, but it is hoped that the commentary will clarify the musical demands made by each piece.

The supplements included under each level are designed to provide good alternatives to the works listed above them.

The second category, concert program material, is devoted to literature that is of primary value on concert programs rather than as subjects for serious study, detailed rehearsal or festival performances. These are listed alphabetically by title under several self-explanatory headings.

A Note on Transcriptions – No subject is more controversial in the band profession than the validity and value of transcriptions. There are those who adamantly refuse to use transcriptions in their programs, taking the view that transcriptions are not "authentic" or "original". Conversely, there are directors who play little original band literature, preferring to deal with the "true masterpieces of classical literature". This book takes a position somewhere in between, being concerned with the effectiveness and validity of the specific transcription being evaluated. As a result, a number of transcriptions are listed, at all grade levels. However, many well-known versions of standard works transcribed from various media are not included, chiefly because they are not effective – or because they make too many alterations of the original (in terms of simplifications, doublings, octave placements, redistribution or textural changes). Some of these are listed under Concert Program Material, where their use is marginally more appropriate.

All titles included either are now, or have been, in print and available for purchase. A number of these are currently out of print; others are available now on rental only. Given the present fluid state of music publishing, it is impossible to keep up with the many changes of status that various works are now undergoing. Similarly, the publisher listed is the original one.

ABOUT THE AUTHORS

A native of Chicago, **Joseph Kreines** came to Florida as associate conductor of the Florida Symphony Orchestra, where he served for four years. Subsequently, he was conductor of the Brevard Symphony, associate conductor of the Florida Orchestra in Tampa, and musical director for several opera and musical theatre productions. He has served as clinician and guest conductor with some 300 bands, orchestras and choruses throughout the nation and also appears as piano accompanist at numerous recitals and festivals.

In addition, Mr. Kreines has composed a number of original works for various media, and has made numerous transcriptions for concert band and brass choir, and other chamber ensembles, being particularly well-known for those of the music of Percy Grainger. He is also the author of Music for Concert Band, a selective annotated guide to band literature.

Kreines received a Masters degree in Music from the University of South Florida and a Bachelor of Arts from the University of Chicago. He did additional study at the Tanglewood Music Festival in 1958 where he was chosen to participate in the conducting class with fellow classmates Zubin Mehta, Claudio Abbado, David Zinman, and Gustav Meier. In 2004, he was honored as an inductee to the Roll of Distinction in the Florida Bandmasters Association Hall of Fame, and is currently music director and principal conductor of the Brevard Symphony Youth Orchestra.

Dr. Robert S. Hansbrough is Professor of Music and Music Department Chair at The College of Saint Rose in Albany, NY. Additionally he is Director of The Saint Rose Summer Youth Music (SrSYM) program. His teaching responsibilities include conducting the wind ensemble and chamber winds as well as graduate courses in music education, instrumental conducting and wind band literature. Additionally, he conducts The Empire State Youth Wind Orchestra and The Faculty Camerata Chamber Orchestra. He earned a BA in Music Education from The University of South Florida and the Masters and PhD in Music Education with a concentration in wind band conducting from The Florida State University.

Prior to The Saint Rose appointment, he served for four years on the faculty of Western Kentucky University as Associate Director of Bands and Director of The "Big Red" marching band. He taught for fifteen years in the Florida Public school systems. For twelve years he was Director of Bands at Lincoln HS in Tallahassee where his bands consistently earned "Superior" ratings at The FBA District and State Festival Evaluations and performed at various invitational conferences.

Dr. Hansbrough has conducted honor bands throughout The United States and Europe and has adjudicated bands and orchestras from 26 states, Canada and Mexico. He has served on the National Band Association Board of Directors as the Eastern Division Chair. His articles and research have been published in several professional journals including The NBA Journal, The School Music News, The NYSBDA Newsletter, The Bluegrass News and The Florida Director. He holds professional memberships in MENC, NYSBDA, NYSSMA, NBA, CBDNA, The New York State Association of College Music Programs, Phi Mu Alpha, Pi Kappa Lambda, Kappa Kappa Psi, and Phi Beta Mu and is Lifetime Member of The Florida Bandmasters Association.

MUSIC FOR CONCERT BAND

ANDREWS, James   **CHANTEYS**   Shawnee
4:30

An interesting arrangement of three British sea-songs, set in one continuous movement with contrasting tempos. After a brief majestic introduction, the first, *AWAY TO RIO* (E^b, 3/4 in one) appears in a lilting, jaunty setting, briefly interrupted by a slower episode. A ritard leads into a reflective setting of *SHENANDOAH* (Largo, A^b-E^b, 4/4) first stated in unison clarinets, then in trumpets and alto sax. The third song is a lively and vigorous version of *THE DRUNKEN SAILOR* (Allegretto, C Dorian, 2/4). An allargando leads to a short climactic coda in slow tempo.

ANDREWS, James   **HILL SONGS**   Shawnee
4:30

A medley of three American folk-songs in well-conceived imaginative settings. (1) *CUMBERLAND GAP* (Allegretto, A^b, 2/2) – melody first stated in upper woodwinds, then divided between trumpets, trombones and horns, with a rhythmic accompaniment. (2) *COME ALL YE FAIR AND TENDER LADIES* (Adagio, B^b, 3/4) – melody stated in chorale setting for brass alone, then in upper woodwinds with chordal accompaniment, concluding with a tutti statement. (3) *SOURWOOD MOUNTAIN* (Allegro, E^b, 2/4) opens with an introduction using fiddle fifths, followed by the melody in clarinet and sax with rhythmic accompaniment, followed by trumpets, then low brass, finally in augmentation broadening into a majestic coda.

ABREAU, Thoinot   **TWO FRENCH DANCES**   Shapiro-Bernstein
Arr. Peter Williams   2:35

Excellent settings of two dance-tunes from the classic 16th-century dance treatise "Orchesographie", very well arranged for young band, utilizing both tutti and choir scoring and dynamics editing to great effect. (1) Moderato, B^b, 3/4 – legato, lilting and graceful (2) Allegro con brio, E^b, 2/2 – marcato and vigorous, with a short contrasting slower section more legato in style.

BALENT, Andrew   **TWO SEASCAPES**   Shawnee
3:30

A very attractive and enjoyable work using two American sailing songs. (1) *FAREWELL AND ADIEU* (Andante, B^b, 4/4), a melancholy and plaintive melody in several contrasting settings, including solo cornet and tutti. (2) *CAN'T YOU DANCE THE POLKA* (Allegro, B^b, 2/4), a lively tune with energy and bounce, making effective use of registers for contrast (melodic materials appear in trumpets, low brass and woodwinds and upper woodwinds). The *SAILOR'S HORNPIPE* is used in the introduction and coda.

BARTOK, Bela   **FOR CHILDREN**   Boosey & Hawkes
Arr. Walter Finlayson   2:15

An excellent transcription of three contrasting piano pieces. The first is a lively and rhythmic *DANCE SONG* (Allegro, B^b and G minor, 2/4) featuring abrupt contrasts of dynamics and frequent use of accents and varied articulations. The second, *PLAY SONG* (Andante, B^b, 2/4), is gentle and graceful, scored mostly for woodwinds, with melody in clarinets, flutes and bells. The finale, *REVELER'S SONG* (Vivace, G minor, 4/4), is brilliant and energetic, with use of inverted and dotted rhythms, striking contrasts of dynamics and articulations and effective use of choir scoring.

BARTOK, Bela   **FOUR SKETCHES**   Elkan-Vogel
Arr. William Schaefer   4:30

A very appealing set of four short pieces. (1) *PRELUDE* (Allegramente, B^b, 2/4) featuring simple folk-like tune set in three different ways. (2) *SERENADE* (Allegretto, G minor, 2/4) expressive and somewhat melancholy in character, consisting of 10-bar phrases with interesting contrasts of rhythm and scoring. (3) *DANCE* (Allegro ironico, B^b, 3/4 and 2/4) – well marked, rhythmic staccato, with effective changes of meter. (4) *FINALE* (Vivace, G minor, 2/4) – lively, aggressive, driving, with contrasts of dynamics and articulation (marcato and staccato) and use of inverted and dotted rhythms. (This is the same piece as *REVELER'S SONG* in the *FOR CHILDREN* suite listed above). While the technical demands are light, this piece requires sensitivity to articulations, dynamics, irregular phrases and alternating meters.

BRISMAN, Heskel   **THE ASH GROVE**   Presser
3:00

An unusual and imaginative setting of a lovely British melody, in a rather contemporary vein (Moderato, A^b, 3/4). It begins with the tune in trumpets with interesting textural counter-material, followed by upper woodwinds. The trumpets again take the first phrase, clarinets and flutes the second, followed by unison flutes with a counter-melody in low woodwinds. The melody makes successive appearances in various voices with interesting rhythmic variations and fragmentary contrapuntal lines, with the final statement dissonant yet climactic.

BRISMAN, Heskel   **BUCKWHEAT**   Elkan-Vogel
2:00

An interesting work using an Eastern European tune which is in two contrasting phrases. The opening one (Andante con moto) is moderate in tempo with staccato accompaniment, while the second (Allegro) is lively and energetic. The remainder of the piece presents variations of the two phrases, with interesting rhythmic extensions and obbligato lines and an effective coda. Technically easy, but requires good rhythmic control and sense of subdivision, as well as confidence in lightly scored passages (very few tuttis occur).

BRISMAN, Heskel   **THE GIFT TO BE SIMPLE**   Elkan-Vogel
2:45

A very well-conceived setting of the familiar tune, featuring the melody in different registers and guises, including a canonic passage, rather complex textures and a section using minor mode. An amusing coda with effective use of percussion provides a fresh conclusion.

BRUCKNER, Anton   **TWO BRUCKNER MINIATURES**   Alfred
Arr. Phillip Gordon   3:55

A splendid introduction to the music of one of the great composers. (1) *PANGE LINGUA* (Moderato, C minor, 2/2), slow, dignified, spare yet expressive. Technically easy (mostly half and whole notes) thereby making it easier to concentrate on intonation, blend, balance and tone and dynamic control. (2) *LOCUS ISTE* (Moderato, B^b, 4/4) – more contrapuntal and imitative in texture, harmonically more complex and chromatic and more dramatic in character, yet technically easy.

BROEGE, Timothy   **THEME AND VARIATIONS**   Manhattan Beach
2:30

A masterful original using a simple theme and variations format. The theme contains a diatonic fragment, in tutti rhythm, starting on C (quarter note =76). A short canon ensues using accidentals and then ornamented with eighth notes. Excellent contrasts of dynamics, articulations, rhythm, harmonization and recapitulation bring this simple yet well-conceived work to a very satisfying end. Percussion parts (snare drum, bass drum, triangle, crash cymbals and timpani) are modest but appropriate for this setting. Highly recommended for first year students.

BYRD, William   **ELIZABETHAN MOTET**   Warner
Arr. L. Forsblad & D Livingston   2:00

Though the title indicates a vocal work, this piece was originally composed for keyboard as *PAVANE-THE EARL OF SALISBURY*, (see below under Medium Easy). It is a beautifully expressive work (Adagio, G minor, 4/4) composed of short melodic motives that weave together to form longer song-like phrases and also form the basis of short imitative sections. An excellent piece for young and developing bands to work on for phrase continuity, beauty of tone, expressivity of line and knowledge of late-Renaissance style.

BYRD, William   **LA VOLTA**   Daehn
Arr. Katheryn Fenske   2:50

A very colorful and imaginative arrangement of this seventeenth century "Turning Dance." Opening in 3/4, F major quarter note = 116-126, the dance theme is presented in upper winds with tutti accompaniment (including very smart percussion scoring using 6 instruments including timpani). The use of call and answer by the brass and woodwind choirs provide ample opportunities for dynamic and phrase contrasts. A short percussion interlude introduces a new statement that is more decorated and continues the call and answer form. A concluding tutti coda section brings the dance to a festive close. The individual parts are not demanding for second year students but maintenance of tempo, style and rhythmic independence will be the musically rewarding challenges. Highly recommended.

BYRD, William   **PAVANA AND MARCH**   Presser
Arr. Philip Gordon   2:00
Another good introduction to the music of the English Renaissance master. The *PAVANA* (Andante, C minor, 4/4) is stately yet tender in mood, with a gently flowing melody and simple chordal accompaniment. The *MARCH* (Allegro moderato, C minor, 4/4) is noble but energetic, strongly marked and solid. Technically easy but with ample opportunity to develop basic skills of ensemble and musicality.

CARTER, Charles   **MINIATURE CHORALE AND FUGUE**   Southern
                                                                                                     2:00
A well written and musically attractive use of baroque forms for young band. The *CHORALE* (Moderate tempo, B^b, 4/4) is contrapuntal in texture with rhythmic and melodic interest in all parts; the *FUGUE* further encourages independence of parts while using easy rhythmic and melodic patterns.

CROFT, William   **PRELUDE AND DANCE**   Warner
Arr. Philip Gordon   2:50
Two nicely contrasted pieces by a relatively unknown 17th-century English composer. The opening *PRELUDE* (Andante, C minor, 4/4) is sustained, lyric and expressive, with nice varieties of texture and scoring. The *DANCE* (Allegro, G minor, 2/2) is moderately lively and rhythmic, featuring contrasts of articulation and dynamics as well as scoring.

CURNOW, James   **AFRICAN SKETCHES**   Hal Leonard
                                                                                                     2:45
A realistic and authentic-sounding arrangement of three traditional African songs and dances for young players. The first section is a lively dance in 2/4 (quarter note = 112). The trumpet plays the marcato melody against sustained wind accompaniments in Bb. This is reversed by the upper woodwinds and transitions into the second section (3/4 quarter note = 92 in G minor.) This lullaby is accompanied by various percussion colors. A syncopated second theme is introduced by the flutes and clarinets and the segment segues into the third section. The final "war song" is in F major (4/4, Fast and Energetic quarter note = 120.) It uses punctuated percussion and wind figures that features several repeated sections and pyramiding effects. The coda contains alternating unison rhythms and the use of silence between exchanges as an effective means to bring the work to a powerful close.

CUSTER, Calvin (Arr.)   **A RENAISSANCE FAIRE**   Hal Leonard
                                                                                                     3:10
Two pieces in contrasting styles and tempos, very playable and well-conceived for young bands. (1) *SARABANDE* by Lully (Andante, B^b, 3/4) is slowly flowing, stately music, thoughtfully scored, contrasting upper woodwinds with tutti in opening, later between choir of trumpets and horns and woodwinds. Technically easy but with exposed groups as indicated. (2) *THE KING'S HUNTING JIG* by John Bull (Moderato, E^b, 2/2). Staccato and marcato styles predominate in full-scored opening, followed by legato style scored for smaller groups. A more fully scored transition leads to the return of the opening section, tutti.

EDMONDSON, John (Arr.)   **AMAZING GRACE**   California Music Press
                                                                                                     2:50
This is a very practical and skillfully arranged setting of one of the best-known hymns. After opening in 3/4, F major with tutti scoring the melody is developed in the brass choir. A set of woodwind choir variations follow in B^b major, a little faster (quarter note = 80). A final tutti section (3/4 Maestoso, in E^b) brings the hymn to a full and quiet close. First year bands will find the dissonance and resolution areas challenging as well as excellent training tools. The percussion parts fit the arrangement well but are logically limited to mostly bells and very reserved snare drum and bass drum parts.

EDMONDSON, John.   **ANASAZI**   Queenwood
                                                                        3:10

A wonderful work for very young players. It opens in 4/4, G minor, quarter note =72 with low winds in octaves and simple percussion colors. Unison rhythms and articulations ensue with upper winds and drone-like voices continue in the low winds. Clever use of dynamics and alternations of brass and woodwind sonorities shape this ABCBA form. All winds must have control of pitch in all dynamic spectrums and percussionist's challenges include keeping a steady pulse throughout the work.

EDMONDSON, John (Arr.)   **THREE SCOTTISH FOLK SONGS**   Barnhouse
                                                                        4:30

An effective one movement setting of three contrasting songs. (1) *WILL YE NO' COME BACK AGAIN* (Andante, E^b-F, 4/4) begins with an introduction using "Scotland the Brave". The setting proper states the tune divided between brass and woodwinds in the first phrase, modulating to F in a tutti setting, concluding with a more lyric mood. A short transition using part of the introduction leads to (2) *TURN YE TO ME* (Andante, E^b, 3/4) utilizing a flowing 8th-note accompaniment in upper woodwinds. The second phrase has melody in woodwinds, succeeded by a brass phrase. A transition using the opening phrase leads to (3) *CHARLIE IS MY DARLING* (Moderato, C minor, 4/4) a jaunty tune appearing in solo trumpet first, then upper winds and all trumpets. The succeeding phrase is presented by soft upper woodwinds with bagpipe drone. The final statement of the tune is divided between brass and woodwinds with extension to the climactic 4 bars with tune in low brass.

ERICKSON, Frank   **AIR FOR BAND**   Bourne
                                                                        3:15

A lovely, expressive melodic work, considered a band classic, that provides an ideal medium for developing legato style, beauty of tone, intonation, blend, balance, feeling of phrase and line. It opens softly (slowly, C minor, 4/4) with melody in unison clarinets and sustained accompaniment in lower woodwinds, horns and baritone. The phrase is then repeated with fuller scoring and melody doubled. Subsequently, new melodic material from accompanying lines is developed, leading to a rich, sonorous climax. After further development of the various motives, the key changes to C major and builds to an affirmative conclusion. Should be in all developing band libraries.

ERICKSON, Frank   **NORWEGIAN FOLK SONG SUITE**   Bourne
                                                                        3:30

Three engaging melodies in contrasting style and character form the basis of this excellent work. The first (Moderately, B^b, 2/4) is simple and straightforward with effective contrasting phrases. The second (Slowly, C minor, 3/4) is somewhat melancholy in tone with a nice modulation to E^b in the middle section. The third movement (Quickly, F major, 4/4) is rather hearty and extroverted, featuring the full ensemble contrasted with two rather delicately scored interludes. Highly recommended.

FARNABY, Giles   **FAYNE WOULD I WEDD**   Studio/PR
Arr. R. Dishinger   2:00
A moderately lively and energetic work, with an attractive melody appearing mostly in woodwinds, and simple chordal accompaniment. Rhythm, ranges and technical requirements are modest – what is needed is awareness of articulations and expression marks, and good feeling for phrase and rhythm. Another good introduction to late Renaissance music for young players.

FELDSTEIN, Sandy and O'REILLY, John   **CHANT AND CELEBRATION**   Alfred
                                                                        3:00

A wonderful original beginning band work using two parts as its basic structure. The chant (Andante, 4/4 in G minor) consistently uses a call and response technique between the woodwind and brass voices incorporating very elementary rhythms. The alternations become shorter and the chant ends on a tutti chord in g minor. The "Celebration" (Allegro) ensues in B^b although the key indicates three flats. The flutes and clarinets perform an uplifting theme accompanied by simple chords in the brass and middle voices. The percussion contribution is limited to very simple snare and bass drum parts and only in the "Celebration." The work ends with unison rhythms in a familiar sequence.

FINLAYSON, Walter (Arr.)   **EARLY ENGLISH SUITE**   Boosey & Hawkes
3:30

A real gem for young bands, sensitively arranged and scored. The first movement, *TRUMPET MENUET* by Duncombe (Moderato, E^b, 3/4) features a fanfare-like figure answered by a legato phrase. The second, *SONATINA* by Duncombe (Moderato, B^b, 2/4) features a graceful lyric melody and is scored mostly for woodwinds. The third, *MENUETT* by James Hook (Moderato, F, 3/4) has an attractive melody and effective dynamic contrasts. The finale, *HUNTING JIG* by Duncombe (Allegro, B^b, 6/8) uses contrast between a marcato motive in trumpets and a lilting legato phrase in woodwinds. Highly recommended for all bands.

GAROFALO, Robert   **AHRIRANG**   Meredith Publications
Arr. Whaley   3:00

A wonderful and imaginative arrangement of this Korean folksong. Metal percussion instruments begin the work in E^b (3/4 quarter note = 88-94,Gently), which is followed by the theme in unison played by the upper woodwinds. The color changes to brass instruments with wood and membrane percussion instruments continuing the accompaniment. A short percussion interlude ensues using various colors and preceding rhythmic materials. A canon follows, using solo woodwinds as well as members of the ensemble singing the theme. The final section shifts to a recapitulation of the theme in canon form but this time with full instrumentation. Highly recommended for very young wind and percussion players.

GAROFALO, Robert   **HUNGARIAN FOLKROUND**   Meredith Publications
Arr. Whaley   3:00

A highly effective and flexible work for very young bands based on Hungarian Folk material. Beginning with unison horns (cued in euphonium) and section clarinets with sustained notes in C minor (2/4 quarter note = 88-96, Moderato) the texture slowly thickens using a percussion ostinato. A contrasting section ensues employing accents and more intense rhythmic development. The tempo quickens into a third section using upper woodwinds and metallic percussion. This tempo subsides but quickens again which introduces a percussion feature (6 instruments) while wind players provide clapping and vocalization to accompany this area. An optional Children's chorus joins the woodwind sonorities before a D.S. The coda includes tutti textures with voices and ends with a surprising C major triad. May be out of print but well worth locating!

GORDON, Philip (Arr.)   **ELIZABETHAN SUITE**   Warner
4:00

Tasteful arrangements and abridgements of three lovely keyboard works. The first, *PAULE'S WHARFE* by Giles Farnaby (E^b, 3/4), is a moderately fast, flowing piece with good contrasts of scoring and dynamics. The second, *QUODLING'S DELIGHT* by Farnaby (G minor, 4/4) is slow and expressive, with effective use of solos (oboe, trumpet, horn, baritone) contrasted with choirs and tutti scoring. The last, *NANCIE* by Thomas Morley, (E^b, 4/4,but should be played 2/2) is a rather lively dance-like tune in light, detached style. Again, the scoring and dynamics add greatly to the musical effectiveness of this selection.

GORDON, Philip (Arr.)   **FITZWILLIAM SUITE**   Marks
2:45

An excellent alternative to the above, also using the 16th-century English keyboard repertory. (1) *FORTUNE MY FOE* by William Byrd (Moderato, G minor, 4/4). Stately and broadly expressive with effective echo scoring. (2) *PAVANA* by John Bull (Andante, E^b, 4/4) is another dignified slow dance – simple but beautiful. (3) *A TOYE* by Giles Farnaby (Allegro Moderato, G minor, 4/4 but should be 2/2) is a delightful, rhythmically vital piece with extensive use of staccato articulations.

GORDON, Philip (Arr.)   **FRENCH MASTERS SUITE**   Marks
3:55

Three well contrasted 18th-century pieces. (1) *RIGAUDON* by Couperin (Allegro non troppo, D minor, 4/4 but should be slow 2/2) is a bouncy, energetic dance that offers opportunity to develop staccato playing in both loud and soft dynamics. (2) *SARABANDE* by La Coste (Andante, F major, 3/4) is nobly lyric, requiring beautiful legato tone and feeling for phrase and line. (3) *GAVOTTE EN RONDEAU* by Rameau (Allegro moderato, D minor, 4/4 really 2/2) returns to the staccato and marcato style of the first, but with more weight and deliberation.

GORDON, Philip (Arr.) **ITALIAN MASTERS SUITE** Marks
3:30

Similar to the above, covering 18th-century Italian literature. (1) *HARVEST ECHOES* (Autumn from "The Seasons" by Vivaldi) (Allegro moderato, E^b, 4/4) is a very capable rendering of this lively and exuberant music, with the echo effects well-handled between tutti and brass choir. (2) *SLOW DANCE* (Sarabande from Violin Sonata #8 by Corelli) (Larghetto, C minor, 3/4) is eloquently lyric music, scored fully but clearly. Requires good legato style and feeling for sustained line and long phrase (8 bars, not 4). (3) *COUNTRY ROUND* by Domenico Scarlatti (Allegro non troppo, E^b, 2/2) is rhythmic and energetic, with nice contrasts of dynamics and scoring between segments of melodic material.

GORDON, Philip (Arr.) **THE KING'S MUSICKE** Boosey & Hawkes
2:55

Three appealing 17th-century English pieces, well scored. (1) *MENUET* by Jeremiah Clarke (Allegretto, F, 3/4) features a very attractive melody with simple accompaniment. (2) *SARABANDE* by William Croft (Andante, C minor, 3/4) features an oboe solo with woodwind accompaniment, then melody in upper woodwinds with low brass support. (3) *MARCH* by Francis Piggot (Allegro moderato, F, 4/4) has a hearty and vigorous opening with a contrasting echo-like response. A crescendo leads back to the opening phrase forte. The work closes with a soft statement building in intensity to a climactic tutti conclusion.

GORDON, Philip (Arr.) **A LITTLE SHAKESPEARE SUITE** Presser
2:45

Excellent settings of three tunes popular in Shakespeare's time that were used in his plays. (1) *O MISTRESS MINE* (Allegretto, E^b, 3/4 in one). A dance-like tune, light and lilting in character. (2) *COME LIVE WITH ME* (Andante, C minor, 3/4) Expressive, sustained and legato – rather melancholy in mood. (3) *LIGHT O'LOVE* (Allegro, E^b, 3/4 in one). Lively and jaunty in style, using effective contrasts of choirs and dynamics. One of the best of all the suites Gordon has done. Highly recommended.

GORDON, Philip (Arr.) **RENAISSANCE MASTERS SUITE** Warner
2:50

An exquisitely scored work consisting of three short, well-contrasted pieces. (1) *BALLETTO* by Vecchi (Allegretto, G minor, 2/2) is constructed of contrasting phrases – light, soft, staccato; and energetic, marked, forte. (2) *AGNUS DEI* by Andrea Gabrieli (Andante, B^b, 4/4), legato and sustained in style with beautiful contrasts of choirs, dynamics and textures. (3) *CHANSON* by Janequin (Allegro, B^b, 3/4 in one), buoyant and joyous in character, in chordal texture throughout, maintaining contrasts of choirs and dynamics. Highly recommended.

HANDEL, G.F. **FINALE GRANDIOSO FROM "JULIUS CAESAR"** Alfred
Arr. Philip Gordon 2:20
A majestic and noble work with good contrasts of scoring and key, effectively transcribed. It opens with a full-scored 6-bar phrase (Allegro, F major, 4/4) contrasted with an echo for woodwinds alone. The remainder of the first section uses similar contrasts between choir and groups. The second section, in F minor, begins with the brass softly stating a rather poignant phrase, answered by woodwinds. The greater transparency of scoring in this section is well-covered by cueing. The work concludes with a return of the opening in tutti scoring throughout.

HULTGREN, Ralph **SIMPLE SONG** Brogla Music
2:55

This is a very expressive and original work for young players. The song begins with soft legato swells in C minor (quarter note = 84, Slow and singing in 3/4). Upper winds perform a tertian melody, which is later transformed into a new section featuring trumpet and euphonium. Alternating brass and woodwind sonorities layer the theme with a walking eighth note ostinato in the percussion section. A final rallentando, using short canonic fragments, finishes the song on a soft C major tutti chord. Although the percussion parts are not rhythmically challenging, they are smartly scored and will help young performers understand their role in terms of tempo, balance and color.

JACKSON, Leroy (Arr.)   **LITTLE ENGLISH SUITE**   Warner
3:00

A three-movement set of simple but appealing settings of familiar tunes. (1)(Con Moto, F major, 3/4) – lilting, flowing with straightforward harmony. (2) (Andante, F-B♭, 4/4) – opening in chorale style with a canonic second section. (3) (Moderato, E♭, 2/4) – beginning in dance-like rhythmic and marcato style contrasted with a legato statement.

KABALEVSKY, Dmitri   **SUITE IN MINOR MODE**   MCA
Arr. F. Siekmann & R. Oliver   4:00

A very enjoyable set of three pieces which provide a good introduction to a modern Russian composer and the use of minor mode in contrasting settings. (1) *DANCE* (Moderato scherzando, C minor, 2/4) features a well-marked rhythmic accompaniment to a simple but lively tune in clarinets and trumpets, harmonized with both triads and spicy dissonances. (2) *A LITTLE SONG* (Andantino cantabile, D minor, 4/4) features a nostalgic folk-like melody first stated in unison clarinets with sustained chordal accompaniment, rather transparently scored – later more fully presented with a climactic tutti ending. (3) The finale, *THE HORSEMAN* (Allegro molto, G minor, 2/4) returns to a rhythmic style, including off-beats in accompaniment and dotted-8ᵗʰ-16ᵗʰs in melody. Scoring is mostly full, but with good variety of combinations and doublings. Requires good sense of rhythms and subdivision in first and last sections, while the slow movement demands good legato, tonal beauty, well-focused intonation and sensitivity of phrasing and accompaniment. Highly recommended.

KINYON, John (Arr.)   **BRITISH ISLE BALLADS**   Alfred
4:10

An excellent suite of three settings of well-known melodies. (1) *THE MINSTREL BOY* (Andante con moto, E♭, 4/4) – chorale-like in character with some imitative voicing. (2) *ALL THROUGH THE NIGHT* (Dolce, B♭, 4/4) – rich-textured opening, with melody in trumpets and obbligato in woodwinds; canonic treatment of the second phrase. (3) *LOCH LOMOND* (March tempo, E♭, 2/4, 4/4) – an unusual treatment of this tune, with emphasis on martial percussion and melody in brass. A maestoso section in 4/4 closes the work with resonant full-band sonority. Technically easy but musically interesting for young bands.

KINYON, John (Arr.)   **SET OF EARLY ENGLISH AIRS**   Bourne
4:00

Very well-conceived and tastefully scored settings of three little-known but appealing 17ᵗʰ-century pieces. The first is a sprightly *ALLEGRETTO* by John Adson (B♭ major, 4/4) using dotted rhythms and varied textures, concluding with a more sustained section in 3/4 which contrasts brass and woodwinds. The second, by Henry Purcell (Grave, G minor, 4/4) is rather somber and mournful, dirge-like in character, in legato style throughout. The finale, by Anthony Holborne (Giocoso, B♭, 2/2) returns to a lighter mood using contrasts of scoring, articulation and dynamics and interesting inner-voices.

KREINES, Joseph   **AMERICAN SONG SETTING No. 1: BILLY BOY**   Alfred
3:20

Opening with a full-band unison statement of the melody, "BILLY BOY" offers three varied presentations: 1.) Chorale (B♭ Major) for full band without percussion; 2.) Waltz (3/4, F Major) with the melody in woodwinds and trumpets, accompanied by horns, trombones and percussion; 3.) March (2/4, B♭ Major) with use of dotted-8ᵗʰ-16ᵗʰ rhythm. "BILLY BOY" provides a good showcase for the familiar melody while introducing different styles in eminently playable writing for young bands.

KREINES, Joseph   **AMERICAN SONG SETTING No. 2: SKIP TO MY LOU**   Alfred
2:25

The work begins with the rhythm of the tune providing an introduction. The melody then appears in upper woodwinds and mallets, succeeded by trumpets. Then it is presented in low woodwinds and low brass while upper woodwinds present "LONG, LONG AGO" as a counter-melody. The first phrase of the tune then appears in canon between saxophones and clarinets. Another setting features saxophones and horns while upper woodwinds present contrasting materials. The next statements turn the melody into a 3-bar phrase. The final statement presents a fully-scored, richly harmonized statement as an appropriate climax.

KREINES, Joseph AMERICAN SONG SETTING No. 3: BARBARA ALLEN Alfred
3:00

One of the most beautiful folk songs in a series of contrasting settings, it opens (3/4, E^b Major) with an 8-bar introduction that sets the tone and character of the melody which appears in flute, oboe, and trumpet. A second statement is presented in clarinet, with saxophone and lower woodwind accompaniment. The next statement is more marked in style, utilizing brass and percussion, then full band. The meter then changes to 2/4, the melody appearing in clarinets with staccato low-woodwind accompaniment. The second phrase features trumpets, flutes, and oboe. The 3/4 introduction returns, leading to a climactic concluding statement of the melody.

LAPLANTE, Pierre (Arr.) ALL YE YOUNG SAILORS Daehn
1:30

This is a very colorful and accessible setting of the Sea Chantey known as "Blow the Man Down." The "Rollicking" unison opening in 6/8 (dotted quarter note = 72-80) introduces the theme in the clarinets. This is answered by the brass and a series of color exchanges follow that are never presented in the same form. Very clever use of textures, dynamics, rhythm and harmonization make this simple tune very interesting. A short and fragmented four part canon brings the work to a strong and appropriate close.

LOTTI, Antonio THE GLORY OF VENICE Grand Mesa
Transc. Ken Singleton 3:05

A remarkable transcription of two motets exposing young bands to sacred Baroque music. The first, *Miserere*, begins quietly in tenor voices using a short canon, 4/4, F minor quarter note= 72. Although simple rhythms and notes dominate this motet, tuning dissonances and maintaining lyrical style and rhythmic independence will be the most challenging elements. There are also many places where expressiveness is required, both notated and implied. The second, *Regina Coeli,* 4/4, quarter note = 100 in B^b major, is more majestic in nature and takes advantage of the woodwind/brass color exchanges in the opening section. The final section, "slower and more sustained" begins with a very short canon and segues to unison rhythmic figures and ends on a B^b major triad. The simple percussion parts are limited to mallets, timpani, bass drum and cymbals, but are very appropriate imitative textures for this historic period.

MAGNUSSON, Daniel FROM THE LAND OF FIRE AND ICE Wynn
Arr. Grant Hull 5:30

Very effective and appealing settings of four Icelandic folk-tunes. (1) *LULLABY* (Andante, G minor, 4/4) presents a tender, rather plaintive tune with simple, throbbing chordal accompaniment. (2) *ICELANDIC FOLK SONG* (Con moto ma marcato) uses changing meters in a strongly marked setting, contrasted with a slower, more sustained phrase. (3) *WHERE IS JOHN?* (Allegretto, F minor, 4/4) is a rhythmic tune, mostly staccato and marcato in style with a contrasting legato phrase in upper woodwinds. (4) *FOLK DANCE* (Allegro moderato, F major) again uses changing meters with tutti scoring, suddenly interrupted by a solo clarinet cadenza which leads to a slower, more reflective section in A^b. A return to the opening brings the work to an energetic conclusion.

MARCELLO, Benedetto PSALM 18 Bourne
Arr. Maurice Whitney 2:00

A vigorous, proclamatory work (Maestoso con moto, B^b, 2/2) that expertly exploits baroque echo devices in the band scoring. Technically easy and mostly homophonic in texture with straightforward material, but with opportunities to develop dynamic contrasts, staccato articulation, rhythmic precision and sense of phrase. Ranges are mostly comfortable (though 1st Clarinet goes to high C and Alto Sax to E above staff).

MCGINTY, Anne AFRICAN FOLK TRILOGY Edmonson and McGinty
1:55

This work is a creative setting of three authentic African children's songs. It begins with trumpets playing the melody, Allegro 4/4 quarter note =152-160, while the rest of the ensemble accompanies with foot stomps in rhythm and percussion colors (5 instruments). One by one the winds join the four-measure phrase until the tutti texture is established in B^b major. The second song starts with no pause (a little slower quarter note= 120 in B^b major) with the melody performed in the flutes and oboes and quickly followed by a canon starting in the trumpets. This segues into the third song in E^b major (4/4 quarter note = 152-160). Beginning with simple syncopation in soli brass and percussion, a "call and answer" effect ensues between brass and woodwinds. The two instrumental families come together using their independent phrases, which brings the work to an exciting ending (a foot stomp in E^b!).

MCGINTY, Anne (Arr.)   **JAPANESE FOLK TRILOGY**   Edmonson and McGinty
2:48

This work is a very clever arrangement of three Japanese folk songs for first year students. "Moon Song", the first song, begins in C minor (4/4, quarter note =80) with simple rhythms in upper woodwinds with ample percussion accompaniment. The texture becomes thicker with added brass and hints of the pentatonic scale. This segues into "Festival of Dolls" (a little faster, quarter note=88) using more eighth note patterns centering in F. Solid use of articulative and dynamic contrasts along with alternating colors provide this section with strong musical challenges. "Please Come Spring" is the final song in the form of a march (quarter note =100). Excellent tutti rhythms (centering on C) with colorful percussion accompaniment results in a very satisfying conclusion to this work.

MCGINTY, Anne (Arr.)   **MADRIGAL FOR BAND**   Edmonson and McGinty
2:30

This arrangement of a sixteenth-century madrigal is a terrific contribution to the beginning band literature. Using simple and imitative rhythms the percussion battery (4 parts) opens the work in 4/4 Moderato quarter note = 108. A short canon beginning with upper woodwinds and concluding with brass ensues in B^b. Effective use of elementary counterpoint develops the work, also using dynamic and articulative contrasts coupled with simple and repeated eighth note fragments. The final section uses almost exclusively half and whole notes to slow the harmonic progression into the concluding unison B^b. The use of counterpoint will help young students develop independence and the matching of styles.

MOZART, Leopold   **A LEOPOLD MOZART SUITE**   R. Smith
Arr. Stuart Johnson   2:55

Three attractive short pieces by the father of Wolfgang, very well scored. The opening *MINUET* (Allegro, B^b, 3/4) uses contrasts of scoring on repeat and nice contrasts between small groups and tutti. The *AIR* (Andante, F major, 3/4) also uses changes of scoring for the melodic line, with fuller scoring in the second phrase. The closing *BOURREE* (Allegro Moderato, D minor 2/2) provides a rhythmically vital conclusion, using similar scoring devices. Ample cross-cuing is provided for solos and lightly scored passages.

MOZART, W.A.   **ANDANTE GRAZIOSO**   Shawnee
Arr. James Thornton   3:30

An excellent arrangement of a beautiful wind work (the slow movement of Divertimento in B^b, K.240) Thornton has even retained the sextet layout of the original (Andante Grazioso, E^b, 4/4) with intelligent and sensitive use of doubling and emphasizing contrasts of dynamics. Technically easy, in comfortable ranges, with ample opportunity to develop balance, blend, ensemble precision, phrasing and style. Highly recommended.

MYERS, Theldon (Arr.)   **FROM AN 18TH-CENTURY ALBUM**   TRN
4:30

Three short pieces by relatively unknown composers, nicely scored. (1) *ARIOSO* by C.G. Neefe (Andante, F major, 3/4) presents a simple, flowing melody in straightforward harmonization and mostly chordal structure. (2) *MINUETTO* by J.A. Hiller (Allegro moderato, B^b, 3/4) features a lilting theme with staccato accompaniment followed by a more sustained second phrase. (3) *SCHERZANDO* by J.F. Reichert (Allegretto, E^b, 2/4) opens with a staccato tune, contrasted with a legato section which is more chromatic in content.

NELHYBEL, Vaclav   **BALLAD (THEME AND VARIATIONS)**   J. Christopher
8:30

An imaginative and well-crafted work ideal for young bands. The opening theme is variously scored for percussion, brass, woodwinds and tutti in alternation. Subsequent variations are each scored for different combinations (1) Espressivo clarinet and saxophone, (2) Religioso, for woodwinds and percussion, (3) Marcato, for brass and percussion, (4) Cantabile, for clarinet choir and low brass,

(5) Misterioso, for flute, clarinet and percussion, concluding with a return of the theme. Technically very easy with opportunity to develop intonation (many unison passages), phrasing, sense of color and style.

O'REILLY, John	CHANT AND CANON	Alfred
		2:02

A very simple and well-crafted work using modal materials and forms for beginning bands. The Chant, 4/4 Moderato, opens with lyrical woodwind choir and bells in C minor (but only two flats in concert key). The brass incorporating similar quarter and half note rhythms answers this pattern. The Canon, Allegro, 4/4 in B^b major, also begins with woodwind choir and is echoed by the brass but using two measure phrases in imitative form. The use of unison rhythms and limited ranges make this a solid work for students with one-year experience. There is only a single bell part written for the percussion section; however, a piano accompaniment is provided and leaves the possibility for adding keyboard instruments.

O'REILLY, John (Arr.)	SKYE BOAT SONG	Alfred
		3:00

This charming arrangement of a traditional Scottish folk song is a refreshing addition to the beginning band literature. Opening in F major, (3/4, Moderato, quarter note = 86) the simple melody is appropriately accompanied by sustained low wind sonorities. Much of the melody appears in the upper winds throughout the work but always presented with a color or harmonic contrast. The final setting uses simple and unison articulative contrasts as well as a short counter melody to close the work.

OSMON, Leroy	AMERICAN SONGS	Southern
		4:20

A very effective treatment of three well-known melodies in one continuous movement. Ranges are comfortable and scoring is solid, with melodies taken by sections (All trumpets, horns, etc.) rather than in solo presentations.

PALESTRINA, Giovanni Pierluigi	ADORAMUS TE AND SANCTUS	Elkan-Vogel
Arr. Russell Harvey		3:30

Two beautiful examples of 16th-century contrapuntal style, effectively transcribed. The opening pieces is mostly homophonic in texture, with nice contrasts of scoring between brass and woodwinds and use of wide dynamic range, while the Sanctus is polyphonic in style, using 4-part imitative counterpoint throughout with intelligent scoring choices and effective doublings.

PALESTRINA, G.P.	A LITTLE PALESTRINA SUITE	Elkan-Vogel
Arr. Philip Gordon		2:50

Another beautiful set of works which superbly exemplify the 16th-century style. (1) (Moderato, E^b-C minor, 2/2) - legato and sustained, with short contrapuntal motives that vary the prevailing homophonic texture. (2) (Moderato, D minor, 2/2) similar in style to the first, but with more choir scoring. (3) (Moderato con moto, 3/4) - more lively and rhythmic in character. Technically easy with ample cross-cuing for exposed passages. Emphasizes intonation, tone, blend, balance, feeling of phrase and expressive style.

PALESTRINA, G.P.	THREE HYMNS	Bourne
Arr. Philip Gordon		4:30

An excellent alternative to the above, with similar stylistic content and approach to scoring.

PEARSON, Bruce	AYRE AND DANCE	Kjos
		4:40

A very well scored two-part composition using modal melodies, simple rhythms and a full battery of percussion instruments (7-8 instruments). Opening with a haunting melody in C minor, 4/4 quarter note = 72, the 4-measure phrases are clearly marked by cadences and notation. This is layered by tutti wind and percussion textures that gradually grow in volume and intensity; however, the Ayre never achieves a volume level above mf. The ensuing dance, quarter note = 108 in E^b major, is in stark contrast to the previous lyrical material. The simple and lively melody is first stated by the trumpets and echoed in various setting and wind sonorities. Careful use of volume contrasts gives this dance additional interest and musical content. Although all of this material is simple, the length of this work places it slightly above the beginning band level.

PLOYHAR, James (Arr.) FANFARE, AIR AND TRUMPET TUNE Wynn
3:30

A tasteful musical rendering of three 17th-century pieces. (1) *FANFARE* by William Duncombe (Allegro, B^b, 3/4), featuring trumpets on melody with solid accompaniment in tutti band. (2) *AIR* by de Neufville (Andante espressivo, G minor, 3/4) - a lyric, flowing melody in woodwinds with chorale-like low brass accompaniment (trumpets tacet) and nice use of echo dynamics. (3) *TRUMPET TUNE* by Jeremiah Clarke (Allegro maestoso, B^b, 4/4) again features the trumpets with effective doubling in flutes; later in clarinets, horns and saxes. A majestic yet rhythmic piece with frequent use of dotted 8th-16ths. (N.B. the *FANFARE* is the same as the *TRUMPET MINUET* movement in the *"Early English Suite"*).

PLOYHAR, James KOREAN FOLK MEDLEY Belwin

A fresh-sounding and colorful work using interesting melodies. A short introduction leads to (1) *BETEUL NORAE* (Moderato, C minor, 3/4), a simple tune in two phrases with light accompaniment. The meter changes to 6/8 for (2) *ODOLKI* (Andante moderato, E^b), a gently lilting tune with delicate percussion accompaniment. The work concludes with *ARIRANG* (Allegro, B^b, 3/4) in two phrases, each set twice, closing with an effective coda using the second phrase.

PURCELL, Henry AIR AND MARCH Bourne
Arr. Philip Gordon 2:45

An effective pairing of two contrasting pieces. (1) *AIR* (Moderato, B^b, 3/4), a simple but attractive melody in flowing legato style, opening with tutti scoring, contrasted with use of woodwinds, then brass choir, concluding with tutti. (2) *MARCH* (Moderato, B^b, 4/4), opening with a well-marked and accented tutti statement, then woodwinds alone softly. Subsequent phrases use similar scoring layout.

PURCELL, Henry A PURCELL SUITE Ludwig
Arr. John Boyd 4:15

A charming suite in three movements, intelligently arranged from pieces originally for recorder and keyboard. The opening *PRELUDE* (Moderato, G minor, 4/4) is majestic and expansive in character, with effective variety of scoring from tutti to smaller combinations. The succeeding *ADAGIO* (G minor, 4/4) is expressive and sustained, beginning in brass choir alone, later adding woodwinds, with subsequent phrases using varying textures. The *FINALE* (Allegro, B^b, 4/4) is jaunty and amiable, dominated by dotted-8th-16th rhythm.

RYDEN, William (Arr.) JEANETTE, ISABELLA Manhattan Beach
1:30

A lovely arrangement of this seventeenth-century French carol. Although there are very simple rhythms and articulations, the tempo (dotted half note = 64 in 3/4) will provide rhythmic and precision challenges for very young players. After alternating woodwind and tutti statements of the carol are exchanged, a clever percussion interlude introduces a canon between upper and lower winds. Excellent use of dynamic and color contrasts of the simple theme are utilized and the work ends quietly and slowly with mallet percussion stating the theme accompanied by sustained woodwinds in E^b.

SAINT-SAENS, Camille GLORIA AND ALLELUIA Etling
Arr. Fred Hubbell 3:15

An attractive selection of two excerpts from a *CHRISTMAS ORATORIO*, capably arranged. The *GLORIA* juxtaposes a lively, energetic theme with a more stately lyric motive, while the *ALLELUIA* is broad and majestic in character using contrasts of choir scoring and dynamics. All parts are in comfortable ranges for young players, and rhythms and melodic shapes are basic.

SCHUBERT, Franz THE SONG OF MIRIAM Alfred
Arr. Philip Gordon 2:20

A flowingly lyric work (Allegro moderato, E^b, 4/4), originally for chorus, with contrasts between majestic and intimate moods that Gordon has paralleled with use of tutti and choir scoring. Technically easy, but requires feeling for phrase, sensitivity to subtle harmonic changes, nuances and dynamic shadings.

EASY

SCHUMANN, Robert   **FROM A SCHUMANN ALBUM**   Barnhouse
Arr. Jared Spears

Two attractive pieces from *"Album for the Young"* (*HUMMING SONG* and *SOLDIER'S MARCH*), sensitively scored for young band. Technically easy – the first requires a legato tone and feeling for phrase; the second demands crisp rhythmic style.

SOR, Fernando   **ANDANTINO**   Medici
Arr. Ronald Dishinger   4:00

A tuneful and appealing work (B^b, 4/4), arranged very effectively from the original for classical guitar. Technically easy, yet with musical challenges of articulations, phrasing and dynamic contrasts. Scoring is fairly full, yet not too heavy.

SPARKE, Philip   **SIMPLE SARABANDE**   Angelo Music Press
       2:00

A very creative and original work for very young players using the basic Sarabande form. All of the tenor and bass voice parts use flexible instrumentation and a piano accompaniment is part of the score. Opening in 3/4, (Andante con moto, quarter note =92 in E^b) the work quickly evolves into a tutti texture using slurred eighth notes and quarter note echo-like phrases. The theme develops with added syncopation and imaginative percussion colors. The closing dance phrases are written with unison rhythms and articulations that fade to a soft- staccato final three notes.

STORY, Mike (Arr.)   **SAKURA, SAKURA (CHERRY BLOSSOMS)**   Belwin Mills
       1:30

A very effective arrangement of this familiar Japanese folk song for beginning bands. The unison clarinet first plays the theme after an appropriate challenging temple block introduction. The percussion continues to accompany the clarinet until a canon is formed, this time with the flutes presenting the melody. Layers of wind and percussion colors (6 parts) envelops the theme until it is exposed in tutti form at the forte level. This quiets and leads to the repeated opening textures. The work concludes on a unison F in the low wind registers with an added gong tag.

SWEENEY, Michael   **DOWN BY THE SALLEY GARDENS**   Hal Leonard
       3:05

A technically easy, yet beautifully done sequence of settings. A brief introduction sets the mood – the melody then follows. The first phrase appears in unaccompanied trumpet, continuing with sustained-chord background. The second phrase appears in tenor sax, horn and trombone, with the concluding phrase in flute and oboe. A contrasting middle section features an original melody in the same style as the folk tune. The tune then returns in a different key with full band scoring. A brief contrasting statement is made in clarinet and saxophone, leading to the closing phrase in a climactic presentation. The work concludes with a quiet statement of the melody and a short coda.

TCHAIKOVSKY, P.I.   **TWO SELECTIONS FROM "ALBUM FOR THE YOUNG"**   Kendor
Arr. Philip Gordon   2:00

A very enjoyable pair of contrasting pieces. The opening *MORNING PRAYER* (Andante, F major, 3/4) is slow, sustained, legato in style, reminiscent of a church organ prelude in mood and character. The *SOLDIER'S MARCH* (Allegro marziale, F major, 2/2) is crisp, staccato, rhythmic. Both pieces have effective contrasts of dynamics and color and appealing melodic and harmonic material despite the technical and textural simplicity.

WEBER, Carl Maria von   **PRAYER AND MARCH FROM "DER FREISCHUTZ"**   Belwin
Arr. Philip Gordon

Two of the better known excerpts from Weber's great opera are effectively combined in a serviceable arrangement for young bands with a minimum of simplification. The slow section is fully scored by demands a good feeling for phrase and tenuto style, while the March has effective soli for trumpets and horns contrasting with both woodwind and tutti scoring.

WILLIAMS, Mark   SONGS OF SCOTLAND   Alfred
                                                                         3:35

An excellent potpourri of four well-known Scots songs. After a short 4/4 introduction using part of "Loch Lomond", an Allegretto 6/8 tune appears in flute, then upper woodwinds. The final phrase adds trumpets. The next song, "Annie Laurie" features the first phrase of the melody in the alto saxophone, with flute and oboe in the second phrase. This section is then repeated with tutti scoring. The work concludes with the march tune "Scotland the Brave" providing a stirring climax.

ZINGARELLI, Nicola   CLASSIC MOTET   Alfred
Arr. Ross Hastings   2:45

An attractive short work in two contrasting sections (Slow and sustained, F minor and Moderately fast, F major) which provides a good example of the classical style. The standard contrasts of dynamics and styles are heightened by Hastings' use of choir scoring (tutti, woodwinds alone, brass alone and various mixtures). Technically easy, it requires good sustained legato style and sensitivity to intonation in the slow section, and control of dynamics and articulations in the allegro.

ZDECHLIK, John (Arr.)   IN DULCI JUBILO   Kjos Music
                                                                         2:50

A clever collection of settings of the familiar German melody for young players. After a four-measure introduction, (Moderato, 3/4 quarter note = 100, B^b) the tune is presented by the clarinet and alto saxophone. Metallic percussion colors provide added interest. Low brass are added to the melody and percussion also change texture and rhythmic intensity. This subsides into a quiet closing of this setting. The next setting, in E^b quarter note = 116, is march-like with unison eighth note rhythms and a more even version to the opening melody. The final setting, in C 3/4 quarter note=90 Maestoso, adds the trumpet to the color now back in its original form draped with woodwind and percussion sonorities. The work ends peacefully on a tutti C major triad. Note: alternate (not optional) percussion parts are provided for advanced players.

● ●

EASY SUPPLEMENT

BACH, J.S.   **A LITTLE BACH SUITE**   Warner
Arr. Philip Gordon   3:00
Good examples of lighter Bach, with simple homophonic textures, basic rhythms and melodic shapes - in three movements.

BARTOK, Bela   **TWO SONGS AND A DANCE**   Wynn
Arr. Ross Hastings
More effective arrangement of easier Bartok piano pieces.

BORTNIANSKY, D.S.   **CHERUBIM SONG**   Ludwig
Arr. David Warren
A lovely early-19th century Russian liturgical work, well-scored and technically easy, with opportunity to develop ensemble sonority, intonation, phrasing and control of dynamics.

BENSON, Warren   **GINGER MARMALADE**   C. Fischer
3:00
An utterly delightful and clever work using musically interesting material and treatment within a technically easy framework. Recommended for program material on any level for a refreshing change of pace.

CARTER, Charles   **MOTET FOR BAND**   Hansen
3:00
An attractive original work using 16th-century contrapuntal stylistic features (e.g. passages of motivic imitation followed by homophonic episodes), technically easy.

CORELLI, Arcangelo   **PRAELUDIUM AND GAVOTTE**   Shawnee
Arr. Andrew Balent

CORELLI, Arcangelo   **SARABANDE**   Studio/PR
Arr. Ronald Dishinger
More good 18th-century Italian baroque literature, both capably arranged.

DISHINGER, Ronald (Arr.)   **KEMP'S JIG**   Medici
An attractive 16-th century English instrumental piece, competently arranged.

EDMONDSON, John   **FANTASY ON A FANFARE**   Hansen
3:45
A good original, interesting for its contrasting tempos and moods, while using one main melodic motive in different guises.

ERICKSON, Frank   **TWO NORWEGIAN FOLK DANCES**   Belwin
2:30
An excellent supplement to the *NORWEGIAN FOLK SONG SUITE* listed previously.

GLUCK, C.W. von   **BALLET OVERTURE (DON JUAN)**   Warner
Arr. Leroy Jackson   3:00
An acceptably scored, tastefully done simplification of a delightful 18th-century classic.

GRETCHANINOFF, Alexander   **MINIATURE SUITE**   MCA
Arr. F. Siekmann, R. Oliver   6:00
Six short children's piano pieces, well arranged. The music is simple and straightforward with regular phrase patterns and basic harmonic progressions.

GRUNDMAN, Clare **KENTUCKY 1800** Boosey & Hawkes
3:00

Appealing settings of three early American folk-tunes, intelligently arranged for young players. Scoring is generally full with cross-cuing provided for effective doubling or substitutions.

JACKSON, Leroy **LITTLE IRISH SUITE; LITTLE SCOTCH SUITE** Warner

Two good alternatives to Jackson's *LITTLE ENGLISH SUITE*, similar in format and style.

HANDEL, G.F. **PRELUDE AND FUGHETTA** Ludwig
Arr. Eric Osterling 3:35

Two attractive pieces in contrasting style, capably transcribed.

KABALEVSKY, Dmitri **SIX EPISODES** MCA
Arr. Richard Oliver 4:15

A good alternative to the *SUITE IN MINOR MODE* listed previously, consisting of six short programmatic pieces in contrasting styles.

MCGINTY, Anne **THREE IRISH FOLKSONGS** Barnhouse
3:15

Very appealing and attractive arrangements of excellent folk material, well-scored, with opportunities for all sections of the band to be featured.

MOZART, W.A. **MENUET, K.164** Medici
Arr. Ronald Dishinger

A charming and enjoyable piece. The scoring is somewhat faulty (the melodic line is not effectively doubled) but the music provides worthwhile material for young players.

PLOYHAR, James (Arr.) **SONGS OF THE FJORDS** Belwin

More excellent folk material, tastefully arranged.

PURCELL, Henry **KING ARTHUR'S PROCESSIONAL** Alfred
Arr. Clark Tyler 1:45

A majestic, noble work with considerable contrasts of style, dynamics and scoring within its brief length.

RAMEAU, Jean Philip **TWO COURTLY DANCES** Shapiro-Bernstein
Arr. Philip Gordon

More good French Baroque material, well arranged.

• •

ADLER, Samuel   **MERRYMAKERS**   Ludwig

3:40

A lively, energetic original work for young bands. It begins with a slow, rather majestic introduction emphasizing dotted rhythms and featuring choir scoring (woodwinds, then brass, closing with woodwinds), followed by a fast, happy main section utilizing ostinato rhythmic passages in brass, with a sparkling melody in upper woodwinds. Elements of these two ideas are then developed and varied, brought to an exuberant climax. Despite the technical simplicity of the individual parts, there are rhythmic intricacies (especially after-beat playing in low brass and woodwinds) and somewhat dense chordal structures that provide musical challenges.

ABREAU, Thoinot   **BELLE QUI TIENS MA VIE**   Manhattan Beach
Arr. Bob Margolis   2:45

A truly beautiful work in moderate tempo (G minor, 2/4, quarter = 80), technically easy, which makes considerably musical demands. It takes the form of a stately and dignified pavane that is nonetheless poignant and expressive. Sensitively and intelligently scored with considerable variety of textures and combinations through use of choir scoring, and interesting imaginative dynamics covering a wide range. Snare drum with snares off provides the rhythmic pulsation throughout the piece. Strongly recomme3nded for any group.

BACH, J.S.   **CHORALE PRELUDE ON "SLEEPERS, WAKE"**   Mills
Arr. Philip Gordon   4:10

A straightforward, tasteful arrangement of the opening section of Bach's Cantata No. 140. The woodwinds carry the elaborations and ornamental figurations while the brass provide the chorale melody and chorus parts. Technically modest in difficulty, but requiring good legato style, feeling for phrase, evenness of 16th-note passagework and beauty and blend of tone in brass.

BACH, J.S.   **FUGUE 22**   Kendor
Arr. Francis Caviani   2:20

An excellent introduction to a contrapuntally elaborate fugue for younger players (Moderato, B^b minor, 4/4). Technically rather easy except for minor-9th leap in theme for some voices, with basic rhythms and note values, but requires some musical maturity due to the key and the demands for rhythmic independence, understanding of phrases, awareness of the 5-part texture (especially in the intricate stretto near the end), careful working out of balances and maintenance of tone quality and feeling for style.

BACH, J.S.   **THREE BACH PIECES**   Jenson
Arr. James Thornton   5:45

An excellent selection of three different aspects of Bach's output, all originally for keyboard. The opening *PRELUDE* (Moderato, E^b, 4/4) features a flowing 8th-note melody. The succeeding *SARABANDE* (Slow, A minor, 3/4) is stately, dignified, somewhat mournful, while the finale, *FUGUE* (Moderato, 4/4) is boldly assertive. Requires some technical facility but is not demanding.

BACH, J.S.   **PRELUDE AND FUGUE IN B-FLAT MAJOR**   Warner
Arr. R.L. Moehlmann   3:30

The opening *PRELUDE* is flowing yet expansive in character, demanding good legato, sense of phrase and control of articulation patterns (the slur patterns of the 8th-note figures are challenging to young players). The *FUGUE* is more rhythmic in nature, yet still rather noble and sustained (the main theme tends to be played too detached and choppily. Also requires attention to balance, clarity, and precision.

BACH, J.S.   **PRELUDE AND FUGUE IN F MINOR**   FitzSimons
Arr. R.L. Moehlmann   3:00

The *PRELUDE* is a fine blend of lyrical expressiveness and rich contrapuntal texture, while the *FUGUE*, featuring a simple but rather chromatic theme, becomes more and more intricate, with effective use of inversion and elaboration of texture. The transcription is simple but very effective.

BACH, J.S.   **QUARTETT**   Wynn
Arr. Grant Hull   5:45

A good sampling of four lesser-known works of Bach transcribed generally effectively for younger bands. (1) *CHORALE* "O Sacred Head Now Wounded" (E^b, 4/4), a rich-textured setting from St. Matthew Passion, scored mostly for full band, with repeated phrases given contrasting dynamics. (2) *MENUET* (G minor, 3/4), a rhythmic well-marked tune with flowing 8th-notes in woodwinds providing contrasting texture. (3) *ANDANTE* ("Sinfonia from Christmas Oratorio") (B^b, 3/8), a flowing, gently rocking melody using contrasts of choir scoring. (4) *SICUT ERAT* from *MAGNIFICAT*, an energetic and exalted piece which is technically the most demanding section, requiring good fluency of articulation and evenness of passagework in both bass and treble instruments.

BACH, J.S.   **PRELUDE AND FUGUE IN D MINOR**   FitzSimons
Arr. R.L. Moehlmann   3:00

The *PRELUDE* (Allegro moderato, 4/4) contrasts full sonorities with choirs and mixed colors on unison lines, in broad, sweeping phrases. The *FUGUE* is more angular in character with effective contrast between homophonic and contrapuntal passages. Technically modest in demands, but requires careful attention to blend, refinement, intonation (especially in unison passages), and awareness of long phrases and feeling of line.

BACH, J.S.   **PRELUDE AND FUGUE IN G MINOR**   Warner
Arr. R.L. Moehlmann   3:00

One of the best of the Moehlmann transcriptions. The opening *PRELUDE (*Grave, G minor, 3/2) is slow, stately, regal, with two contrasting ideas - an arch-like quarter-note melody and a long flowing line of 8ths. The succeeding *FUGUE* (Moderato, 4/4) is rather lyric in character, contrasted with a more rhythmic counter-melody, whose closing motive becomes the basis of a rich-textured noble climax. Technically rather easy, but strongly recommended as a superb example of Bach's contrapuntal style, well-matched to the band medium.

BACH, J.S.   **WHO PUTS HIS TRUST IN GOD MOST JUST**   Shawnee
Arr. James Croft   4:30

A beautiful arrangement of a lovely Bach chorale-setting, done so that it can be performed by winds alone, winds and chorus, or with members of the band singing the choral part with the remainder of the band playing. Technically easy but highly recommended as an excellent way to develop musicianship, tone, phrasing, pitch, blend, balance and overall musical sensitivity.

BANCHIERI, Adriano   **RENAISSANCE CANZONA**   Carl Fischer
Arr. by Carl Strommen

This highly effective arrangement of a lesser-known Renaissance composer is an exemplary model for this historic period and genre. A one-measure imitative theme in 4/4 quarter note = 150 (half note =75) defines the work from the opening measure. These fragments join the original theme in canonic form until a tutti sonority is established. A second section starting with low winds uses a similar style that eventually exchanges the momentum to the woodwind choir. Simple counterpoint and logical sequences prevail until the texture returns to the tutti voices. The coda brings the work to a full conclusion arriving on a tutti G major incomplete triad. This is a wonderful work to expose young students to Renaissance instrumental forms. The percussion parts are simple yet appropriate for this level.

BARNES, James   **YORKSHIRE BALLAD**   Southern Music
                                                          3:40

A well-written work (slow, B^b major) featuring an original folk-like melody presented in several settings. It opens with the melody stated in clarinets, alto saxophones and horn, and a counter-melody in lower woodwinds and euphonium. The second setting features the flutes followed by oboes and clarinets. The tempo increases along with a modulation to E^b major featuring the trumpets, reaching a tutti climax. The music then subsides into a gently lyric coda, closing quietly.

BARTOK, Bela FOUR PIECES FOR BAND Sam Fox
Arr. Benjamin Suchhoff 3:10

A very appealing group of pieces from the set *"FOR CHILDREN"*. (1) Poco Vivace (G minor, 2/4, 3/4) contrasting staccato 2/4 and legato 3/4 and using effective scoring. (2) Allegro (G minor, 2/4), lively and energetic, with melody appearing throughout the band at various times, concluding with a fast coda. (3) Adagio (D minor, 4/4), mournful and dirge-like in character, with legato melody in saxes, clarinets and flute, and sustained or after-beat accompaniment. (4) Molto Allegro (B^b, G minor, 2/4), quite fast and lively, with flowing legato 8th-note melody, quarter and half-note slurred accompaniment, and rhythmic percussion.

BARTOK, Bela HUNGARIAN FOLK SUITE Marks
Arr. Philip Gordon 2:00

Three more excerpts from *"FOR CHILDREN"*, tastefully and sensitively arranged. The first (Allegro moderato, 2/4) is rhythmic and marcato in character with contrasts of tutti and solo scoring and dynamics in short irregular phrases (3-bar groups). The second (Andante molto espressivo, 2/4) is slow and lyric, featuring solo trumpet with sustained chordal accompaniment in the first section. Later the melody is shared with upper woodwinds while the accompaniment is more active. The finale (Allegro, 2/4, half=72) is dynamic and driving, opening with woodwinds alone on the melody answered by brass punctuations, followed by a short tutti section. The opening melody returns in cornet and baritone soli, gradually building to a brilliant, spirited climax.

BARTOK, Bela THREE HUNGARIAN SONGS Bourne
Arr. Philip Gordon 2:20

Very enjoyable and engaging pieces effectively set and scored. The first (Allegretto, B^b, 2/4) features a simple tune in 4-bar phrases, stated first by oboe (cued flute) and clarinet, then flute, clarinet and alto sax; flute and muted trumpet; finally oboe and clarinet, with light, delicate accompaniment. The next 8 bars use full scoring, and the piece closes with contrast between solo and tutti. The second (Andante, D minor, 4/4) opens with a lovely horn solo (cued trumpet) accompanied by clarinets. The melody is then taken by trumpets and upper woodwinds with full-scored accompaniment. The third (Allegro con brio, G minor, 2/4) is lively and rhythmic, featuring woodwinds and punctuating brass chords followed by a staccato trumpet melody with two horns accompanying (cued 2-3 trumpets). The melody is then stated by flute and E^b clarinet (cued Cl.1), finishing with a fully scored statement accompanied by staccato bass line. Though much of this work is technically easy, the transparent scoring and emphasis on solo voices demands a degree of musical maturity.

BIEBL, Franz AVE MARIA Boosey and Hawkes
Arr. Robert Cameron 5:30

This is a beautiful arrangement of a lesser-known choral work, which was originally scored for seven-part men's choir. Beginning with the brief opening chant, sung by the ensemble or male solo voice, the work moves into a colorful backdrop of alternating low brass and woodwind sonorities (*Sostenuto*, quarter note =69) using simple harmonies and rhythms. This section is repeated but with an extended chant being sung at the conclusion of the repeat. The ensuing section is brighter in nature using many swells in volume and less soli scoring. A melismatic "Amen" brings the work to a very emotional and satisfying ending. Highly recommended for ensembles at all levels.

BOHM, Carl STILL WIE DIE NACHT Byron-Douglas
Arr. Charles Spinney 3:00

A sensitive, beautifully scored arrangement of a 19th-century vocal classic, (Andante, E^b, 3/4) this offers an excellent example of legato style, flowing phrases and sostenuto playing in accompanying voices. Fundamentals of intonation (unisons, octaves, chords), blend (doublings of melody), balance (melody against accompaniment) and range of dynamics (pp-ff) are all required. Highly recommended for more advanced groups as well, for use on concerts.

BRAHMS, Johannes MEDITATIONS ON A CHORALE Bourne
Arr. Earl Slocum 2:10

At the very end of his life, Brahms wrote a set of chorale-preludes for organ, of which this is one *("LO, HOW A ROSE E'ER BLOOMING")*, (Larghetto, E^b, 6/4). It is one of his most beautiful inspirations, in which the simple melody is embroidered by a long, flowing line of 8th-notes. This work demands above all a true legato style along with beauty of tone and well controlled intonation.

The arrangement is an intelligent one with simple but effective contrasts of choirs and range. Recommended for all levels capable of handling the musical requirements.

BROEGE, Timothy	**SINFONIA VI**	Manhattan Beach
		6:00

An excellent original work in four short movements. (1) Andante (quarter=72). This features a solo group of three clarinets which state all the musical material, answered by both small groups and tutti. Rather reflective and melancholy in character. (2) Allegretto (quarter=112), featuring solo baritone in a somewhat humorous marching tune in changing meters, with transparent, light, simple accompaniment. (3) Andante (quarter=76), featuring solo alto saxophone and trumpet in a simple, nostalgic phrase, answered by a soft, pulsating rhythm in the accompaniment. (4) Allegro (quarter=144), featuring percussion. A dramatic and aggressive movement with effective contrasts of dynamics and rhythmic figures. Highly recommended for younger bands. The solo needs will prove a strong aid to developing musical, tonal, and projective skills of the players involved.

BRISMAN, Heskel	**UGANDA LULLABY**	Elkan-Vogel
		1:45

An unusual and intriguing setting of a very simple but haunting tune. Technically easy and melodically elemental, this work challenges young players with the use of asymmetrical meters (5/8, 7/8) which constantly appear, and with rhythmic patterns, frequently repeated, which go against the meter.

BROEGE, Timothy	**DREAMS AND FANCIES**	Hal Leonard
		5:45

A technically modest but aurally challenging work for young players, the harmonic content is rather dissonant and the melody shapes are frequently irregular. It is in four short movements with contrasting tempos and moods.

1. First Dream: slow and atmospheric with tasteful use of percussion
2. First Fancy: moderately fast with staccato 8th-notes providing rhythmic background
3. Second Dream: featuring short melodic ideas over a sustained chordal accompaniment
4. Second Fancy: fast, lively, and energetic in 5/4 meter featuring syncopated rhythm

BRUCKNER, Anton	**HYMN OF PRAISE**	C. Fischer
Arr. Philip Gordon		4:30

This short but very expressive work has been well-adapted from the choral original. While it is technically easy, with basic rhythms and comfortable ranges, the piece requires more developed musical and aural comprehension. There are many abrupt changes of harmony and tonal direction (e.g. D minor to B^b minor; A major to F minor), though the key signature remains constant throughout (D minor). Also requires good intonation, beauty of tone and feeling of phrase. Strongly recommended as a worthwhile addition to any group's concert program.

BRYANT, Steven	**DUSK**	Gorilla Salad Productions
		5:15

This charming yet somewhat thinly scored chorale setting is a refreshing addition to the repertoire. Beginning in 2/4 (quarter note = 44) and centered around F, the work incorporates an arch structure. The climax is located in the middle using both texture and harmony to convey its expressive qualities. Many moments of unresolved dissonances make this a challenge for young performers. Control of legato style and dynamics in all registers are paramount, but well worth the effort.

BYRD, William	**THE EARL OF SALISBURY**	Sam Fox (Kalmus)
Arr. Arthur Frackenpohl		3:00

A great keyboard work, expertly scored. The opening *PAVANA* (Allegro moderato, B^b minor, 4/4) is noble and dignified, with a tinge of poignant sadness. The contrapuntal texture is simple but effective, and scoring uses both choir and tutti sonority. The succeeding *GALLIARD* (Moderato, B^b minor, 3/4) is stately yet rhythmic, with frequent dotted-8th-16th patterns and subtle interplay among voices and choirs.

CARTER, Charles	**POLYPHONIC SUITE**	Ludwig
		3:40

A fine work consisting of three pieces, each of which exemplifies a polyphonic form used in Renaissance of Baroque music, but which is composed of original material. The first, *MOTET*, uses imitative counterpoint throughout, thus helping to develop sense of rhythmic independence. The second, *CHORALE*, is written in a broad, flowing legato style. The third, *MADRIGAL*, is more lively and rhythmic, with both homophonic and polyphonic episodes. Technically easy, requiring rhythmic security, sensitivity to style, good intonation and balancing of voices.

COPLAND, Aaron	**DOWN A COUNTRY LANE**	Boosey & Hawkes
Arr. Merlin Patterson		3:30

A very moving (and authorized) transcription of an original Copland piano work. Faithful to the archetype , the work begins with treble voices (woodwinds) using 4-measure phrases (4/4, quarter note = 88, F major) in a legato style. The texture thickens and thins while varying the opening material by tempo, key (F minor) and harmony before a transition back to the original F major, this time employing tutti scoring (ff) in a triumphal mood. The work closes quietly and slowly on an F major triad scored in mid-range winds. Although not technically challenging, this short work requires tonal maturity in all ranges for the winds and a clear understanding of the colorful harmonies for proper balance and style. Only an optional vibraphone part is provided for percussion.

DAEHN, Larry	**AS SUMMER WAS JUST BEGINNING**	Daehn
		4:50

A beautiful and original instrumental song as a tribute to the late James Dean. The saxes and horns open with a somber yet heroic lyrical statement (Andante con moto, 4/4, quarter note = 68-74 in B^b). An answering theme is introduced by the flutes and oboes with simple clarinet accompaniment. Several cadences are outlined clearly with suspensions that naturally resolve. The A and B themes are repeated but with more elaborate instrumentation and decorated harmonies. A logical modulation leads to a final *maestoso* section in C major, which concludes with a satisfying "amen." This is a very practical and expressive work for teaching younger students legato style, dissonance and resolution and direction of line.

DAEHN, Larry	**BRITISH ISLES SUITE**	Daehn
		7:00

A masterful suite using Welsh, Scottish, Irish and British folksongs. The first movement, "March Song" is a clever combination of "Britons, Raise Your Banners High" and "March for the Men of Harlech." It opens with a drum cadence (Moderato, 4/4, D minor) as winds enter softly and thinly using simple rhythms and dotted eighth-sixteenth notes. The melody is embellished and given an imaginative counter-melody in low brass before a shift to legato style and tonality to B^b *(L'istesso* tempo). This also builds to a powerful tutti section before subsiding into a quiet fade of the opening drum cadence. A very expressive setting of "Barbara Allen" follows (3/4, *Andante espressivio*, in E^b major) using effective colors, dynamics, moods, movement and legato style in all of the wind families. A final "poco piu mosso" section in B^b followed by a relaxation of the tempo, which quietly ends this movement. "Farewell, Dundee" opens with a fife and drum-like texture using material from the Scottish folksong "Adieu, Dundee" (6/8, Moderato, D minor). A surprise transition into "Auld Lang Syne" quietly ends the work as the drum patterns fade into the final unison F. Highly recommended. Requires 5 competent percussionists appropriate to this level of difficulty.

DAQUIN, Louis Claude	**NOEL SUITE**	C. Fischer
Arr. Philip Gordon		3:00

A set of three charming pieces in early 18th-century style. The first (Andante, E^b, 3/4) is stately and dignified, with a nice contrast of dynamics and scoring. The second (Allegro, E^b, 4/4 - should be 2/2) is lively and dance-like, featuring passages of both choir and tutti scoring. The finale (Allegretto, E^b, 4/4) is more weighty and marked in character, beginning rather softly in woodwinds and building to a sonorous tutti climax.

DAVIS, Albert Oliver	**FROM SHIRE AND SEA**	Byron-Douglas
		5:00

An attractive, well-scored three-movement suite of English folk-tune settings, perfectly suited to young bands. The opening movement (Allegretto, G minor, 3/4) uses two contrasting tunes - the first in moderate tempo, scored mostly for woodwinds; the second more lively, featuring the brass. The second movement (Lento, F major, 4/4) presents four differently scored settings of *BARBARA ALLEN* in lyrically expressive mood. The third, *HIGH BARBARY*, begins in G minor (6/8 March tempo) leading to a climactic setting of *RULE BRITTANIA* (B^b major, 2/2) featuring some interesting counter-melodic lines in upper woodwinds.

DAVIS, Albert Oliver   **LADIES, LORDS AND GYPSIES**   Belwin
5:30

An excellent alternative to the above, using similar material. (1) *HENRY MARTIN* (Moderato, C minor-A^b major, 3/4 in one) opens with a tutti introduction, followed by three statements of the tune, each time with an added counter-melody or doubling. The tune is then state in A^b major with other obbligati and accompaniment figures. (2) *SWEET KITTY* and *O SALLY MY DEAR* (Lento, C minor, 3/4) Very lyric, rich textured, with flowing lines and counter-melodies, and use of choir and section scoring most of the time. (3) *LORD THOMAS* and *WRAGGLE-TAGGLE GYPSIES* (March tempo, E^b, 2/2), with interesting uses of legato and staccato styles, both separately and together.

DAVIS, Albert Oliver   **RHENISH FOLK FESTIVAL**   Ludwig
4:00

Another fine suite of settings, this one tapping the vast source of German folk material. The first movement, *O YOU BEAUTIFUL RHINE* (Waltz tempo, B^b, 3/4 in one) is lilting yet energetic, containing a number of attractive melodies. The second, *THE LORELEI* (Lento, E^b,6/4) is nostalgic and poetic in mood, with beautiful flowing lines and choir scoring. The finale, *WHAT DOES THE GRAPEVINE BRING?,* (March-like, B^b, 2/4) is a lively polka that utilizes effective dynamic contrasts and changes of key. Highly recommended.

DAVIS, Albert Oliver   **SONGS OF WALES**   Ludwig
7:30

The rich resource of Welsh folk-song provides the melodic material for this excellent suite, which features abundant contrasts of texture and scoring while remaining technically in the grasp of young developing bands. The opening movement features two tunes – the first (Moderato, E^b, 3/4) is gently flowing with sustained background, while the second (Andante, C minor, 3/4) is somewhat faster with a more dance-like accompaniment. The second movement (Andantino, B^b, 4/4) opens with short introduction leading to the melody in horns and baritone. It is then passed around to other sections with phrases often divided between choirs. The finale (Allegro Marcia, E^b-B^b-A^b, 2/2) features three tunes in a march-like rhythmic setting.

DAWSON, Jay   **AMAZING GRACE**   Arrangers Publishing Co.
4:30

A very creative and emotional setting of this traditional hymn. Beginning with pyramiding fragments of the three-note hymn theme the work exposes the full Hymn first in woodwind choir (F major, quarter note =80). This quickly and effortlessly becomes a well-scored tutti chorus in G-flat major. A short and logical development section ensues using various solo groupings and harmonies. A clever transition using simulated bagpipe color (also effective with real bagpipes) performs the hymn, soli, including a bass drone in E-flat major. This leads to a final chorus, now tutti, in F Major with full percussion battery. Highly recommended.

DEL BORGO, Elliot   **IMAGINARY LANDSCAPES**   MSB Publishing Co.
3:00

This is an excellent, well-crafted work using simple modal melodies and harmonies. The opening (4/4 quarter note= 72, Cantabile) begins in the flutes and clarinets. Layers of percussion and brass sonorities interrupt the preceding lyrical statements. This becomes very agitated and leads to a fast section, with vigor (quarter note = 126). A full battery of percussion accompanies the two contrasting statements into an ostinato-like transition. A short canon ensues before the D.S. The coda section exposes more percussion activity, both rhythmically and tonally, and a restatement of the opening motif, now augmented by the winds, brings the work to an enthusiastic end. The percussion parts may be more challenging than the winds, but they are important colors and not extra fodder for educational purposes.

DEL BORGO, Elliot **MODAL SONG AND DANCE** William Allen
2:50

A well-crafted work for young ensembles in two parts using modes for its melodic and harmonic content. The first movement is in D minor (Smoothly, quarter note =88) and contains very clever scoring of the melodic material with drone-like accompaniment. This segues into the "dance" (Quickly, quarter note = 132) beginning with a short percussion interlude as a prelude to the rhythmic motives which ensue. The dance is punctuated with several colorful canonic and contrapuntal passages, concluding with a very strong ending. Percussion parts are very creative for this level and are vital to the texture, drive as well as the melodic content.

DVORAK, Antonin **ANDANTE from AMERICAN SUITE** Presser
Arr. Philip Gordon 3:30
A lovely lyric work, with the folk-like melody appearing in various voices (including clarinet, flute, trumpet, horn and oboe). Though it is technically easy, it requires good control and maturity due to transparent scoring, and balancing of accompaniment with solo voices.

ERICKSON, Frank **SONATINA FOR BAND** Belwin
3:45

This piece provides an excellent opportunity to develop several aspects of musicianship. The first movement has changing meters and contrapuntal imitation; the second has a simple melodic line doubled in octaves; the third develops contrasts of full band and choirs, melody with accompaniment, sense of continuity with ability to maintain tempo (it tends to slow down and lose flow of line).

FENSKE, Katheryn (Arr.) **MUSIC FROM THE GREAT HALL** Daehn
2:40

Two brilliantly scored and creative settings of Renaissance dances forms. The first dance, *A Toye,* in B^b (although the concert key indicates three flats) 2/2 quarter note =116-144 or "as fast as possible", begins with arpeggiated figures in the flute and mallet percussion. A second statement ensues in tutti form using eighth notes and simple accompaniment. The penultimate measure features a decorative bell solo in free time before the ensemble settles on an incomplete B^b major triad. The second dance, *The Kings Morisco*, opens "boldly" in 4/4 quarter note=108-126. The band is asked to use footsteps and jingle bells to accompany the percussion colors of the first four measures. Using the same key signature, the tutti ensemble presents simple melodic and harmonic materials appropriate to this style period. This is developed with color exchanges and leads to a quiet section in 3/4 for brass choir now in C major. Layers of winds join in to return to the tutti ensemble and the work ends with a C major echo by the upper winds. Very excellent scoring for 5 percussionists using nine instruments.

GOULD, Morton **MINI-SUITE** Chappell
4:30

A delightful and appealing set of three pieces with well-defined moods and simple construction. (1) *BIRTHDAY MARCH* (Moderate march-tempo, B^b-E^b, 2/4), with a declarative tune stated in trumpets, supported by percussion, using a phrase from "Happy Birthday" - contrasted with a more lyric trio section featuring clarinets. (2) *A TENDER WALTZ* (Slowly moving, B^b, 3/4) a gentle, warmly lyric piece featuring a dotted-rhythm melody, emphasizing woodwinds. (3) *BELL CAROL* (Energetic, B^b, 2/4), using an accented bell-like motive stated in brass. Technically modest in its demands and rhythmically straight forward (except for a tricky off-beat syncopation passage in the "Bell Carol"), the emphasis is on attractive musical content, with opportunities to develop style, dynamics, articulation and contrasts of mood and character.

GOUNOD, Charles **TE DEUM** Columbia
Arr. Lloyd Conley 3:00
A beautiful work in slowly flowing tempo (Andantino, quarter = 88, F major, 4/4), written in simple contrapuntal style with attractive imitation and interplay between voices, it is technically quite easy (mostly quarter and half-notes in comfortable ranges) but demands sensitivity of phrasing, feeling of line, relationships between voices, as well as beauty of tone, blend and intonation. Scoring is fairly full most of the time but has some transparent passages (e.g. oboe solo - cued trumpet - saxophone trio cued into clarinet and baritone). Highly recommended.

GRAINGER, Percy **YE BANKS AND BRAES O'BONNIE DOON** G. Schirmer
2:00

A band classic that poses challenges for any group. Though technically quite easy (apart from some range extension in horns and upper woodwind flexibility), this work demands beauty of tone, ensemble sonority, intonation, balance, blend, long-phrase playing, feeling of line, expression and flexibility of tempo and nuance. Every library should contain this work – a real gem of the literature (Slowly flowing, F major, 6/8 - 8th =104).

GRUNDMAN, Clare **AN IRISH RHAPSODY** Boosey & Hawkes
7:00

A superb medley of Irish folk-tunes, beautifully scored and imaginatively worked out, it opens with a fanfare-like introduction (Bb, 4/4) based on "Rakes of Mallow", leading to *THE MINSTREL BOY* (F major) with the melody variously scored. A short transition leads to *I KNOW WHERE I'M GOING* (Andante moderato, Eb, 2/4) with melody in horn, trumpet and upper woodwinds and rich-textured counter-melodic lines. *THE SHEPHERD'S LAMB REEL* follows (Allegro, F, 2/4 – 4/4), lightly articulated and rhythmic in character. The lovely *COCKELS AND MUSSELS* (Quietly, Bb, 3/4) follows with lush harmony and effective modulations. Another reel-tune, *THE RAKES OF MALLOW,* now appears (Allegro, F, 2/4), with delicate and colorful scoring to match its gaiety. The opening fanfare section returns, leading to *KATHLEEN O'MORE* (Con moto, F, 3/4) which is stated in horns. This leads to a concluding section which combines parts of several of the tunes and weaves the whole fabric into a warm-hearted climax. Technically modest in demands but requires a good solo and section talent (horns, trumpet, flute and piccolo, clarinet, baritone), rhythmic security and precision, clarity and balance of parts, beauty of tone and expressive style in lyric passages. Highly recommended for bands at all levels as an excellent concert number.

GRUNDMAN, Clare **LITTLE ENGLISH SUITE** Boosey & Hawkes
5:00

An attractive work in four movements using English folk-tunes. (1) *THE LEATHER BOTTEL* (Allegro moderato, Eb, 6/8) opens with a short introduction using the rhythm of the tune, leading to the tune itself in upper woodwinds, then stated several times in varied settings, including a 2/4 version as a coda. (2) *ROVING* (Freely with motion, F, 4/4) begins with an 8-bar introduction using a fragment of the tune, followed by a broad, noble version of this well-known chantey. (3) *WE MET* (Moderato, Bb, 3/4) a lovely legato melody with simple accompaniment, interrupted by a 4/4 variation in the middle, closing with the original tune in two settings – upper winds and tenor voice (saxes, baritone, horn). (4) *THE VICAR OF BRAY* (Moderato marcato, Eb, 2/2) a vigorous, sturdily rhythmic tune treated in several guises, with a short but effective coda.

GRUNDMAN, Clare **LITTLE SUITE FOR BAND** Boosey & Hawkes
4:30

An excellent work using original material in fresh and interesting ways. (1) *PRELUDE* – fanfare-like and emphatic with a short contrasting gentle phrase. Mostly fully scored with effective doublings. (2) *BALLAD* – reflective and nostalgic in character, with melody first stated by solo muted trumpet (cued several instruments) accompanied by soft woodwinds. The melody is further developed and extended by upper woodwinds with accompaniment continuing in lower woodwinds and low brass, and rhythmic counter-material in muted trumpets. (3) *FESTIVAL* – lively and energetic, with a short introduction leading to the melody in muted trumpets with an ostinato rhythmic figure in woodwinds and horns. Later, the melody is in trombones, baritones and horns, with trumpets and saxes playing ostinato. The concluding section features upper woodwinds, horns and baritone in a variation of the melody, leading to a coda based on the introduction. Technically easy, but requires care in balance, blend, intonation (especially doubled parts), musical details of dynamics and articulation.

GRUNDMAN, Clare **WELSH RHAPSODY** Boosey & Hawkes
4:00

Similar in format to the *IRISH RHAPSODY* listed above, though the emphasis is more lyric and expansive, with importance placed on beauty of tone, flow of line, sensitivity to nuance and flexibility of tempo. Several passages are delicately and transparently scored, requiring security of pitch and ensemble and tonal support. Technically rather easy, but with appealing musical value.

GUILMANT, Alexandre · **PRELUDE & ALLEGRO** · Etling
Arr. Fred Hubbell · 4:45

An eminently playable example of 19th-century organ music. The opening *PRELUDE* (Andante sostenuto, F, 4/4) is sustained in character yet requires a feeling of flow and forward motion, while the *ALLEGRO* (Allegro maestoso, B[b], 4/4) is more jubilant and vital in mood. The dotted rhythms and 8th-16th figures require good rhythmic precision, while the bass line is smooth-flowing yet covers a wide range (1½ - 2 octaves). Exposed passages are effectively doubled or cross-cued.

HANDEL, G.F. · **CARE SELVE from "ATALANTA"** · Associated
Arr. Erik Leidzen · 3:30

A thoughtfully conceived and effectively nuanced arrangement of a beautifully expressive aria. Clarinets play the melody in unison throughout, variously doubled by other instruments (Largo, G[b], 3/4). Requires well-controlled legato playing, refinement of tone, feeling for long phrases and security of key.

HANDEL, G.F. · **AN OCCASIONAL SUITE** · Ludwig
Arr. Eric Osterling · 5:40

A generally good transcription of three contrasting excerpts from Handel's vocal works. The opening *MARCH* (B[b], 4/4 – should be 2/2) is festive yet regal in character, with nice contrasts of choirs and dynamics. The second, *ARIA* (Larghetto, E[b], 3/4) has great dignity and repose with a broadly expressive melodic line. The finale (Allegro moderato, B[b], 4/4 but should be 2/2) is a chorus that contains both contrapuntal and homophonic textures.

HANDEL, G.F. · **TWO HANDEL MINIATURES** · Studio/PR
Arr. Andrew Balent · 2:00

Two familiar keyboard works, intelligently arranged. The *SARABANDE* (Andante, D minor, 3/2) has great breadth and majesty and requires good feeling of line and rhythmic shape. The *SONATINA* (Allegro, B[b], 4/4) requires good rhythmic awareness, precision, fluency, and clarity of articulation.

HASTINGS , Ross · **TUNE AND TOCCATELLA** · Bourne
· 3:00

An interesting and imaginative work, opening in graceful, lyric mood. (Adagietto semplice, B[b], 2/4), scored for woodwinds and bells alone, featuring a flowing 8th-note figure. The *TOCCATELLA* (Con Brio, quarter=104, 2/4) succeeding without interruption from a timpani roll, features brass and percussion in a nervous rhythmic figure of 16th-notes and rather dissonant harmonic content. At the climax the *TUNE* appears in maestoso tempo in brass, with the *TOCCATELLA* rhythm in woodwinds. A short coda returns to the faster tempo and Toccatella material in brass. Requires good tonguing facility in brass, discriminating ear for rather complex harmonic material and good rhythmic awareness (e.g. 2 bars of syncopated triplets and numerous 16th-note entrances after 16th-rests).

HOGG, Brian · **LLWYN ONN** · Brolge Music
· 4:05

An imaginative, colorful setting of "The Ash Grove." It begins with a short introduction utilizing fragments of the melody, along with delicate percussion. The melody itself is then stated in the clarinets, followed by trombones and euphonium, leading to the closing phrase in flutes and trumpets. A number of developmental variants of the melody are then presented, with a climactic statement of the closing phrase, in full band. The work concludes with a tranquil presentation of the introductory material. Highly recommended for development of tonal refinement, blend, phrasing sensitivity and nuance.

HOLSINGER, David · **ON A HYMN SONG OF PHILIP BLISS** · TRN
· 5:00

A well-crafted and effective setting of a lovely hymn tune in chorale-prelude format. It opens with the decorative material for the tune in clarinets and saxophones leading to the tune itself presented by solo horn and flute. The last phrase appears in the brass. After a short transition, the opening material returns, then the tempo increases as the brass choir makes a climactic statement of the closing phrase. The final section presents the short introduction and closes with the decorative material from the opening measures.

HOOK, James   SUITE FOR BAND   Wimbledon
Arr. William Schaefer   4:35
A very appealing set of three keyboard pieces by a little-known 18th-century English composer. (1) *OVERTURE* (Moderato, E^b, 3/4), stately yet energetic in clearly marked style, with effective use of echo dynamics. (2) *GAVOTTE* (Andante con moto, E^b, 4/4), a short movement with emphasis on woodwinds. (3) *FINALE "THE* HUNT" (Allegro, E^b, 6/8), a lively piece with fanfare-like hunting call figures, featuring trumpets and horns, contrasting choirs with tutti scoring; excellent for developing rhythmic precision in 6/8 meter.

HULL, Grant   CONTRASTS ON A THEME OF CORELLI   Wynn
                                                                                                   5:30
A very interesting, well-crafted work ,using a theme from a Violin Sonata. The theme is stated at the beginning in a slow, solemn setting (Largo, C minor, 3/4, quarter =76). The first variation is rather fast, flowing, agitated in mood. Variation 2 (Pesante, C minor, 4/4) is sustained and dirge-like in character. Variation 3 (Tempo rubato, E^b, 3/4) has the feeling of a minuet, with grace and restraint. The final variation (Allegretto, E^b, 3/8 in one) begins as a lilting scherzo, leading to the climax where the theme in 3/4 is combined with the scherzo in 9/8, providing a satisfying conclusion.

KARG-ELERT, Sigfrid   LITTLE ORGAN SUITE   Wynn
Arr. William Rhoads   4:30
An unusual and interesting set of three short pieces. (1) *SARABANDA* (Slowly, very sustained, F major, ¾), demanding legato playing, containing flowing lines with simple but well-textured counterpoints. (2) *SCHERZO* (Allegro, G minor, 2/4) – light, rhythmic, mostly staccato, with contrasting slurred 8th-16th figures and interesting use of percussion (temple blocks and tambourine) in a clock-like ostinato of 8th-notes. (3) *FUGHETTA* (Andante, poco marcato e maestro, E^b, 4/4) in broad, dignified style with effective use of dynamics and scoring contrasts.

KIRNBERGER, J.P.   BAROQUE SUITE   Ludwig
Arr. Eric Osterling   4:00
A fine example of Baroque dance forms by a relatively unknown composer-protégé of Bach. The opening movement, *RIGAUDON* (Animato, E^b, 4/4) is moderately fast and rhythmic with effective use of echo dynamics and varied articulations. The succeeding *MINUET* (B^b, 3/4) is graceful and dignified, with a lovely melody scored for flutes (solo oboe or trumpet on the repeat). The finale, *LA LUTINE* (Allegretto, F, 2/4) is light and staccato in style with a few rhythmic intricacies (e.g. dotted 8th-16th against 8th-two 16ths).

LA PLANTE, Pierre (Arr.)   A LITTLE FRENCH SUITE   Bourne
                                                                                                   6:15
Very attractive settings of several French folk-songs in three contrasting movements. (1) *MARCH* (Moderato, E^b, 2/4), utilizing "J'ai du bon tabac" and "Sur le pont d'Avignon". Technically simple, but with some intricacies of texture, especially counter-melodies. (2) *SERENADE* (Slow, E^b, 3/4). A gently flowing melody (Cadet Rouselle) appearing first in solo flute, joined by oboe and alto sax, then in tutti scoring, with short-long rhythm in accompaniment (in the manner of Satie's "Gymnopedies"). (3) *FINALE* (Allegro moderato, A^b-B^b, 6/8) – a jolly setting of the humorous song "Il etait un bergere".

LA PLANTE, Pierre   MUSIC FOR THE KING'S DELIGHT   Daehn
                                   (A Suite from Centuries Past)
A well-written and enjoyable suite based on four diverse piece. The first section is a rigaudon by Purcell – a sprightly, rhythmic dance using brass and woodwind in alternation, along with a brief tutti. The second uses an air from "The Beggar's Opera," opening with a flowing melody, then contrasted with a more detached and articulated idea. The third is a beautiful Irish melody set in flowing lines, while the finale is a 6/8 jig with the appropriate lilt and bounce. Highly recommended for all bands as an excellent example of varied settings.

LOTTI, Antonio   GRANT US THY MERCY   Southern
Arr. Charles Spinney   3:00
A very beautiful and expressive Renaissance motet (Largo, D minor – F major, 4/4), exquisitely scored. It opens with a short motive in lower woodwinds which is imitated in clarinets, saxes and flutes, reaching a homophonic conclusion in full woodwind choir. A second

phrase begins in trombones, answered by trumpets, then baritones and basses, concluding with a cadence in woodwinds. The opening music then returns in varied scoring, reaching an imposing climax in full band. The work concludes with a final statement of the second phrase, subsiding into a tranquil and serene conclusion. This work provides an excellent medium for developing all the fundamentals of tone, intonation, blend, balance, phrasing, dynamics and feeling of line within a technically simple yet musically rewarding framework. Highly recommended.

LUKE, Ray	**PRELUDE & MARCH**	Ludwig
		4:30

An appealing work for developing bands. It opens with an imposing, majestic prelude that utilizes well-conceived contrasts of scoring and style. The march features a marcato melody in trumpets with rhythmic accompaniment in horns and saxes, contrasted with a more aggressive phrase featuring dialogue between upper and lower voices. A short transition leads to the trio - a flowing legato line in lower-register clarinets. The break strain uses the contrasting phrase from the first section, and the march concludes with the opening melody in slower tempo.

LULLY, Jean Baptiste	**THE KING'S MUSICIANS**	Ludwig
Arr. Robert Barr		5:00

An excellent introduction to the music of the French Baroque and a fine transcription, this work provides numerous contrasts of style, mood, tempo and character. The opening *OVERTURE* (in G minor) is in two sections - a slow, stately introduction (Lento, 4/4) leading to a moderately fast, rhythmically marked allegro (3/4), more contrapuntal and technically demanding. At the end, the Lento returns, providing a strong, emphatic conclusion. The second movement, *FANFARE* (Allegretto, F major, 3/4) is like a minuet in character, with the feeling of both lift and weight that dance exemplifies. A short trio follows, scored for contrasting choirs in phrases (brass, woodwind, tutti, brass).

MARGOLIS, Bob (Arr.)	**FANFARE, ODE AND FESTIVAL**	Manhattan Beach
		4:00

A superb work in three well-contrasted movements. (1) *FANFARE* (Bright, B[b], 2/4) features a spirited, rhythmic 8th-note tune in 1st trumpets accompanied by brass choir, followed by a second phrase that is played by upper woodwinds. The first phrase returns in trumpets punctuated by woodwinds and percussion, concluding with a 4-bar coda featuring percussion. Requires good rhythm and clean articulation. (2) *ODE* (Gentle, G minor, 3/4) - a lovely, lyric slow movement scored in choirs - first trumpets, then upper woodwinds, then brass, etc. Technically very easy but demands well-focused pitch and tonal beauty and blend. (3) *FESTIVAL* (Happy, F major, 2/4) - a short introduction on unison F with timpani rhythm leads to a well-marked melody in unison trumpets with background material in woodwinds. The next phrase features a rhythmic staccato line with sustained notes in low brass and winds. The third phrase begins in clarinets (with short answers in flute, piccolo and oboe), concluded by trumpets, leading to the initial phrase in trumpets and upper woodwinds, second phrase tutti, then in brass with woodwinds answers. The coda, in faster tempo, features the opening phrase in full choir and tutti, closing with the beginning timpani rhythm and a soft, delicate cadence. Technically rather easy but requires good control of articulation, dynamics, and tone.

MCGINTY, Anne	**SEA SONG TRILOGY**	Boosey & Hawkes
		2:30

This is a creative and interesting set of three sea songs appropriate for those with one or two years' experience beyond the beginning band level. "Johnny Come Down to Hilo" opens the medley in Eb (4/4, quarter=132) with imaginative use of rhythm, articulation, contrasts, dynamics, tonal shifts and texture. A very smooth transition into "The Sailors Alphabet" (3/4, quarter=100) gives this work an effective contrast in both meter and style. The final song, "Sailing at High Tide" returns to the opening tempo but in 2/4 with a smart and snappy fife and drum-like introduction. This transitions into a march (now in F) with the trumpets performing the theme. Several color exchanges set up the conclusion with a strong percussion pattern essential to the final measures.

MENDELSSOHN, Felix	**CANTUS CHORALIS AND FUGUE**	Chappell
Arr. Louis Brunelli		3:30

A well-conceived transcription of an organ original (Sonata No. 6), this offers an excellent introduction to the early-Romantic Mendelssohn, along with his creative approach to Baroque idioms. The *CHORALE* (Moderato assai, D minor, 2/2), slightly abridged from the original, is broad and majestic in character, homophonic and chordal in texture, demanding good blend of tone, balance of voices and intonation; while the *FUGUE* (Poco allegro ma sostenuto, D minor, 3/4), moderate in tempo and technically easy, provides experience in playing independent melodic lines with shape, style and direction.

MOZART, W.A.	**ALLEGRO MOLTO (from DIVERTIMENTO, K.270)**	TRN
Arr. James Thornton		3:00

Another excellent realization of an original Mozart wind work by Thornton, technically somewhat more advanced than the *Andante Grazioso* listed previously. Requires good light staccato, some fluency in both legato and staccato passagework, sensitivity to dynamics and line, and good rhythmic control. (B^b major, 4/4 – should be played as 2/2, half=72-80).

MOZART,W.A.	**ALLELUIA**	Ludwig
Arr. Clifford Barnes		3:00

Another musical gem from Mozart's early career (he was 17 when he composed it, for soprano and orchestra), acceptably transcribed. It is jubilant and exultant in character, yet must be played with lightness and fluency. There are a few technical passages (16th-notes in woodwinds) and numerous dynamic contrasts in the customary classic manner. The solo vocal line is divided between cornet and upper woodwinds. It requires both beauty of tone and facility.

MOZART, W.A.	**AVE VERUM CORPUS**	Boosey & Hawkes
Arr. J. Kreines		3:15

Unlike other transcriptions of this beautiful work ,this version seeks to closely parallel the original by using the trumpets and trombones as a choir to duplicate the choral parts. Although not technically difficult, it requires control, beauty of tone, feeling of long phrases and sensitivity to blend and balance, while maintaining a slow but flowing tempo.

MOZART, W.A.	**VIENNESE SONATINA**	Ludwig
Arr. Walter Beeler		4:00

Two movements from an original wind work (Divertimento, K. 439b) excellently expanded for band, providing another classical-period work for young players. The *ANDANTE* (B^b, 4/4) is stately, dignified and legato, while the *ALLEGRO* (B^b, 3/4)is sparkling and light, but with both lyric and serious elements providing effective contrasts. Technical demands are limited - what is required is sense of style (particularly classical staccato articulation), control of dynamic contrasts, legato in lyric passages, refinement and sensitivity to phrasing, as well as well-focused pitch and tonal centers.

NELHYBEL, Vaclav	**RITUAL**	Theodore Presser
		5:30

A remarkable and rare work in which the challenge of the percussion parts match the difficulty of the winds. It is very unusual for a composition of this quality and level to contain such characteristics. The first sixteen measures are for percussion alone (4/4 quarter note =144) in which layers of colors entering at varying times build until the first brass unison on B-flat. Woodwind and brass colors alternate rhythmic themes with quick and appropriate percussion punctuations. Although there are several families of textures with unison rhythmic ideas, the rhythmic independence of the brass, woodwind and percussion choirs are paramount. Strong accents, color contrasts and simple syncopation permeate this score. An extended *Vivo* section, using similar contrasts of texture, brings this clever work to an exciting and thunderous close. May be out of print but well worth the effort to locate and perform for young to medium-level ensembles.

NELHYBEL, Vaclav	**SUITE FROM BOHEMIA**	Canyon
		8:00

A very colorful and effective work which evokes medieval Bohemia in four strongly contrasted movements. (1) *PROCESSION TO THE CASTLE* (Allegro marcato, C minor, 4/4), alternating brass and percussion with woodwinds in simple quarter-note material articulated three different ways. (2) *FOLK TALE* (Moderato, Bb mixolydian, 4/4) – soft legato woodwinds contrasted with forte marcato brass. (3) *TOURNAMENT* (Con fuoco, 2/2) – fast, driving, intense, featuring brass and percussion contrasted with woodwind interludes. At the end both brass and winds are combined in a thrilling climax. (4) *ROUND DANCE* (Allegretto, Bb mixolydian, 3/4 in one) beginning softly in percussion alone, then clarinets in a lilting, graceful melody answered by a declamatory brass phrase. The two ideas are then restated in different scorings, culminating with the marcato idea in a final burst of speed and energy in full band. Demands a wide variety of style, dynamics, articulations, within technically modest limits – and adept, intelligent percussion capable of playing rhythmically independent parts (including mallets).

PLOYHAR, James	**CASTLE, LOCH AND HEATH**	Wynn
		4:20

A very tasteful, musically sensitive setting of three English folk-tunes. (1) *THE BONNY LIGHTER-BOY* (Allegretto, D minor, 6/8) – a jaunty, lilting tune presented in two settings, the second of which is in canon, with a pulsating rhythm and a slower coda. (2) *SCARBOROUGH FAIR* – not the popular one but the authentic old tune – (Andante moderato, G minor, 3/4) – a very flowing legato setting with melody in upper winds, then in trumpet and baritone. (3) *HIGH GERMANY* (Alla marcia, D minor, 4/4) – a bold declamatory melody (used in Vaughan Williams' Folk Song Suite) in marked style, with melody in brass and counter-melody in woodwinds, concluding with a short climactic coda.

PRAETORIUS, Michael	**TERPSICHORE SUITE**	Ludwig
Arr. Conrad Ross		4:30

A worthwhile transcription of five short movements from a 16th-century collection of instrumental dances, in contrasting styles and tempos. The first, a stately *BRANSLE*, is followed without pause by a lively and energetic *PHILOU* which utilizes dynamics and scoring contrasts. The third movement is a stately *GALLIARD* which uses scoring changes on the repeats. The fourth, *BALLET DES BACCHANALES*, reprises the character of the *PHILOU*. The work closes with a majestic and noble *BALLET*. Technically not difficult, but requires sensitivity to the contrasting styles, balance and clarity of rhythm and texture.

PURCELL, Henry	**SONGS AND DANCES**	Boosey & Hawkes
Arr. Arnold Freed		4:00

An excellent selection of four contrasting excerpts from the stage work "Dioclesian". The first (Con brio, B^b, 2/2) is a vigorous rhythmic dance featuring numerous dynamic changes and contrasts of choir scoring. The second (Allegretto, E^b, 3/4) is a flowing and melodic *COUNTRY DANCE*. The third (Andante espressivo, D minor, 3/4) features a poignantly lyric melody with a contrasting phrase using dialogue scoring. The finale (Spirited, B^b, 3/4 in one) is a lively fanfare using both choir and tutti scoring. Technically modest in requirements but excellent for developing all aspects of musicianship.

REED, Alfred	**CHORALE PRELUDE IN E MINOR**	Southern
		4:00

A worthwhile introduction to the chorale-prelude form and style for young players. Reed uses a Bach chorale ("Meine Seele Erhebet") as the basis for the work, which is slow and sustained in character (Lento, 4/4, quarter=54), but which also contains flowing legato contrapuntal lines. The emphasis is on musical continuity of line, balance of voices and blend and beauty of tone. Technically rather easy, with comfortable ranges, but demands intelligent musicianship and sensitivity.

RHOADS, William (Arr.)	**THREE RUSSIAN CAMEOS**	TRN
		6:30

A very attractive and interesting set of lesser-known works, tastefully arranged. (1) *FOR COSSACKS ONLY* by Glinka (Allegretto, G minor, 2/4), is a lively dance using dynamic contrasts. (2) *ELEGY FOR A FALLEN COMRADE* by Maykeper (Slowly, G minor, 4/4), a dirge-like piece, emphasizing low-register sonorities in the opening but building to a heroic and intense climax. (3) *GAMES PEOPLE PLAY* by Kabalevsky (Allegro moderato, G minor, 2/2), like a scherzo in character, with contrasts between a block-chord accented motive in brass and a flowing figure in woodwinds.

ROOT, Thomas	**POLLY OLIVER**	Kjos
		5:00

An interesting and imaginative work using a lovely British folk-song, in an approach that combines the rhapsody and variation format. After a short introduction (Andantino, Eb), which uses the closing phrase of the tune, the melody is stated in solo clarinet with a sustained-chord accompaniment. The closing phrase again appears as at the beginning, leading to the second statement with melody in clarinets and oboe, counter-melody in horns and alto sax and accompanying harmony in low woodwinds and brass. The next setting

(Allegretto, 3/4) features an ostinato rhythm in low brass and percussion while trumpets present an embellished version of the melody. A new idea derived from segments of the theme now appears in horns, sax and baritone and is developed and elaborated to a climax, subsiding into the next setting (Freely), more tranquil and reflective in character, with upper woodwinds stating harmonized melody over F pedal in bass instruments with horn and sax counter-melody. This builds to a final statement of the tune, now in its original form with rich harmony and texture. The final phrase is extended, leading to a short poetic coda with a sustained C chord over which flutes ramble using a fragment of the melody. Technically rather easy but requires intelligent listening and rhythmic accuracy in fast sections, good tone and balance in lyric ones.

SHELDON, Robert (Arr.)   **BLACK IS THE COLOR**   Alfred
2:50

A very moving arrangement of a familiar Appalachian folk song most likely transplanted from Scotland. The work is very expressive with several shifts of mood and contrasting textures. Valuable for those with very limited experience with legato style shaping phrases and matching tonal centers. Expertly scored, it contains appropriate percussion battery along with alternating wind families who perform the melody. It ends tutti, but very quietly with a surprise harmonic shift. Highly recommended.

SHELDON, Robert   **WEST HIGHLANDS SOJOURN**   Birch Island
5:30

An attractive 3-movement suite featuring folk-like tunes (all original). It opens with "Stow-on-the-wold" – a moderately fast 2/4, the first theme of which appears in flute, clarinet, and trumpet – contrasted with a dotted-rhythm motive. The second movement, "Bradford Ballade", is slow and gently lyrical, with a simple but appealing melody made very interesting by effective contrasts in scoring, texture, and mood. The final movement, "On Derwentwater" is a lively 6/8 comprised of two contrasting ideas.

SMITH, Charles   **SUITE FOR BAND**   ProArt
4:30

An excellent piece with good variety of style, mood and character, using modality to great effect. The first movement, *PASTORAL*, is very slow and serene (2/2, half=40) with transparent scoring (no trumpets, limited low brass), requiring good control of tone and legato style. The succeeding *MARCH* (6/8) is vivacious and lively, with a lilting rhythm and jaunty tune in woodwinds and a brilliant "street march" episode featuring brass. The third, *SONG*, is slow and lyrical (4/4, quarter=60) with the melody first in the trumpet, then the bass instruments. The finale, *CAPRICCIO* (Jocosely, quarter=126) is brilliant and animated, with some technical 16th-note passages in upper winds and rhythmically active brass.

SPEARS, Jared   **A WIND RIVER PORTRAIT**   Southern
3:30

A well-organized work with effective use of motivic construction and development. The opening section is in fast tempo (mostly 2/4, quarter=120), emphasizing a three-note motive and its rhythmic shape, developed at some length and leading to a slow, expressive section (3/4, quarter=60) with a long flowing melody, stated first in woodwinds, then brass, rising a rich-textured climax leading to a return of the opening section, varied in shape. The introductory measures return to provide a short but emphatic coda.

STALTER, Todd   **TWO RENAISSANCE SKETCHES**   Alfred
2:30

This glorious and original Renaissance-like work is very appropriate for ensembles with students possessing one or two years of experience. In two parts, the first section is a courtly dance (F, 4/4, quarter note= 88), which begins with a percussion introduction and leads to alternating tutti and sectional wind presentations. Simple quarter note and eighth note patterns using skillful dynamics, articulations and percussion scoring complete this section centering on G. The second section, a jig (C minor using modal harmonies, quarter note =104), is lively and offers each family of instruments a fragment of the theme. Superb material for introducing young students to Renaissance-style music. Requires six percussion players.

STANDRIDGE, Randall **DANSE BOHEMIEN** Grand Mesa

3:00

This is a terrific showcase for medium-level ensembles inspired by the Pas Redouble style. Opening in unison rhythms (f minor, quarter note = 160+) this dance uses several volume and color contrasts to vary the theme. Important euphonium and xylophone solos contribute to this exciting melody. A short shift to d minor using woodwinds colors acts as segue back to f minor. A recapitulation of the A theme ensues and a short coda brings the work to a thrilling finale. Modestly demanding in all parts but skilled euphonium and mallet players are required.

STARER, Robert **FANFARE, PASTORALE AND SERENADE** Marks

2:40

One of the finest works written for younger players, using technically easy materials in imaginative and fresh ways. The opening *FANFARE* (Fairly fast, B^b, 2/4) features a legato but rhythmic melody in upper winds, lightly accompanied by brass and saxes. This is followed by a section featuring a delicate staccato figure in upper winds answered by a legato motive in low winds and brass. The opening section then returns to conclude the movement. The *PASTORALE* (Gently flowing, C minor, 3/4) presents a short lyric phrase in woodwinds answered by a cadential closing in the brass. These two ideas are extended with an imitative treatment of the first phrase building to a climax using the two ideas. The *SERENADE* (Fast and light, B^b, 4/4), features the percussion section providing a ground bass with light staccato brass and a simple legato phrase in woodwinds, varied in length and rhythmic shape.

STONE, David (Arr.) **THREE ENGLISH DANCES** Boosey &Hawkes
Transcr. John Boyd 4:20

A superb transcription and arrangement of three lovely dance-movements from John Playford's 17th-century collection *"The English Dancing Master"*. (1) *ALL IN A GARDEN GREEN* (Moderato, F major, 2/2). Rather stately and dignified, yet well-articulated and rhythmic, making excellent use of terraced dynamics and choir scoring. (2) *DRIVE THE COLD WINTER AWAY* (Andante con moto, D minor, 6/8). A beautiful lyric mood-picture, requiring flowing legato, refinement of tone and intonation, musical sensitivity. Scoring is transparent, with important solos for clarinet and horn. (3) *NEWCASTLE* (Allegro moderato, F, 2/2). Rhythmic and vital, opening in staccato style requiring clean but refined articulation, contrasted with a legato idea. The opening idea returns in marked tenuto style, leading to a final statement of the legato idea in climactic fashion. While this piece is technically fairly easy, it nonetheless demands considerable sensitivity to dynamics, articulation, phrasing, style, and nuance. Highly recommended for all levels and worthy of performance on any concert.

STUART, Hugh **THREE AYRES FROM GLOUCESTER** Shawnee

4:15

A delightful and appealing suite of three contrasting pieces in English folk-song style. The first (Allegretto, F, 2/2) demands a light, lilting approach and features solo clarinet and trumpet with lightly-scored accompaniment alternating with more full-scored passages. The second (Andante, B^b-E^b, 3/4) features a warmly lyric melody in horns (cued alto sax), with a faster full-scored middle section. The last (Allegro, D minor, 6/8) is a well-marked, rhythmic peasant dance with nice contrasts of scoring between woodwind and brass choirs. An excellent piece for development of all musical fundamentals and sense of styles.

SUSATO, TIELMAN **A RENAISSANCE REVEL** Grand Mesa
Arr. Kenneth Singleton **(GREATER DANCE HITS OF 1550)**

An excellent compilation of five contrasting dances popular in 16th-century Europe; well-scored and edited for the modern band.

1. La Morisque – a moderately fast dance with well-marked rhythm
2. Pavane – a moderate legato-style dance with nice contrasts of scoring between woodwinds and brass
3. Ronde – a lively, energetic dance scored for brass and percussion.
4. Saltarello – a triple-meter variant of the Ronde scored for woodwinds and percussion
5. Another Ronde in faster tempo featuring a bright, energetic melody

| SUSATO, Tielman | BATTLE PAVANE | Manhattan Beach |
| Arr. Bob Margolis | | 3:00 |

A marvelous piece, simple yet epic and dignified, with elemental musical motives and harmony, put together to create an intense buildup and stunning climax. Margolis' scoring makes the musical effect possible - it is a brilliant job. Requires beauty of tone, well-focused intonation, legato tonguing style, solidity of rhythm and sensitivity to dynamics. Highly recommended, (B^b, quarter=76).

| SWEENEY, Michael | ANCIENT VOICES | Hal Leonard |
| | | 3:25 |

A very interesting and effective piece using a number of contemporary devices and techniques (including blowing air through the instrument and tapping on music stands), and extensive yet expressive use of percussion. It opens with a slow, mysterious section presenting short chant-like motives accompanied by clusters and modal harmony, then proceeds to a fast, driving rhythmic section. The opening mood returns briefly, leading to a climactic statement of the fast section.

| SWEENEY, Michael (Arr.) | CELTIC AIR AND DANCE | Hal-Leonard |
| | | 3:05 |

A very imaginative and colorful arrangement using Celtic material for younger bands. Opening in C minor slowly quarter note = 80 in 4/4 a short tutti introduction is established. The percussion introduces a sorrowful melody played by the flute and accompanied by the woodwind choir. Tutti sections incorporating dynamics, phrase and articulative contrasts answer this. A faster section ensues, (quarter note =116), again using percussion as a transition but evolving into a pipe-and-drum-like setting. After a four measure soli drum cadence the final and even faster section is presented in G minor (quarter note = 126-132). This march becomes more intense both rhythmically and harmonically and concludes with a driving percussion line into the unison rhythmic tag.

| TCHAIKOVSKY, P.I. | ALBUM FOR THE YOUNG OP. 39 | Curnow Music |
| Arr. James Curnow | | 5:00 |

A delightful arrangement of four movements of the original twenty-four movement piece for young pianists by the Russian master. "Morning Sun" (3/4, Sustained, quarter note=72 in F) is very expressive and lyrical containing simple rhythms, articulations and dynamics. "Winter Morning" is 'Fast' (quarter note=120) and light with transparent scoring using exchanges of colors for contrast. "Mama" is very similar to the opening movement (key, meter and style) but uses new material, which is more contrapuntal and incorporates several shifts of tonality with accidentals. The final movement, "*Winter March,*" is a short and majestic march in B^b (2/4, quarter note = 112) using dotted eighth sixteenth notes and an appropriate DC and Coda. It is the only movement that ends loud. Percussion scoring is intelligent (5-6 players on 8 instruments) and adds to the interest of this simple work. Although the technical aspects are certainly within most first year students' ability, the length of all four movements may elevate this to the next level of difficulty. However, the musical and educational aspects make this selection a very good choice.

| VAUGHAN WILLIAMS, R. | THREE DORSET SONGS | Daehn |
| Arr. Douglas Stotter | | 6:30 |

Three original songs written in folk-tune style, originally for voice and piano, sensitively and intelligently scored for band.
1. BLACKMORE ON THE STOUR – A jaunty rhythmic tune with a straightforward accompaniment. Good contrasts of scoring between woodwinds and brass
2. THE WINTER'S WILLOW – a nostalgic lyrical song with a beautiful, simple melodic line and richly-varied harmonic accompaniment
3. BOY JOHNNY – a martial yet rather somber song in a minor mode with changing meters and rhythmic configurations

| VINSON, Johnny | THREE CZECH FOLK SONGS | Hal Leonard |
| | | 5:25 |

A very refreshing and richly imaginative arrangement of three Czech folk songs. I. "Walking at Night" begins quietly with tutti scoring in legato style (4/4, quarter note = 72 in B^b). The theme evolves into several color combinations with clear expressive phrase patterns. A contrasting gallop alternates (2/4 quarter note = 144) with the opening passage before concluding the movement with a crisp and exciting coda. "Meadows Green" is a lyrical and expressive movement (quarter note = 63, in E^b) with clearly marked phrases using alternating wind choirs and sensitive dynamics. The final movement, "Spring, The Madcap" is an energizing gallop

(2/4, quarter note = 144, in F) using driving themes accompanied by contrasting march-like fragments. A glorious setting for percussion and flute soli introduces several treatments of the theme including a short canon. The final section (Joyously, quarter note=160-168, in A^b) brings the work to a sparkling finish! Expertly scored percussion requiring 6-7 players.

VINSON, Johnny (Arr.)	**TUDOR SUITE**	Musicworks
		3:10

This wonderfully orchestrated suite features three important composers from the British royal dynasty - Thomas Morley, William Byrd and Giles Farnaby. The first movement, "My Bonnie Lass," begins in E^b major, 4/4 quarter note = 144 with a tutti rhythmic statement. A short syncopated and imitative brass statement leads back to the tutti sonority using sustained lines with percussion repeating the opening rhythmic material. This is repeated and leads to a colorful 3/4 section that cadences on an incomplete E^b major triad. "Fortune," the second movement, is slower (4/4 quarter note =116) and more sustained. Beginning in F minor, the brass choir and percussion perform short imitative statements that are augmented by the entire wind section. This subsides into sustained woodwind choirs and metallic percussion with simple harmonic and melodic ideas. The brass rejoins the ensemble color maintaining the sostenuto style to end the movement. "A Toye," the final movement in F minor quarter note = 144, is more joyous in nature. The opening melody is performed by the upper winds with tutti accompaniment (including simple but full and very smart percussion scoring). Shifts of brass and woodwind sonorities ensue and an eventual return to a tutti texture but using syncopation to ornament the melody. Overlapping eighth notes and a quickly moving progression bring this work to an exciting close. A terrific work to develop style, independence and execution of simple syncopation for younger bands.

VAUGHAN WILLIAMS, Ralph	**FLOURISH FOR WIND BAND**	Oxford
		1:40

A very short and technically simple work that has considerable grandeur, sweep and majesty, as well as real beauty of harmony, richness of texture and effective dynamic contrasts. Excellent for development of ensemble sonority, balance, blend, dynamic control, intonation and feeling of line, phrase and style within technically easy material. Highly recommended for all levels - particularly good for opening concerts. (N.B. Trombones 1&2 are in tenor clef).

VAUGHAN WILLIAMS, Ralph	**WELL MET, MY OWN TRUE LOVE**	Daehn
Arr. Larry Daehn		3:55

An expertly arranged setting of this charming Vaughan Williams original folksong. A weeping statement in the opening woodwind choir, 4/4 in C minor, quarter note= 54, provides the character for the entire work. This gem offers ensembles of all levels opportunities for expression in colors, volume and harmonic motion. All phrases are clearly notated and contain logical contrasts. Simple counterpoint, as outlined by the melodic content, is almost exclusively assigned to various wind families. The alterations of the repeated melody are authentic and separate this work from many arrangements of folksongs. The result is a lyrical picture of simple rhythms and melody shapes that vary in color and volume to produce a satisfying expressivity. The final section evolves into a short canon that eventually arrives on a tutti C major triad. Highly recommended.

VERDI, Giuseppe	**LAUDE ALLA VERGINE MARIA**	Barnhouse
Arr. Barbara Buehlman		4:00

A fine transcription of a beautiful choral work (Andante, F major, 4/4). The music is well-balanced between chordal and contrapuntal textures, while scoring uses small groups, choirs and tutti in varying fashion. Technically easy, with comfortable ranges, it demands good control of tone, legato phrasing and wide dynamic range (*ppp - fff*) as well as careful listening for intonation (especially the numerous unisons and octaves), sensitivity to balance and awareness of relationships between voices. Highly recommended.

VINSON, Johnnie	**NETTLETON**	Hal Leonard
		3:30

A beautifully scored, attractive setting of the American hymn tune. It opens with an introduction featuring parts of the tune, leading to the first statement of the melody in horns, with the concluding phrase in tutti scoring. The next setting is in upper woodwinds with brass accompaniment. A short contrasting passage using materials from the introduction follows. The next setting features solo oboe with clarinet choir accompaniment, followed by woodwind choir in the closing phrase. The final section features trumpets on the first half of the tune and woodwinds on the second half. The concluding coda uses the opening phrase with a slow tag. Highly recommended for any band to perform as an excellent example of hymn-tune setting appropriate for any concert.

WATKIN, Andrew   **THE CITY OF LIGHTS**   Scherzando
                                                                              2:30

This is a wonderful showcase (2/4, E^b major, quarter=168) using simple rhythms and scale-like figures to create a "Can-can" effect. Various passages using contrasting volume combined with colorful scoring make this a welcome addition to the literature. A short and easy xylophone feature, doubled in flutes, acts as a segue back to the opening theme. This is a very exciting yet relatively easier Gallop (depending on tempo).

● ●

BACH, J.S.   **IF THOU BE NEAR**   FitzSimon
Arr. R.L. Moehlmann   3:00

BACH, J.S.   **BIST DU BEI MIR**   Barnhouse
Arr. Alfred Reed
Two different but equally valid treatments of Bach's famous melody.

BARTOK, Bela   **RHAPSODY (FROM "FOR CHILDREN")**   Alfred
Arr. Frank Erickson   3:00
A very attractive alternative to other works from the same source, using two contrasting ideas – a slow, flowing lyric line and a lively staccato tune.

BUXTEHUDE, Dietrich   **ARIA AND GIGUE**   Kendor
Arr. Philip Gordon   3:35
The Aria features a lovely slow melody, simply harmonized; the Gigue is light, lilting and graceful. A good example of lesser-known Baroque literature by a major pre-Bach figure.

CARTER, Charles   **THREE PIECES IN ANTIQUE STYLE**   C. Fischer
                                                                      3:45

A set of pieces written in various styles of 16th-century contrapuntal music. Technically easy, but demands rhythmic independence and ensemble precision.

DAVIS, Albert Oliver   **FANTASIE ON A DANISH THEME**   Byron-Douglas
An attractive work providing interesting and imaginative treatments of a lovely folk-song.

ELGAR, Sir Edward   **AS TORRENTS IN SUMMER**   Ludwig
Arr. Albert Oliver Davis   3:00
A lovely choral work, well-transcribed. Very lyric and poetic in character, with emphasis on tone, phrasing and expressive style.

GORDON, Philip (Arr.)   **LOUIS XIV SUITE**   Belwin
                                                                      5:10

A somewhat more advanced alternative to the *FRENCH MASTERS SUITE* listed previously, also using three contrasting pieces (by Couperin, Lully and Campra).

GRUNDMAN, Clare   **AMERICAN FOLK RHAPSODY NO. 1**   Boosey &Hawkes
                                                                      6:15

A very effective and appealing medley, technically modest but requiring sensitivity and taste.

GRUNDMAN, Clare   **ENGLISH SUITE**   Boosey &Hawkes
An interesting suite of folk-tune settings, longer and somewhat more challenging than the *LITTLE ENGLISH SUITE* listed earlier – both technically and musically.

HANDEL, G.F.   **FUGHETTA**   Boosey &Hawkes
Arr. Lloyd Conley   2:00
A good example of the fugue form for younger bands, acceptably scored. (N.B. Indicated tempo seems too slow – should probably be half=80 rather than quarter=120).

HODKINSON, Sydney   TOWER   Presser
7:00

A valuable contribution to the new-music repertory, using contemporary notational devices. Technically not difficult, but requires willingness to approach the new, with fresh ears and minds.

HULL, Grant   EUROPEAN FOLK TUNE SUITE   Shawnee
4:30

A very enjoyable and imaginatively arranged set of three contrasting folk tunes.

HULL, Grant   VARIATIONS   Wynn
7:00

A somewhat inconsistent and lengthy work which nonetheless has much interest and value for young bands. Worth investigating.

KABALEVSKY, Dmitri   KABALEVSKY SUITE   Wynn
Arr. Grant Hull   4:00

Three short piano pieces, well-arranged , with effective contrasts of style. (N.B. The third one is the same piece as the third movement of *SUITE IN MINOR MODE* previously listed).

LULLY, Jean Baptiste   PRELUDE TO ALCESTE   Warner
Arr. Marcel Frank

Another excellent example of French Baroque, serving as a fine alternative or supplement to *THE KING'S MUSICIANS*.

LATHAM, William   DODECAPHONIC SET   Barnhouse

Valuable for introducing the 12-tone technique to young players, though the music is somewhat contrived and stilted.

MUFFAT, Georg   SARABANDE AND FANTASIA   Ludwig
Arr. Eric Osterling

A good example of German late-baroque style. The transcription is somewhat heavy on doubling but is acceptable.

OSMON, Leroy   HEBREW FOLK SONG SUITE NO.2   TRN

Very attractive and well-scored settings of lovely melodies.

RHOADS, William (Arr.)   TWO NOVELLAS   Ludwig
4:00

Two contrasting pieces *(Song of the Creuse* by Franck; *Hobby-Horse* by Tchaikovsky), well arranged.

ROOT, Thomas   THE LONE WILD BIRD   Kjos

A lyric, rich-textured work that demonstrates imagination and taste, though a bit long.

SCHUMANN, Robert   LITTLE SCHUMANN SET   Manhattan Beach
Arr. Doug Hartzell

Two lovely song-settings, sensitively scored. Technically easy but musically subtle, especially the first one.

STUART, Hugh   A HYMN FOR BAND   Shawnee
3:30

An effective work, designed to develop legato, expressive and sustained long plying for younger bands, emphasizing development of intonation, ensemble sonority and phrase feeling. No percussion.

STUART, Hugh   THREE SONGS FROM SUSSEX   Shawnee

A good alternative to *THREE AYRES FROM GLOUCESTER* listed previously. Similar in style and character.

41

TCHAIKOVSKY, P.I.

Arr. Jim Curnow	**ALBUM FOR THE YOUNG**	Jenson
Arr. Bob Margolis	**TCHAIKOVSKY ALBUM**	Manhattan Beach
Arr. Andrew Balent	**TCHAIKOVSKY SUITE**	Studio/PR

These short suites are all taken from a children's piano collection *(Album for the Young)*. Some of the pieces are duplicated, but all three are excellent arrangements of charming and attractive literature.

TELEMANN, G.P.   **DANSES ELEGANTES**   Presser
Arr. Philip Gordon   3:45

Three contrasting dance-movements by the prolific Baroque master, well-arranged.

TICHELI, FRANK   **SIMPLE GIFTS**   Manhattan Beach

Very well-written and enjoyable settings of four shaker melodies.

TYRA, Thomas   **TWO GAELIC FOLK SONGS**   Barnhouse
5:20

Attractive settings of two well-known Irish melodies *(Molly Malone; Wearing of the Green),* both providing musical and technical challenges to this level (key signatures, exposed solos, etc.).

WAGNER, Richard   **TRAUME**   Rubank
Arr. Barbara Buehlman   3:20

A good example of the Wagner style for this level, with rich harmony and expressive melodic line, requiring beauty of tone, pitch support (for long-sustained note values) and legato phrasing.

WHITNEY, Maurice   **PRELUDE ON "GREENSLEEVES"**   Alfred

An imaginative setting of the familiar tune, using a wide variety of styles and scorings.

• •

ADLER, Samuel **A LITTLE NIGHT AND DAY MUSIC** C. Fischer
7:00

An interesting attempt to merge contemporary compositional techniques and notations with technically modest materials. The opening *Night Music* is highly atmospheric, slow, mysterious, with cluster effects, improvisatory passages and imaginative use of color and tone. The succeeding *Day Music* is fast, energetic, primarily rhythmic in character, with many contrasts of dynamics and scoring. Effective cross-cuing and scoring substitution suggestions are provided. Requires musical intelligence and receptiveness to contemporary sounds and style from both conductor and players.

BACH, J.S. **PRELUDE AND FUGUE IN E MINOR** Studio/PR
Arr. Carroll DeCamp 4:00

This is the same work as the Prelude and Fugue in F minor listed above (Medium Easy), but left in its original key. This transcription is equally valid and effective, but the key of E minor poses a challenge that is worth attempting, since the music is superb.

BACH, J.S. **COME, SWEET DEATH** **THUS DO YOU FARE, MY JESUS** Barnhouse
MY HEART IS FILLED WITH LONGING **MY JESUS! OH, WHAT ANGUISH**
Arr. Alfred Reed 3:00 – 5:00

These settings of chorale-melodies are among the most beautiful and affecting in the literature and have been superbly arranged and transcribed. They are technically not difficult, but demand great control of intonation, attack and release; tonal beauty, sustained slow playing, sensitivity to phrase, line, and expression and great care for blending of tone and balancing of voice. All are strongly recommended.

BACH, J.S. **JESU, JOY OF MAN'S DESIRING** C. Fischer
Arr. Erik Leidzen 4:00

A familiar chorale-prelude (from *Cantata #147*) with the chorus parts scored for brass choir very successfully. Requires smoothness and flowing legato style in the 9/8 woodwind line, and richness of sonority, balance and blend in brass.

BACH, J.S. **O MENSCH, BEWEIN DEIN SUNDE GROSS** Jenson
Arr. Percy Grainger 3:00

A magnificent work, intensely poignant in its sorrow, yet profoundly eloquent (Slowly flowing, E^b, 4/4), in one of the greatest transcriptions of any Bach work made for any medium. Provided with "elastic scoring" (any combination of instruments can be used provided that each voice is covered - detailed in the preface to the score), this work requires the utmost in legato style, beauty of tone, blend, intonation, flow of line and phrase, and expressiveness. Should be played by all groups capable of handling its musical demands. Strongly recommended. (N.B. Bach's ornamentation is written out very intelligently and musically).

BACH, J.S. **FESTIVAL PRELUDE** Manhattan Beach
Arr. Bob Margolis 3:00

A very creative and imaginative transcription of one of Bach's "Little" Preludes that make striking use of instrumentation, doublings, articulations and dynamics. Though technically not difficult, the musical subtleties and nuance are challenging – especially phrase continuity and control of dynamics. In particular, requires good control in brass, care in balancing and blend , timpani with a good sense of pitch.

BARNES, James **TRAIL OF TEARS** Southern
6:15

A very emotional and moving work depicting the tragic death of 4,000 Native Americans who were marched, by force, 1,500 miles from their sovereign land. The work opens in 4/4, d minor, with a slow and solemn timpani and flute solo. Saxophone and bassoon solos (cued tenor sax) ensue, using a similar Native American motive both singularly and harmonized. Muted brass and metallic percussion introduce a new theme by woodwinds and French horns. A fast contrasting section (Allegro vivo non troppo, quarter = 120-128) follows, using a variation on the opening theme including mixed meters. A field drum signals a third section, which climaxes into a Meno Mosso. Two off-stage trumpets, in a cadenza-like format, alternate with echoes of the bugle "charge calls."

Members of the ensemble are directed to speak specific passages of a prayer in the Native American language. This builds into a very powerful Adagio, which is much more sonorous and optimistic in nature, into the final chords in D major. Although not technically demanding, it does require rhythmic independence, adept soloists and a competent and sensitive percussion section of five to eight members.

BARTOK, Bela	**PETITE SUITE**	Boosey & Hawkes
Arr. Charles Cushing		10:00

A very attractive selection of seven short piano pieces, idiomatically scored. They include: (1) *WALACHIAN DANCE* – lively and energetic. (2) *MOURNING SONG* – slow and sad, delicately scored, with many solos and unaccompanied parts (3) *UKRANIAN SONG* – moderately fast and rhythmic, with varied articulations (4) *SLOW MELODY* – using a syncopated melody and legato ostinato (5) *BAG PIPE* – very fast and rhythmic (6) *MELODY* – for clarinet choir alone (7) *HUNGARIAN DANCE* – fast and marcato, with sudden changes of tempo and dynamics. Though technically not difficult, this work requires a 1st trumpet with good upper register, strong secure solo playing (oboe, trombones, saxes, etc.) in *MOURNING SONG*, good rhythmic understanding and control (inverted rhythms, offbeat playing, syncopations, etc.), and general good musical sensitivity that transcends the technical demands.

BENSON, Warren	**NIGHT SONG**	Chappell
		6:30

A highly atmospheric, evocative and poetic work, with fine sense of color and texture. While the parts are technically easy, much of the musical content is carried by solo players (baritone, clarinet, horn, flute) playing in sustained, expressive style; the tempo is extremely slow (eighth=80-90) and the dynamic level is very soft most of the time. Also there is considerable demand for delicate, sensitive percussion playing, and accompanying parts must play sostenuto at soft levels. Can be played by any group capable of fulfilling its musical demands.

BOYCE, William	**OVERTURE TO THE NEW YEAR 1758**	Shawnee
Arr. William Schaefer		6:15

This is an attractive and enjoyable work that has been generally neglected. The first section (Fast, spirited, C major, 2/4) is lively and rhythmically vital, requiring good facility and control for clarinets and trumpets and sensitivity to balance and dynamics. The second section opens with a slow, short introduction (Larghetto, 3/4) that leads to a bright, spirited allegro (C major, 6/8), requiring a lightness and buoyancy of rhythms and clarity of articulation (especially in bass instruments). The third movement (a march that actually belongs to another work by Boyce) is festive yet regal in character (Allegro moderato, E^b, 2/2), featuring dotted rhythms.

BRAHMS, Johannes	**TWO CHORALES**	Associated
Arr. Arthur Christman		5:30

A sensitively scored, effectively presented transcription of two organ chorale-preludes. The first, "O World I Now Must Leave Thee" (Moderato, F major, 4/4), uses the echo effect to great advantage by shifting between large and small groups. The second, "Lo, How a Rose E'er Blooming" (cf. *MEDITATIONS ON A CHORALE* listed previously – Medium Easy) (Moderato, F major, 6/4) uses contrasts between choirs. Both demand considerable musical sensitivity, careful attention to blend and balance, and a fine horn section with full range and flexibility.

BRUCKNER, Anton	**ANTIPHON**	Presser
Arr. Philip Gordon		4:30

A beautiful, rich-textured, harmonically subtle, expressive work in slow tempo (Moderato misterioso, C minor, 4/4) superbly scored. The opening section is scored for brass alone, beginning with a soft chorale-like phrase in trombones, baritone and tuba which is answered by a short dotted-rhythm call in trumpet and trombone, with a closing phrase in trumpet and horns. This leads to another chorale phrase, more dramatic in character, with abrupt change from pp to f, gradually fading into a quiet cadence from which the woodwinds emerge. The rest of the work deals with all these ideas, reaching an intense climax for full band with brass in chorale style and woodwinds playing 8ths embroidery. The mood subsides to one of hushed mystery, in transparent scoring. This work requires both musical maturity and technical control of sustained, soft playing, gentle attacks and feathered releases, as well as finesse of tone, ability to sustain phrase and line, security in exposed passages (there are few tuttis). Highly recommended as an excellent example of Bruckner's mature style.

BRUCKNER, Anton   **AVE MARIA (1882 SETTING)**   Daehn
Trans. Joseph Kreines   4:10

A very moving and effective transcription of a sacred work from Bruckner's matures years. The simple opening is dark (Andante Sostenuto, 2/2, half note =42-46, F major) yet rich and imitates the original solo voice in clever grouped and solo textures. Although technically simple the extreme use of long phrases and legato style are paramount. Several phrases contain sequential dissonant and resolutions, which lead to firm cadences. Brass and woodwind choir alternations combined with accidentals and shifting tonal centers create simple lines that possess poignant character and contrast. Most phrases begin soft and build to louder volumes and others remain at the quiet level. The work subsides in volume and harmonic progressions and ends "pp" on an F major triad. Highly recommended for ensembles of all levels that can master sostenuto style, respond to balance and are able to control tone quality throughout the volume spectrum. Reviewed by RH.

CARTER, Charles   **SYMPHONIC OVERTURE**   C. Fischer
5:00

An enjoyable and effective band standard, with vital rhythms and attractive tunes that are well-scored. Incorporating a traditional three-part form, the work opens with a vigorous and well crafted "A" section using tutti sonorities. This is followed by a slow and somewhat somber "B" section introduced by the flute followed by layered woodwind and brass textures. The snare drum begins the return of the A theme but this time it is treated in a canon-like setting. This spins into a coda section using previous rhythmic materials into a very exciting conclusion.

CLARKE, Jeremiah   **JEREMIAH CLARKE SUITE**   Shawnee
Arr. William Schaefer   8:00

An excellent transcription of five pieces by the great 17th-century organist-composer. (1) *DUKE OF GLOUCESTER'S MARCH* (Moderato, B♭, 2/2), stately but rhythmic, featuring dotted 8th-16th rhythms and varied scoring and dynamics. (2) *SERENADE* (Andante grazioso, B♭, 3/4), a gently flowing movement, lightly scored, using echo dynamics on repeats. (3) *CEBELL* (Tempo di Gavotte, B♭, 2/2), bouncy and energetic, well-marked in style. (4) *MINUET* (B♭, 3/4), using both varied scoring and echo dynamics on repeats. (5) *PRINCE OF DENMARK'S MARCH* (Allegro moderato, B♭, 2/2) (also known as "*Trumpet Voluntary*" and often attributed to Purcell), broad, majestic and festive in character, with nice contrasts of scoring and texture, brought to a noble, resonant conclusion.

DEL BORGO, Elliot   **ADAGIO FOR WINDS**   Shawnee
3:45

A lyrically expressive work in slow tempo (Legato e sostenuto, E♭, 4/4, quarter=54), with flowing melodic lines and sustained legato accompaniment. Technically rather easy, but demands beauty of tone, well-focused intonation, refinement and control of attacks and releases, and above all, command of legato style and feeling of phrase.

DELIUS, Frederick   **THE WALK TO THE PARADISE GARDEN**   Aeolus Music
Transc. Joseph Kreines   9:30

A very effective transcription of this beautiful interlude. Beginning soft and slow (4/4, Lento, quarter note = 54, Eb major) the work moves as if it were a slow dance with several long phrases, rubato settings and shifts of colors. A shimmering rhythm introduces the solo oboe with answers from the lower winds. This leads to a logical key change to C major (quarter note=63) with additional triple figures by the solo English horn and oboe later echoed by the flute. An agitated accelerando section (quarter note =88) follows using tutti sonorities, which build into fortissimo passages including an important harp part. This subsides and a quiet section follows (quarter note =60) using accidentals and various woodwind sonorities. There are several dissonant and resolution cadences as the chromatic harmonies drape the woodwind solo interjections into volumes of pianissimo and pianissiissimo. The chromatic harmony progresses into a very expressive section (B major) that builds and builds until a final release of tension into a new section (Broadly) results. This begins to thin and soften while still retaining several rubato shifts until the concluding woodwind solos, followed by the clarinet choir (pianissiissiissimo), whose sustained notes empty into silence. A superb work for those ensembles that are capable of maintaining long phrases, executing lyrical style, possess solo oboe and English Horn and a conductor who can master the many shifts of motion and emotion required of this music. Reviewed by RH.

DVORAK, Antonin   SERENADE, OP. 22   Volkwein
Arr. R.L. Moehlmann   6:15

A superb example of the Romantic style, splendidly transcribed from the string orchestra original. It is moderate in tempo (E^b-G^b-E^b, 4/4) with beautiful melodies, rich-textured harmonies and simple but effective counter-melodies. The opening section features a flowing legato idea in solo oboe and trumpet, answered by bassoon and bass, soon expanded into a longer phrase. A transition leads to a repeat of the opening, expanded further and varied in treatment. This leads to the second section in G^b major, featuring a gently lilting melody in trumpets with dotted-rhythm accompaniment in low brass. This too is varied and expanded, returning in clarinets with a new counter-melody in saxophones. The tag of the melody is used for a transition that leads back to the first section while the tag continues as a rhythmic accompaniment. The second re-statement now appears as a horn duet, building to a glowing climax. The coda which follows is based on the opening theme, transparently scored like the beginning but with melody in bass instruments, ending serenely. Requires solo trumpet and oboe with ensemble intonation, good horns, blended saxophone section, secure and fluent baritone – and total ensemble tonal beauty, blend, refinement and sensitivity to phrase, line and nuance. Strongly recommended for its outstanding musical value.

FARNABY, Giles   GILES FARNABY SUITE   Oxford
Arr. Bram Wiggins   5:30

Excellent arrangements of five short late-16th-century keyboard works. (1) *A TOYE* (Allegro con brio, G minor, 2/2). Light, delicate and rhythmic, featuring staccato brass at beginning, then woodwinds and horns followed by trumpets and trombones, closing with woodwinds. (2) *GILES FARNABY'S DREAM* (Lento sostenuto, 4/4) Beautiful, slow, lyric woodwinds melody with low brass accompaniment, followed by subtle textural doublings and mixed combinations. (3) *HIS REST* (Tranquillo, 3/4) Choir scoring in first two phrases (brass, woodwinds) followed by mixed doubling in imitative closing section. (4) *GILES FARNABY'S CONCERT* (Allegretto, 2/4), with effective use of contrasting choirs and register changes. (5) *HIS HUMOUR* (Allegretto, 2/2), using contrasts between legato and staccato, dynamics and scoring between phrases. Cf. also *GILES FARNABY SUITE* by Gordon Jacob, listed below.

FAURE, Gabriel   CANTIQUE DE JEAN RACINE   Alfred
Arr. Monty Musgrave   5:30

A well-scored, sensitive rendering of a French choral classic. The vocal parts throughout are scored for the brass choir, while the woodwinds present the string and wind parts of the original. Requires a well-defined sense of line, careful balancing of part, and close attention to the many dynamic nuances. Highly recommended as an excellent introduction to the French Romantic style for developing players.

FRESCOBALDI, Girolamo   CANZONA IN QUARTI TONI   Kendor
Arr. Valentine Anzalone   3:40

A good example of an authentic Frescobaldi keyboard work, effectively transcribed. Texture is quite contrapuntal throughout, with intricate rhythm patterns in the opening Andante and Allegro sections, and the 6/4 subdivision in the succeeding Allegro moderato. Technically not difficult, but demands good rhythmic sense and control of subdivisions, and careful working out of balances between voices and projection of contrapuntal lines.

FRY, Tommy   TRIPTYCH   C. Fischer
                                                                        5:00

A very good one-movement work with effective contrasts between its three sections. The opening is declamatory in character (Allegro, 4/4) with tutti scoring, leading to a reflective and poetic slow section (3/4), featuring flutes and soft percussion followed by brass choir. The final section is fast, driving and brilliant in character, requiring fluent staccato style in bass instruments as well as treble.

GLAZUNOV, Alexander   INTERLUDIUM   Warner
Arr. R.L. Moehlmann   4:00

A lovely lyric work in slow tempo, sensitively scored. (Andante, 4/4, quarter = 58) featuring two main ideas – a horn melody at the beginning and a flowing 8th note line which is developed to an eloquent climax. Technically rather easy, but requires good ensemble concepts (pitch, tone, blend, balance) due to extensive choir scoring, and feeling for long line legato. (Ensembles used: trumpets, clarinets, horns).

GORDON, Philip (Arr.)   **VENETIAN MASTERS SUITE**   Marks
4:45

An excellent sampling of the music of three 18th-century Italian composers who worked in Venice. (1) *ALLEGRETTO* by Giovanni Grazioli (E^b, 3/4) is in gently flowing style requiring sensitivity to dynamic and balance. (2) *ADAGIO* by Benedetto Marcello (C minor, 3/4 in 6), the slow movement of an oboe concerto, demands great care in balancing the accompaniment to the solo line (oboe, cued into clarinet, later doubled by flute) and a feeling for long, sustained and expressive line. (3) *THE HUNT* by Antonio Vivaldi (excerpt from "*Autumn*" of The Four Seasons) (Allegro con brio, E^b, 3/4) is in emphatic and vigorous style which nevertheless demands continuity of phrases. Also contains several passages of 16th-note scales for upper woodwinds and trumpets.

GOSSEC, Francois   **MILITARY SYMPHONY IN F**   Presser
Arr. Richard F. Goldman and R. Leist   6:00
A fine original work from the French Revolutionary period in three short movements, capably arranged for modern instrumentation. (1) (Allegro Maestoso, F, 4/4) – contrasting an epic, marked theme, staccato rhythmic figures and short melodic motives of 8ths and 16ths in well-crafted classical form; requiring rhythmic precision, clean staccato articulation, fluent legato and careful attention to balance. (2)(Larghetto, F, 6/8 in 6) – a gently flowing 2-bar idea containing dynamic and scoring contrasts forms the basis of this very short slow movement. Requires beauty of tone, blend, balance, legato style and control of soft dynamics. Scoring is rather transparent with emphasis on woodwinds, though horns are also exposed. (3)(Allegro, C major, 2/2) – opens with a heroic, martial statement succeeded by a more graceful, delicate phrase. The remainder of the movement juxtaposes the two ideas and their stylistic counterparts, concluding with a triumphant statement of both ideas. Requires clear articulation, control of tone in full-scored passages, and sense of classical style.

GRAINGER, Percy   **AUSTRALIAN UP-COUNTRY TUNE**   G. Schirmer
Arr. Glenn Cliffe Bainum   2:00
The brevity and technical simplicity of this beautiful work belie its deeply expressive emotional musical content. It provides a model vehicle for developing beauty of tone, refinement of intonation, legato style, flexibility of ensemble, range of dynamics and expression. Strongly recommended for any band.

GRAINGER, Percy   **HARVEST HYMN**   Barnhouse
Arr. Joseph Kreines   3:00
A rich-textured chorale-like work with lash harmonies supporting an original melody (not a folk-tune). It opens with the woodwind choir stating the first part of the phrase, followed by full band presenting the second part. The second phrase utilizes soprano saxophone solo (cued in 1st clarinet), followed by oboe with clarinet choir accompaniment. A development-like section follows, leading to a return of the opening melody with an obbligato line in upper woodwinds. The concluding measures provide a broadly triumphant climax.

GRAINGER, Percy   **SPOON RIVER**   G. Schirmer
Arr. Glenn Cliffe Bainum   4:20
A rhythmically vital and imaginative setting of an old American fiddle-tune, excellently scored. Requires great clarity of articulation and rhythmic precision (especially in dotted-8th-16th figures, which are the basis of the tune), woodwind fluency (they present the melody throughout) and secure mallet players. An important harp part which accompanies flute and piccolo solos can be played on piano – an optional cut is provided should there be no keyboard player.

GRAINGER, Percy   **WALKING TUNE**   Daehn
Arr. Larry Daehn   4:10
Grainger loved walking, and the tune on which this piece is based is the result of walking through the Scottish highlands when he was 18. He first set it for woodwind quintet, but later did a version for the orchestral wind section, which is the basis for the present version.

It is a lyric gem, with rich-textured accompanying harmony and counter-melodic lines that are trademarks of Grainger's style. Highly recommended for its lyric and textural beauties. (Note: the solo oboe carries the melody – cued in flute and clarinet)

GRIEG, Edvard   **THE LAST SPRING**   Kendor
Arr. Robert Bardeen   4:00

A tasteful, generally effective rendering of one of Grieg's *Elegiac Melodies* for strings. The tempo is slow and sustained, the mood intensely poetic and lyric (Andante cantabile, F, 4/4). Emphasis is on woodwind sonority most of the time, with much transparent scoring (only 8 bars of tutti). Requires considerable sensitivity to nuance, ebb and flow of line and phrase, beauty of tone, blend, balance and well-focused pitch center - so that, despite its technical simplicity, there are considerable musical demands on both players and conductor.

GRIEG, Edvard   **TWO NORDIC MELODIES OP. 63**   Aeolus Music
Transc. Joseph Kreines   12:30

This is an excellent transcription of two lesser-known gems by Grieg. The ominous opening of part 1, "In Folk Song-Style" (4/4, Andante, quarter note = 69, F major) is followed by additional declamatory successive statements performed by solo French horn, low winds, alto sax until the tutti woodwind choirs enters with a very haunting and lyrical melody. These contain both logical and surprising harmonies almost reminiscent of Grainger. This is traded by several sonorities until a clever segment using off beats blurs the meter in a chamber setting. This becomes much more developed leading to a unison rhythmic halt before the return of the theme. This time, however, it is fortissimo and well-marked until the final sounds drift off into a pianissimo D major triad. Layering colors of clarinets open part 2, "Cow-keeper's Tune and Country Dance (6/8, Andantino, eighth note = 126, G major). Several shifts of brass woodwind sonorities ornament the enchanting and expressive melody. This is treated by several colors interactions until it subsides into a pianissimo close. A familiar fiddle-like announcement starts the Country Dance (Allegro molto vivace, quarter note = 144, C major), which leads to a very syncopated tune played by the solo clarinet and later joined by oboe and traded to the flutes. This spins itself into a fermata followed by a soft repeat of the tune in its simple form. A subito shift of volume and a tutti-Fortissimo gasp of the theme brings the work to a convincing close. Very well-orchestrated, this transcription will provide ensembles of various levels a wonderful musical experience. Reviewed by RH.

GRUNDMAN, Clare   **AMERICAN FOLK RHAPSODY NO. 3**   Boosey &Hawkes
                                                                                7:00

Perhaps the most interesting of Grundman's American folk rhapsodies, with the balance between unity and contrast well-handled. Four tunes are featured – *COLORADO TRAIL* (Moderato, E^b, 4/4 modulating to C major); *GIT ALONG LITTLE DOGIES*(Allegro moderato, C-B^b-F-G, 6/8 and 2/4); *CARELESS LOVE* (Moderato cantabile, C, 4/4), featuring woodwinds; and *TURKEY IN THE STRAW* (E^b, 2/4), in leggiero style with some attractive variations in phase length and rhythmic shape. The piece closes with a combination of all the tunes (Con Moto, 4/4) with a short coda recalling the very opening. Very effective for concerts, with interesting parts for all players.

GRUNDMAN, Clare   **HEBRIDES SUITE**   Boosey &Hawkes
                                                                                7:00

An excellent suite of folk-tunes in four movements. (1) *THE PEAT-FIRE FLAME* (Allegro moderato, C minor, 2/3-4/4) takes the form of two contrasting settings – one lively and rhythmic, the other sustained and majestic –each of which utilize phrase extensions and interruptions with counter-material; considerable variety of scoring and texture adds to the musical effect. (2) *AN ERISKAY LOVE-LILT* (Quietly with motion, G-C-F major, 3/4) – a lovely melody set four different ways (solo trumpet; upper woodwinds; horns and baritone; horns, baritone and trumpet) with a return to the first setting and key for a coda. Excellent scoring and rich textured contrapuntal and harmonic treatment. (3) *MILKING SONG* (With simplicity, F, 2/2) – a gently humorous, rather light and transparent setting, using a segment of the melody as a rhythmic motive and a flowing bass and tenor line as accompaniment. In the middle section the key modulates to A^b and the melody appears in augmentation. A short transition using the rhythmic motive leads to a return of the first setting, ending softly and staccato. (4) *THE ROAD TO THE ISLES* (Moderate march tempo, B^b, 4/4) features a march melody with dotted rhythms (regular and inverted) and using a variation and a thematically-rated counter-melody, all three of which are combined to form an imposing climax. One of Grundman's finest works, calling for good solo piccolo, flute, clarinet, trumpet, horns, baritone, low woodwinds – and requiring musical maturity and sensitivity within the modest technical requirements.

HAYDN, Franz Joseph ST. ANTHONY DIVERTIMENTO G. Schirmer
Arr. James Wilcox 11:00

One of Haydn's most engaging and popular works, originally for wind octet, in four contrasting movements not unlike those of a symphony except for their relative brevity. (1) *ALLEGRO* (B^b, 4/4) – lively and spirited, with emphasis on rhythmic energy (including effective use of rests). (2) *CHORALE ST. ANTONI* (Andante, B^b, 2/4), well known for Brahms' version in his Haydn Variations – noble but gentle, utilizing a 5-bar theme. (3) *MINUET* (F, 3/4). The opening is hearty and vigorous in character, with a transparently scored trio containing important horn parts (partly doubled in trumpets). (4) *RONDO* (Allegretto, B^b, 2/4) – light-hearted and sparkling with frequent dynamic contrasts and variety of articulations and rhythmic figures. Requires a light touch, some solo capability (though most parts are effectively cued or doubled), rhythmic accuracy and precision, control of articulations, care in balancing sustained and accompanying parts to melodic interest. Strongly recommended.

HAZO, Samuel SOLAS ANE Musicworks
4:30

Truly a wonderful setting of Gaelic inspiration utilizing all original themes. The work begins in A^b major, incorporating a flowing piccolo solo, accompanied by bass clarinet, quarter note =70. This major theme is later presented by various solo and tutti lines (including oboe) with phrases defined by meter contrasts. The second theme ensues with the full ensemble in E^b. Percussion begins a syncopated "pipe rhythm" against jig figures in the upper woodwinds, which is simultaneously colored by a lush brass drone in C minor. After a short bridge section, the work closes very peacefully in F. Requires several woodwind soloists and a French horn section with accurate pitch control. Percussionists will need to define a steady tempo through various contrasts of colors and styles containing the melody in a Rubato style. The texture thickens with embellishments including woodwind ornaments and builds to a tumultuous climax and then subsiding and building again to the final tutti "FFF" before a short subito-pianissimo-A^b- triad is finally performed by the low winds. Although there are few technical challenges, all winds must possess maturity of tonal and pitch focus, legato style and sensitivity to balance. The rubato style leaves much room for musical expression and expansion.

HIDAS, Frigyes MERRY MUSIC Editions Music Budapest
5:00

A fresh-sounding, thoroughly enjoyable work in neo-classic style by a contemporary Hungarian composer. The opening section (Allegretto giocoso, 4/4) is rhythmic, accented, detached in style, with a bouncy theme. The contrasting middle section is slower and more sustained, rather nostalgic in character. The work concludes with a varied recapitulation of the opening section. Technically not difficult, but requires clean staccato tonguing, rhythmic precision and attention to balance and clarity.

JACKSON, Tim PASSACAGLIA Maecenas Music
6:00

This imaginative and original work, using the Passacaglia form in 4/4, was initially written for French horn choir. It opens with a simple ground (Lento Assai, quarter note = 72) in low woodwinds using a variety of accidentals but fixing on F. The mood is somber and the textures thin as the early variations are introduced. As the textures thicken the harmonies become more intense and dissonant as each variation leads to a rhythmic and textural contrast. An augmented form of the ground unveils a series of rapidly growing ornamented rhythms, which climax into the final chord in F major. Highly recommended.

JACOB, Gordon (Arr.) GILES FARNABY SUITE Boosey &Hawkes
19:00

Superb transcriptions of 11 short but musically worthy keyboard works by the 16th-century English master with excellent variety of style, color, character and texture. (Cf. *Giles Farnaby Suite*, arr. B. Wiggins, listed previously). (1) *FANTASIA* – in two sections: Maestoso,4/2 – contrapuntal and imitative in texture using two motives; Allegretto, 6/4 in 2 – with a flowing legato line of 8th-notes and quarter-note rhythmic accompaniment. (2) *THE OLD SPAGNOLETTA* (Allegretto, 6/4 in 2 – a gently flowing legato piece requiring skill in subdivision. (3) *GILES FARNABY'S DREAME* (Poco lento e tranquillo, 4/4) – serene and lyric, melodic yet simply contrapuntal. (4) *FARNABY'S CONCEIT* (Allegro, 2/2) – energetic and vital, requiring precision and clarity of rhythm . (5) *HIS REST* (Andante molto tranquillo, 3/4) legato, melodic, flowing, with simple but effective imitative texture. (6) *HIS HUMOUR* (Allegro scherzando, 2/2) – light staccato and strongly marked tenuto, further contrasted with long legato phrases dominated by a rising and falling scale motive. (7) *TELL MEE, DAPHNE* (Andante con moto, 4/4) – melancholy in mood, using choir scoring (opening with woodwinds, closing with brass). (8) *ROSASOLIS* (Alla marcia, 4/4) A dignified brass motive contrasted with a staccato woodwind reply, succeeded by variations and embroideries of both. (9) *A TOYE* (Andante con moto, 4/2) – scored for woodwinds alone in choirs (saxophones, then clarinets) – lyric and flowing in style. (10) *LOTH TO DEPART* (Andante espressivo, 3/4) – a beautiful, eloquent, lyric statement, using a mixture of choirs and tutti scoring. (11) *TOWER HILL* (Allegro, 2/2) – Vital, energetic, rhythmic; using a well-marked tune and embroidering it with rhythmic and melodic figuration, brought to a vibrant and exuberant conclusion.

JADIN, LOUIS **SYMPHONIE FOR BAND** Shawnee
Arr. William Schaefer 5:00

An original wind-band work from the French Revolution, this single-movement work captures perfectly the classical style. In a lively Allegro throughout (F major, 3/4, feeling in one), it follows the form of an overture, opening with a vigorous marcato phrase dominated by dotted 8th-16th rhythm; contrasted with a more legato, gentle idea. These two phrases and their extensions and variations are the chief materials of the entire movement, which contains some striking harmonies and abrupt modulations as well as effective contrasts of dynamics and scoring. Not difficult technically, but demands good understanding of the classical style (especially in terms of light, fluent articulation) and sensitivity to contrasts.

JOHNSON, Stuart **RHAPSODY ON AN OLD ENGLISH SEA SONG** G&M BRA
4:30

An enjoyable, rather clever series of variants on "THE DRUNKEN SAILOR." After a short introduction, the tune is introduced in clarinets and saxophones, followed by a more martial statement by full band. The next setting features trumpets alternating with flutes and oboe, then flute and clarinet. The next two variants use 3/8 meter thrown into the 2/4 context. A waltz version is next – flute solo accompanied by clarinets. The waltz mode is brought to a tutti climax subsiding into an andante featuring solo oboe followed by muted trumpets and flutes. An allegro introduction leads to the final section – a brilliant vivace using the rhythms and fragments of the tune.

KARRICK, Brant **CUMBERLAND FALLS OVERTURE** Daehn
5:30

A colorful and programmatic work with Copland-esque shadows. The work begins very quietly (Expressivo, quarter=72) with solos for oboe, cued flute, and trumpet accompanied by percussion and woodwinds. The theme is presented in tutti forms with various embellishments and textures. A lively Allegro spiritoso (quarter=144) is introduced by a vibrant percussion ostinato followed by solos for flute, oboe, and clarinet. An interesting mixed-meter phrase ensues and acts as a repeated bridge to the various settings and interludes of the theme. A charming Cantabile section, followed by the bridge theme, leads to a brief exposition of the familiar "Gifts to Be Simple" melody. A Meno Mosso section prepares a broad (Maestoso, quarter=72) and heroic coda. The work is very well-scored with interesting parts for all wind and percussion instruments.

KARRICK, Brant **SONGS OF OLD KENTUCKY** Alfred
6:00

A very enchanting setting of five Cumberland Mountain folk songs. "John Riley and Wayfaring Stranger" (quarter note = 66 in D minor) open the work in a lyrical style using a brief alto saxophone solo and occasional meter shifts of four and two but generally remaining in triple time. A middle section (quarter note =72) creates a pleasant contrast before the return to the opening tempo. Very skillful scoring and imaginative harmony choices complete part one of this two-movement work. Part II, Barn Dance, which contains "Sourwood Mountain, Frog Went-a- Courtin', Loving and Hannah" begins with a short introduction (2/2, half note = 104, in Bb) and then quickly to the melody performed in clarinets with bass line and hand clap accompaniments! Several color exchanges take place including intelligent and appropriate percussion scoring. A lovely soft and expressive section (with regimental distant drums in a 6/8 contrasting meter) provides a refreshing contrast to the return of the opening theme for a very energetic conclusion. Highly recommended. Requires five able percussionists performing on 13 instruments.

KIRCK, George T. (Arr.) **EARLY MUSIC SET** Shawnee
5:00

A welcome transcription of three superb Renaissance works, intelligently scored and arranged. The opening piece *ALLONS, GAY, GAY* by Costeley, (Allegro moderato, 2/2) is lively and animated in staccato, rhythmic style, alternating homophonic and imitative contrapuntal writing. The second, *WHAT IF I NEVER SPEED* by Dowland, (Andante Cantabile, G minor, 4/4) is poignantly expressive and mostly homophonic in texture, with a more intricate middle section. The final piece, *PASE EL AGOA* (3/4 in one) is a lively dance, rhythmic yet lilting in character.

KISTLER, Cyrill **PRELUDE TO ACT III OF "KUNIHILD"** Aeolus Music
Transc. Joseph Kreines 5:30

A very effective transcription of one of the most expressive Preludes from this era. Beginning (Slow and dark, 4/4) with a very somber and sensitive bassoon solo (ably cued for bass clarinet) the work climbs chromatically with gentle antecedent responses. A new section emerges (Expressively without dragging) featuring clarinets and French horns exposing a beautiful and poignant melody. Shifting tonal centers and various sonority groupings develops the theme. A very emotional and broad transition follows (More and more passionately) into a breathtaking climax (Very broad, yet not dragged) now with the lower winds (FFF) presenting the theme. This is echoed by the upper woodwinds (FFF) and eventually subsides into a final "Ever calmer" section. The concluding measures cascade into the ultimate and waning unison F. Although not overly technical, all winds must have tonal control in all registers and have command of lyrical style. Recommended for all level ensembles that can meet the musical demands of this masterpiece. Reviewed by RH.

LA PLANTE, Pierre **A COWBOY SYMPHONY** Daehn
9:30

A brilliant suite of American folk songs using symphonic forms for parts of its structure. Movement one, "The Chishom Trail", opens with a short euphonium solo in recitative style (quarter note = circa 70 in E^b). The theme is stated briskly (2/4 quarter note =104-110) by the upper woodwinds and further developed by several shifts of instrumentation (including rapid syncopated trumpet parts which require mature tonguing). A sustained lyrical section ushers in the second theme, "The Girl I left Behind Me" in the dominant key, featuring additional color exchanges. There is a quick return to E^b and a more accented style follows using previous material to end the movement with solo French horn remaining. Movement II, "The Cowboy" is much slower (eighth note = 92 in 6/8) and reflective in nature. Several solo and soli colors are dominant throughout this expressive movement. The final movement, "At The Cowboy Dance," contains many familiar folk songs including, "Buffalo Gals", "Golden Slippers", "Soldier's Joy" and "Skip to My Lou." The opening theme (2/4,Lively, quarter note = 120-126 is presented in the low winds and quickly answered and ornamented in various wind families. The dance continues with fiddle-like passages and colorful percussion. A middle lyrical section of "Skip to My Lou" (quarter note =90-100) provides a comfortable contrast to the lively dance themes before the final coda section (Fast and Boisterous, quarter note = 132-136) explodes into a raucous finale.

LA PLANTE, Pierre **AMERICAN RIVER SONGS** Daehn
7:10

An excellent work containing settings of four contrasting American songs. It opens with a lively $^6/_8$ version of "DOWN THE RIVER," utilizing contrasting dynamics and scorings. A poetic setting of "SHENANDOAH" follows, with the melody appearing in different instruments throughout. This leads to a rhythmically vital setting of "THE GLENDY BURK," featuring trumpets, then upper woodwinds. A creole Bamboula tune in ragtime rhythm then appears, which then is combined with a reprise of "GLENDY BURK," driving to a vibrant conclusion.

LA PLANTE, Pierre **ENGLISH COUNTRY SETTINGS** Daehn
7:05

A well-conceived, imaginative work featuring three Enlish folk tunes. It opens with a delicately scored statement of "MAY DAY CAROL" – first in solo woodwinds, then trumpets. More fully scored passages follow, leading to the first statement of "O WALY WALY" (THE WATER IS WIDE) in F minor. Some development follows, leading to a climactic section where the tune is stated in B^b Major. This leads without a break into "THE ASH GROVE," featuring a variety of instruments playing the tune in a lively 6/8 jig-like rhythm, building to a short coda in faster tempo.

LA PLANTE, Pierre   LA BONNE AVENTURE   Daehn
"VARIATIONS ON AN OLD FRENCH SONG"   6:04

A very imaginative theme in theme-and-variation format based on a childrens song of the same title. It opens with a sparkling introduction (Allegro, quarter=124-128, 2/4, B^b major) leading to the theme presented first in the upper woodwinds. This quickly and smoothly leads to the first variation, which offers more sustained material with canonic exchanges between upper and lower winds (4/4, quarter note = 112). Variation III is march like (2/4, quarter note = 116-120) using more syncopated rhythms that begin on the off beats and incorporate accidentals. The texture thins and introduces Variation IV, which is more reflective and lyrical (4/4, F major, quarter note = 72). Variation V begins light and quietly (Tempo Primo, 2/4, quarter note = 124-128 in B^b) while shifting both the agogic accent and the texture to create rhythmic interest and contrast. A very clever transition leads to Variation VI (quarter note =138) which contains very short articulations in unison rhythms and subito dynamics. The final variation is a thrilling Gallop (quarter note = 140-144) that uses syncopation, color exchanges (including appropriate percussion writing) and articulative contrasts to resolve into a very exciting conclusion. Musically and educationally very rewarding.

LA PLANTE, Pierre   LEGENDS AND HEROES   Daehn
8:00

Skillfully written, well-crafted settings of three folk songs.
1.   PATRICK ON THE RAILWAY (G minor, 6/8) – a lilting, rhythmic tune (reminiscent of "When Johnny Comes Marching Home") with nice contrasts of scoring between solo and tutti passages.
2.   SWEET BETSY (3/4, E^b Major) – a graceful waltz with a short contrasting episode in C minor- dark and agitated in mood.
3.   LITTLE DAVID PLAY ON! – A short introduction for E^b clarinet solo (cued in flute) leads to an energetic 2/4 with cake-walk and syncopated rhythms. (Note: the closing section is in concert G Major)

LATHAM, William   COURT FESTIVAL   Summy-Birchard
5:30

A fine evocation of the Renaissance style in an original four-movement work. (1) *INTRADA* (Allegro Moderato, G minor, 2/2), effectively contrasts brass and woodwinds choirs as well as terraced dynamics, unified by a 4-note motive (melodic and rhythmic). (2) *PAVAN* (Andantino, G minor, 2/2) offers a simple melody comprised of legato and staccato elements scored several different ways. (3) *GALLIARD* (Allegretto con gracia, Bb, ¾), a lively but graceful dance, again uses the echo effect with contrasting scoring on repeats. (4) *THE HORSES BRANLE* (Vivace, G, 2/2) is sparkling and brilliant, featuring piccolo solo, followed by brass in a "galloping" motive and woodwinds in a staccato echo. These are developed and brought to a festive conclusion. Highly recommended.

LATHAM, William   THREE CHORALE PRELUDES   Summy-Birchard
6:30

Excellent original settings of three chorale-melodies using the chorale-prelude format developed by Bach. The first (F major, 6/8 in moderate 2) uses a flowing 8th-note line to decorate the melody *"HOW BRIGHTLY SHINES THE MORNING STAR"*. The second is a somber, brooding setting of "O SACRED HEAD NOW WOUNDED" (D minor, 3/4), while the finale is a jubilant version of *"NOW THANK WE ALL OUR GOD"* (F major, 2/2), using fanfare-like trumpet figures to decorate the melody which appears in trombones. Requires considerable musicianship in terms of phrasing, style, refinement of tone and blend, balance, solo and section voices (oboe, clarinet, trumpet, trombone) and some technical facility in trumpets (3rd movement). Highly recommended.

LIADOV, Anatol   LETTERS FROM LIADOV, Op. 58   Grand Mesa
Transc. Jim Mahaffey   7:30

This very charming transcription of a lesser-known Russian composer is a wonderful addition to this level and genre. It contains 5 short movements, each displaying wide contrasting material. The opening "Round Dance" (2/4, quarter note = 108-120 in F major) is a self-contained uplifting dance using various eighth-note patterns incorporating the repeated round motif. "Cradle Song" (3/4, quarter note =60-68, in G minor) begins with a somber melody in oboe and clarinet. This leads to a tutti section using swells for dynamics and chromatic harmony, quickly subsides into conclusion of the movement on a G minor triad in the soli clarinets. "The Humorous Song" opens with trill-like figures trading swells (2/4, quarter note = 86 in B^b) which lead to embellished figure exchanges (including a challenging euphonium and trumpet passage). The introductory rhythms return to a satisfying close. The "Chant" opens with solo bass clarinet, capably cued **,** (2/4, Moderato; quarter note =63-66 in B^b) followed by echoing woodwinds. A brass interlude ensues before a tutti section appears using similar modal material. This movement subsides using only clarinet choir for the ending measures. The final movement, "Village Dance-Song" (2/4, quarter note = 144-152) opens with a brilliant tutti statement followed by repetitive dance themes and appropriate accompaniment. Accidentals and texture contrasts using more elaborate rhythms give the melody more interest. Overlapping phrases with unison dynamics build to a very celebratory ending. Appropriate percussion scoring using 5-7 players. Although much of this work uses simple rhythms and keys, the length will stretch most ensembles with three to four years' experience. However, the musical benefits far outweigh the endurance challenges.

MCBETH, W. Francis	CHANT AND JUBILO	Southern
		6:45

An effective, well-scored work with strongly delineated contrasts of mood and style. The opening *CHANT* (4/4, quarter=72,60,51) is modal in harmonic content, influenced by early church organum complete with parallel triads and flowing, melismatic lines. The *JUBILO*, which follows without pause, is rhythmic and driving (quarter=96), featuring brass and percussion in fanfare-like writing, with a melody treated several ways and brought to a strongly marked climax (quarter=108), leading to an impulsive, forceful fast section (quarter=144) with the main *Jubilo* theme in augmentation in horns and baritone and a fragment of it in diminution in upper winds, treated as an ostinato. A surging climax built on bi-tonal formations (G and E^b) leads to a short but eloquent coda (Maestoso, quarter=84), bringing the work to a grand conclusion. Requires good clarinets, flutes and baritone in opening section, which demands well-focused pitch and tone; and trumpets with solidity of articulation, rich toned, full-sounding horns and low brass, flexible and adept percussion; with strongly controlled rhythm and stability of tempo in fast section.

MOZART, W.A.	MENUETTO AND RONDO	Shawnee
Arr. Jack Snavely		8:30

Mozart's Serenade #10 for 13 winds, from which these movements are taken, can easily be called the foundation of wind music repertory. It is a great masterpiece that all who are interested in wind music should know. The transcription is remarkable in its fidelity to the original – even the sonority is well-delineated. The *MENUETTO* (Allegretto, B^b, 3/4) has both grace and weight, while the two trios serve as perfect foils – the first is dark and somber (B^b minor), while the second (F major) has the character of a Landler (country dance). The *RONDO* (Allegro molto, B^b, 2/4) is brilliant, boisterous and energetic, demanding fluency and rhythmic precision.

MOZART, W.A.	IL RE PASTORE OVERTURE	Ludwig
Arr. Clifford Barnes		4:00

A delightful, lively work with attractive themes and the usual effective contrasts between rhythmically energetic and gently melodic materials. Though most of the passage-work is technically not difficult, it does demand agility, light-ness and flow, especially in woodwinds and bass instruments. There are two short but important passages scored for two solo oboes (though cued into muted cornets, they are more effective in oboes that can play them in tune). This transcription tends to be somewhat heavy in places, but it is serviceable and provides bands with an excellent example of fine Mozart repertory.

NELHYBEL, Vaclav	CHORALE	Belwin
		5:00

A powerful, intensely dramatic work based on a medieval Bohemian chant, developing it through various settings from the evocation of fear to that of hope at the end. It opens with a statement of the first phrase of the theme, one note at a time, with a crescendo on each note built from successive entrances - all presented over a sinister and menacing snare drum rhythm. This leads to an accented tutti statement of the first phrase in unison, followed by the second phrase in bass trombone and baritone with obbligato lines in trumpets and trombones. This is succeeded by a varied statement of the first phrase in clarinets, then saxophones and bassoons. The second phrase is then taken up in canon by clarinets and baritone. The tempo now changes(Allegro, 3/4, quarter=138) with a contrapuntal and canonic treatment for cornets, trumpets and horns, punctuated by low brass and woodwinds playing the theme one note at a time at irregular intervals, with a strong rhythmic underpinning by snare drum. Another contrapuntal treatment follows, with upper winds playing the theme in canon while horns and sax play it in augmentation. The meter now changes to 4/4, with the second phrase now taken up by brass choir and percussion. This is followed by a Meno Mosso with homophonic chordal statement of the first phrase in full band, followed by a soft contrapuntal statement of the second phrase, brought to a climax leading into a Piu Vivo, presenting a canonic statement between upper and lower voices along with an 8th-note obbligato. This leads to an allargando using the final segment of the theme, which brings the work to a powerful conclusion. Requires excellent brass (trombones with security in upper register, saxes and lower woodwinds with richness of tone and control of intonation, and intelligent, rhythmically solid percussion. The very opening requires good control of soft entrances and crescendos, while the end demands control of sonority in loud, intense playing. Highly recommended.

NELSON, Ron **COURTLY AIRS AND DANCES** Ludwig
12:00

Nelson's homage to Renaissance song and dance forms in a six movement suite. It opens with a fanfare-like INTRADA, followed by a dignified BASSE-DANSE featuring chamber-ensemble scoring with a tutti passage at the end. A stately, lyrical PAVANE follows, succeeded by a lively SALTARELLO with a bright, bouncy 6/8 rhythm. A poetic SARABAND is next, featuring singing by the band members in unison. The work ends with an ALLEMANDE, utilizing the melodic materials from the INTRADA as well as new ideas. This piece provides an excellent introduction to Renaissance style with Nelson's own musical ideas.

NELSON, Ron **PASTORALE: AUTUMN RUNE** Ludwig
7:30 M

A very skillfully scored work of color and evocation. After a subtle and delicately textured sostenuto opening (3/2 half note =56), the flute and oboe exchange floaty-like fragments which leads to a mysterious atmosphere in the upper woodwinds and French horns. This is further developed in brasses using the lower end of the volume spectrum (ppp to mp). Interesting and contrasting clarinet ostinato figures (traded by parts 3/4 and 5/6) pervade much of the work. A challenging and thickly scored percussion battery as well as harp and celeste colors are very important to the effectiveness of this work. Although reminiscent of Nelson's other works, it is not a duplicate, but a satisfying creation very worthy of mature ensembles. Winds must have tonal control in all registers and complete proficiency in sostenuto style, rhythmically independent clarinets (six separate parts) and very skilled mallet percussion players.

PALMER, Robert **OVERTURE ON A SOUTHERN HYMN** Shawnee
5:30

An interesting, imaginatively conceived work using *"Wonderous Love"* as its basis. Opening with a slow introduction (quarter=152) featuring the brass in sustained legato style with fragments of the tune, the mood shifts to fast and energetic, featuring the woodwinds, with brass supplying rhythmic underpinning. After several contrasting episodes using different aspects of the melody, the work comes to a triumphal conclusion using the last phrase of the tune. Requires good brass (especially trumpets and horns), fluent woodwinds and intelligent percussion.

PERSICHETTI, Vincent **SO PURE THE STAR** Elkan-Vogel
4:00

A beautiful, lyrically expressive work based on an original chorale melody. It begins quietly (Religioso, 4/4, quarter=66) with a short introduction followed by a statement of the chorale in clarinets, baritone and tuba (later with saxophones). The remainder of the work treats segments of the melody and expands on them, interrupts phrases with comments by contrasting choirs, uses overlaps of rhythmic figures and melodic fragments, building to a noble climax, then subsiding into a full statement of the chorale as it is at the beginning.

PERSICHETTI, Vincent **CHORALE PRELUDE: TURN NOT THY FACE, Op. 105** Elkan-Vogel
4:30

A highly expressive, technically simple work, which begins with the chorale stated by solo flute in very slow tempo, gradually building in momentum, texture and dynamics to a powerful, climactic dissonant chord. From this climax the tempo becomes gradually slower and the character returns to the serenity and tranquility of the opening. Despite the technical easy of the parts, this work requires great musical sensitivity, with careful attention to dynamics, intonation, blend, phrasing, flow of line. The conductor must have a good command of slow, undivided beat.

PERSICHETTI, Vincent   SERENADE FOR BAND, Op. 85   Elkan-Vogel
5:30

A fine example of the Persichetti style set in a suite of five short movements. (1) *PASTORALE* (Commodo, 2/2, half=88). A lovely lyric piece with a flowing melody accompanied by sustained bi-tonal chords, in transparent scoring, requiring tonal refinement and nuance. (2) *HUMORESKE* (Grazioso, 2/4, quarter=96), a graceful legato melody in woodwinds with staccato bass and chord accompaniment. (3) *NOCTURNE* (Doloroso, 4/4, quarter=63). An expressive, melancholy piece using simple materials and bi-tonal formations. (4) *INTERMEZZO* (Amabile, 4/4, quarter=112). Two melodic ideas used together - a quarter-note line and an 8th-note figure, again with simple but effective bi-tonal chords. (5) *CAPRICCIO* (Spiritoso, 6/8, dotted-quarter=100), The most challenging movement, thanks to tied-8ths followed by legato or staccato-8th, and the general problem of playing 6/8 with rhythmic precision. Bi-tonal and extended triadic formations provide harmonic content, which is more demanding on the ear due to the more rapid tempo. Dynamic contrasts and stylistic niceties also provide musical demands. This is a challenging work due to the transparent scoring with its emphasis on small-group and sectional writing (very few tuttis) and the consistent use of bi-tonal and expanded chordal formations - but, well worth the effort required. Highly recommended.

PIERNE, Gabriel   A L'EGLISE (IN THE CHURCH)   Daehn
Arr. Monty Musgrave   4:30

A well-scored, generally faithful rendering of a short piano piece. It opens with a unison statement of a chorale-like phrase, answered by a fully harmonized setting, then continues with short phrases using alternating scorings (brass, woodwinds, brass and low woodwinds, then tutti), reaching a climactic statement of full-voiced chords in rhythmic unison. The final section states the chorale material over a flowing 8th-note line, concluding with the final chorale-section phrase and a tutti full-chord tag.

PROKOFIEFF, Serge   MARCH AND GAVOTTE (OP.12, NO.1-2)   Presser
Arr. John Tatgenhorst   3:45

An excellent example of Prokofieff's style, with its tonal yet dissonant harmony, unusual melodic turns and interesting inner-voices and textural embroidery. (1) *MARCH* (Andante, F minor, 4/4, quarter=126) – using frequent dotted-8th-16th patterns and crisp, light staccato style. Scored rather fully most of the time. (2) *GAVOTTE* (Adagio, F minor-F major, 4/4), using both legato-8th passages and staccato quarters, with a more sustained style in the major section, and closing with a return to minor and marcato style. Requires good command of articulation styles, rhythmic precision, dynamic contrasts and ear for dissonant harmony and textural details.

PURCELL, Henry   SUITE FROM "DIDO AND AENEAS"   Kjos
Arr. Mark Walker   5:15

Three beautiful excerpts from a great masterpiece, excellently transcribed. (1) *OVERTURE* – begins with a slow, sustained introduction (Moderato, C minor, 4/4) using expressive chromatic harmony, followed by a lively allegro moderato in imitative contrapuntal style. (2) *PRELUDE FOR THE WITCHES* (Moderato, F minor, 4/4), slow and somber ,using chromaticism and dissonance and building to an intense climax. (3) *ECHO DANCE* (Allegro, F major, 4/4), brilliant and fluent, with tongued-16th note passages and a series of short phrases which are echoed. Both the allegro of the overture and the *Echo Dance* demand fluent fingers and tongue, as well as rhythmic precision and control of dynamic contrasts.

RACHMANINOFF, Serge   VOCALISE   Warner
Arr. R.L. Moehlmann   7:30

One of the most beautifully expressive orchestral works, given a sensitive and thoughtful transcription. (Slowly, C minor, 4/4). The melody is given to the trumpets (in unison throughout) which demands great beauty of tone, accurate intonation and sensitivity to phrasing, blend and balance. The accompanying parts require attention to ensemble sound and flow of line. Musically demanding, but worth the effort.

RACHMANINOFF, Serge   VOCALISE   Kendor
Arr. Jack Snavely   7:30

Another excellent transcription of the above, interesting for its very different scoring, in which the 1st and 2nd clarinets carry the melody (except for the last statement, taken by solo trumpet). The key here is D minor. The comments for the above version are equally applicable here despite the differences of scoring and key.

REED, Alfred   **A SYMPHONIC PRELUDE**   Marks

5:45

A highly expressive and poetic treatment of the folk-tune *"Black is the Color"*. Reed uses the chorale-prelude format, opening with a subdued yet rich-textured introduction that leads to the first elaboration on the melody, featuring woodwinds. The second elaboration uses flowing 8th-notes while the melody appears for the first time, in bass voices, leading to a climactic statement with the melody in upper brass. The cadence is extended, then gradually diminishes in intensity to a gently melodic final statement of the tune and its elaboration in clarinets. A short coda, really a variation of the introduction, brings the work to a tranquil conclusion. Requires beauty of sonority, control of woodwind pitch and muted trumpets, good horns and baritone with rich sonority and pitch focus, and overall ensemble blend and finesse with feeling for long phrase and line.

SCRIABIN, Alexander   **NOCTURNE, OP. 9, NO. 2**   Marks
Arr. Alfred Reed   6:45

This is an ingenious, remarkably effective adaptation of a lush, richly colored and intricate piano work, in slow tempo (Molto moderato, E^b, 3/4). The keyboard figurations have been altered to suit the medium, but without affecting the essential musical content. Technically not demanding (except for two moderately showy and short clarinet cadenzas) but calling for great beauty of tone, well-controlled and focused intonation, blend of sonority, refinement of attack, balance of sustained voices with moving parts, and poetic feeling of line and flow of phrase. Highly recommended.

SCRIABIN, Alexander   **PRELUDE, OP. 9, NO. 1**   Marks
Arr. Alfred Reed   3:00

The companion to the above work, but darker and more subdued in mood (Molto andante e sostenuto, D minor, 3/4 in 6). The melodic lines are more flowing in motion but also more angular in shape. As in the Nocturne, the emphasis is on woodwinds, but the horns and baritones also have important roles. Requires good control of tone and ability to sustain slow tempo.

SHELDON, Robert   **A LONGFORD LEGEND**   Alfred
6:00

Subtitled "A Collection of Irish Street Ballads," this is a brilliant work of craft and imagination. The three movements are written as tributes to Grainger, Holst and Vaughan Williams. The first movement, A Longford Legend (Eb major, quarter note =92) opens with bouncy-dance-like rhythms in the woodwinds. This is followed by a lyrical trumpet melody that introduces fragments of the opening theme now using a "Scottish snap." A surprising saxophone ensemble ensues and layers of winds, with restatements of various syncopated rhythms, bring the movement to a close. The next movement, Young Molly Bawn, is a tender song in C minor quarter note = 60. Opening solos traded by flute and clarinet introduces the alto saxophone, which is featured in much of the movement. The movement ends quietly and peacefully with shades of the opening statements. Killyburn Brae begins with a jaunty clarinet soli section in F major, 6/8, dotted quarter note= 138. The motive is transferred several times using various wind colors, augmentation and articulative contrasts. The mood becomes very agitated and boils into a short statement (FFF) of the "Dies Irae" motive. A brief coda-like section, now stated in the trumpet, spins into a flurry of sound that brings the work to a very climactic close. Expertly scored and technically modest, but the winds must have rhythmic independence and percussion must understand their role within the ensemble.

SOR, Fernando   **RONDO**   Shawnee
Arr. James Sharp   4:15

A musical gem by one of the great guitar composers, sensitively scored. Emphasis is on rather transparent and delicate sonorities, in keeping with the nature of the original instrument and the classical style. Technically not difficult, but requires some fluency in 16th-note passages, delicacy of staccato 8ths, good feeling for phrase, rhythmic buoyancy, and security in playing in concert C major.

SPINNEY, Charles Richard   **AN IRISH SUITE FOR BAND**   Byron-Douglas
5:30

An interesting and creative three-movement suite of folk-song settings. (1) *AS I ROVED OUT* (Giocoso, C minor, 2/4-4/4) is fast and energetic, with a good deal of rhythmic interest and staccato articulation contrasted with a legato-style framework in the middle section. (2) *RISING OF THE MOON* (Misterioso, G minor, 4/4) is lyric and sustained, opening with a short, poetic horn solo and gradually building to an eloquent climax. (3) *JOHNNY I HARDLY KNOW YOU* (the original of *"When Johnny Comes Marching*

Home") (Agitato, D minor, 4/4) is in the form of a fantasy, including reminiscences of the first two movement, growing more and more agitated, arriving at a climactic passage featuring three different rhythmic patterns simultaneously.

STEVENS, Halsey   **UKRANIAN FOLK SONGS**   TRN
Arr. William Schaefer   11:30

A wonderful collection of 11 imaginative and colorful settings, superbly transcribed. (1) *FAMILY GATHERING* (Andante, F, 4/4) Flowing, gentle, lyric. (2) *REPENTANT WIFE* (Allegro vivace, B^b, 2/4) Fast, lively and energetic. (3) *EASTER SONG* (Moderato, G minor, 3/8). Reflective and nostalgic, scored for smaller group. (4) *UNDER THE CHERRY TREE* (Andante, G, 2/4). Lightly scored, with solos for oboe and bassoon (cued). (5) *THE SUN HAS SET* (Lento moderato, E minor, 7/4). Scored for brass choir –dark and somber. (6) *MOTHER'S CONCERN* (Allegretto, E^b, 3/8). Scored for woodwinds, two horns and bells – gently flowing legato. (7) *TROUBLE WITH HEMP* (Pesante, C minor, 2/4). Heavy and ponderous. Accompaniment in brass with melody in horns and clarinets (later trumpet and flute). (8) *A MERRY WIDOW* (Lento, G minor, 5/4) Slow and mournful with solos for oboe, horn and English horn. (9) *LOVE SONG* (Andante con moto, E^b, 3/2) Lyric, flowing legato with melody in different registers and groups. (10) *WHY DO YOU POUT, DEAR* (Allegretto, A^b-C-A^b, 2/4) Rich-textured with contrasts of scoring. (11) *WIFE WHO BEAT HER HUSBAND* (Allegro Moderato, F, 2/4) Marcato and rhythmic with light-tongued passages.

STEVENS, John   **BENEDICTION**   Hal Leonard
3:30

An inspirational work originally written for tuba/euphonium quartet and re-scored for wind band by the composer. A sorrowful euphonium solo opens the work (quarter note=72, Freely, in E^b). The theme is echoed and harmonized by the brass choir before the tutti ensemble is exposed. A slightly quicker section (quarter note = 76-80) ensues and the harmony is further developed in a tutti presentation using accidentals and cross rhythms cadencing on a B^{b7} chord. Next, the woodwind choir states the theme in the original tempo followed by the return of the euphonium solo. The work concludes with a fully scored "amen". Although not technically challenging, this work requires a mature euphonium soloist and wind players that can execute legato style in various ranges and are sensitive to pitch center. Ample percussion scoring includes texture responsibilities for timpani, marimba and suspended cymbal.

STRAUSS, Richard   **ALLERSEELEN**   Ludwig
Arr. Albert Oliver Davis   6:40

A glorious-sounding, richly lyrical work, beautifully scored and expanded from the original song for voice and piano. It opens with a serene, tranquil introduction using the main motive of the song. The first phrase of the melody features unison clarinets followed by trumpets. Later a subordinate phrase is presented in solo oboe and baritone. The development uses the opening motive stated in unison by various instruments, gradually building to a sonorous climax with the melody harmonized in brass choir, and arpeggio decoration by upper woodwinds, gradually subsiding to a calm conclusion. Requires beauty of tone, sensitivity of nuance and phrasing well-focused pitch center in both unison and harmonic passages, solo and section talent (oboe, clarinets, horns, low woodwinds, trumpets, low brass) and overall ensemble sound. Strongly recommended.

STRAUSS, Richard   **ZUEIGNUNG**   Ludwig
Arr. Albert Oliver Davis   4:30

Strauss' eloquent and noble song forms the basis for this beautiful tone poem, intelligently expanded (to 91 bars from the original 39) and well-scored. It opens with a poetic introduction featuring contrasts of scoring and dynamics between upper woodwinds and lower voices. The melody then appears in solo cornet, later in horns, baritone and saxophone – supported by rich-textured harmony and various accompaniment figurations. Technically not demanding, but requires considerably musical sensitivity and care for pitch, tone, balance, blend and feeling for long line and phrase shape.

STRAVINSKY, Igor   **A STRAVINSKY SUITE**   Chappell
Arr. Frank Erickson   4:30

An excellent introduction to the style and character of neo-classical Stravinsky, this work offers three short movements taken from pieces for piano duet. The first movement, *MARCH*, is constructed of short contrasting phrases unified by an "oom-pah" march rhythm. The second, a lyric, *ANDANTE*, features a simple melody with an undulating accompaniment. The finale is a lively *GALOP* in humorous vein, with a bouncy tune accompanied by dissonant chords. The transcription is well-scored and faithful to the original. It demands a good trumpet soloist, flexible upper woodwinds, and ears well-tuned to the dissonant harmonic content.

TCHAIKOVSKY, P.I. **SYMPHONY NO. 2 – FINALE** Alfred
Arr. Frank Erickson 9:00

Erickson has done an excellent job of transcribing this lovely, dynamic finale, though he has followed a tradition of making several cuts. What remains, however, is an exciting work which provides considerable challenges to players and conductor. The major problems relate to rhythmic and ensemble precision, particularly with regard to playing after-beats. The conductor must keep a good sense of phrase continuity while maintaining incisiveness of articulation and rhythmic accuracy. It also requires good control of dynamics, balances and tonal blend.

TICHELI, Frank **SHENANDOAH** Manhattan Beach
6:45

A highly effective setting and variants of this nineteenth-century American folk song. Beginning in E^b (4/4, quarter=50), the melody is exposed in the euphonium and French horns (low register) with gentle woodwind accompaniment. A new theme enters in the form of a variation by the flute and saxophone (quarter=63). A short development section follows with a transition into G^b and B^b. The melody is treated in several manners, including textural shifts, a three-part canon for flutes and a 're-transition' back to E^b through a short G^b restatement. The coda (E^b, quarter=ca. 58) is brilliantly scored for brass choir into a final tutti E^b unison played by clarinets and bassoon (niente). Limited, but very appropriate and important percussion scoring using six instruments.

VAUGHAN WILLIAMS, Ralph **RHOSYMEDRE** Galaxy
Arr. Walter Beeler 4:00

A beautiful chorale-prelude (Andantino, F major, 4/2), originally for organ, sensitively transcribed. It opens with a gently flowing melodic line in clarinet, with counter-melody in bassoon and alto clarinet; later doubled in flutes with saxophone doubling clarinet lines. The chorale-melody proper soon enters in horns and baritone while the clarinet choir continue the melodic embroidery with other contrapuntal voices and their doublings. The trumpets present the second statement of the chorale, answered canonically in horns and trombones, while other voices continue the contrapuntal decorations, reaching a rich-toned and noble climax in a unison statement of the last phrase of the chorale by trumpets, horns and trombones, gradually subsiding in volume and intensity as the horns alone conclude the chorale statement. Requires legato style, beauty of tone, careful attention to intonation and blend (all lines are doubled throughout), and feeling of phrase and line. Most important, players must keep feeling of quarter-note subdivision even as conductor gives half-note beat (music should not be subdivided until final ritard in the last two bars).

VERDI, Giuseppe **AVE MARIA** Ludwig
Arr. Barbara Buehlman 4:00

A wonderful choral master work very well transcribed. One of Verdi's last compositions, it nonetheless breaks new ground in using a scale of Verdi's own devising, which produces a mystical, other-worldly effect, with the resultant chromatic harmony and unusual progressions and voice-leadings. Technically not difficult and rhythmically straight-forward, with typical vocal-style suspensions and elemental contrapuntal imitations, but requiring sensitive, rather mature ears for pitch and subtle harmony. Strongly recommended for any group capable of handling its musical requirements.

WARLOCK, Peter **CAPRIOL SUITE** G. Schirmer
Arr. Walter Beeler

A superb string-orchestra original in neo-classical style, combining 16th-century dance tunes with contemporary harmony, in six short movements. (1) *BASSE-DANSE* (Allegro moderato, 3/4), very rhythmic and well-marked, with a forceful and energetic tune. The scoring uses contrasts of choirs. (2) *PAVANE* (Allegretto ma un poco lento, 2/4) – the tune *"Belle Qui Tiens Ma Vie"* by Arbeau; (see under Medium Easy) – slow, dignified, sustained with a wistful melody and transparent scoring (solos: trumpet, alto sax, English horn – cued, tenor sax, horn). (3) *TORDION* (Allegretto con moto, 6/4 in 2) – a lilting but delicate movement in staccato style, requiring lightness and refinement. Emphasis is on woodwinds. (4) *BRANSLES* (Presto, 2/2) – opening with very soft staccato playing in brass choir, followed by woodwinds. This is contrasted with a legato melodic figure, and later a short slurred dotted-rhythm motive. The tempo speeds up to an exciting Prestissimo at the end, requiring both fluency and power. (5) *PIEDS-EN-L'AIR* (Andantino tranquillo,

6/4 in 2) – a complete contrast to the preceding, with soft, gentle legato, long-flowing phrases in woodwinds with important solos for trumpet, baritone, and oboe. (6) *MATTACHINS* (Allegro con brio, 2/4) is a joyous, exuberant, rhythmic movement featuring an ostinato rhythm (quarter-two 8ths).

WHITE, Donald   **DIVERTISSEMENT NO. 3 FOR BLUE LAKE**   Ludwig

A very interesting original work in four movements. (1) *DECLARATION* (4/4, quarter=50), a slow, dramatic piece opening with solo trumpet melodic line punctuated by percussion followed by bi-tonal chords. The horns then take up the melody, then the upper woodwinds, with the chordal accompaniment providing the conclusion. (2) *INVENTION* (Allegro giusto, 2/4), lively and rhythmic, utilizing imitation, inversion and cross-rhythms, with effective choir scoring – requiring good staccato style and intelligent percussion. (3) *REFLECTION* (Molto legato e sostenuto, 3/4, quarter=50). Very slow and intense using bi-tonal and quartal chord formations and long, sustained melodic lines. (4) *ROMP* (Allegro spiritoso, 2/4 and 3/8). Fast, brilliant, dynamic. Staccato 8ths and two-note slurred figures abound, in varying rhythmic and metrical configurations, culminating in a vibrant coda. This piece provides a useful source for much musical training (style, articulation, bi-tonality, contrapuntal and technical devices, etc.) and is also viable for concerts.

● ●

MEDIUM SUPPLEMENT

APPLEBAUM, Stan **IRISH SUITE** European-American
4:30

An appealing and colorful work, composed of original material in Irish style, in three movements.

BACH, J.S. **FUGUE IV (FROM "WELL-TEMPERED CLAVIER")** G. Schirmer
Arr. C.K. Wellington 4:00
A great work, highly contrapuntal (in 5 voices), well transcribed.

BACH, J.S. **ORGAN CHORALE SUITE** Bourne
Arr. Thomas Duffy 5:00
A group of three beautiful settings, well arranged. The third, for full band, is somewhat difficult (being in concert D major and having intricate technical passages); the first two (scored for brass and woodwinds respectively) are more accessible for this level.

BACH, J.S. **SINFONIA NO. 9** Canyon Press
Arr. Cecil Effinger 3:30
A highly expressive, intricate work in chromatic style, very well-scored.

CURNOW, Jim **HYMN AND ALLELUJAH** Studio/PR
5:00

A well-crafted work with good contrasts of mood, style and scoring.

DELIBNES, Leo **LE ROI S'AMUSE** C. Fischer
Arr. L.W. Chidester 4:30
An enjoyable suite of three stylized dances, written for a play, capably scored.

ERICKSON, Frank **TOCCATA FOR BAND** Bourne
5:10

A well-known band standard, effectively written and enjoyable to play, with enough technical and musical challenges to provide value.

FRACKENPOHL, Arthur **AMERICAN FOLK SONG SUITE** Shawnee
An interesting, fresh-sounding and imaginative treatment of good folk material.

FRSCOBALDI, Girolamo **PREAMBULUM AND CANZONA** Belwin
Arr. Justin Gray
A rich-textured contrapuntal keyboard work, effectively arranged (and authentic Frescobaldi!).

GOSSEC, Francois Joseph **SUITE FOR BAND** Belwin
Arr. Douglas Townsend
Another French Revolution original, well scored for modern instruments, in five short, contrasting movements (including three marches in different tempos and styles, a Passapied and a Finale).

GABRIELI, Giovanni **CANZONA NO. 1 (CANZONA PRIMI TONI)** Manhattan Beach
Arr. Bob Margolis 4:20
A very effective and imaginative scoring of a great brass original. Technically modest but requires careful working out of balances, rhythmic precision and textural clarity.

GRIEG, Edvard **SOLEMN PROCESSION** Bourne
Arr. Maurice Whitney 6:30
A moving and eloquent funeral march originally scored for brass alone, effectively arranged (though some textual liberties are taken).

GRUNDMAN, Clare   **FANTASY ON ENGLISH HUNTING SONGS**   Boosey & Hawkes
5:00

Another excellent Grundman work with sensitive scoring and well-judged contrasts of tempo, mood, style and texture.

GRUNDMAN, Clare   **A SCOTTISH RHAPSODY**   Boosey & Hawkes
6:00

A very enjoyable and effective medley of both well-known and less familiar tunes.

JACOB, Gordon   **FANTASIA ON AN ENGLISH FOLK SONG**   R. Smith
5:00

An appealing, well-organized work with nice mood and scoring contrasts. Technically modest in difficulty, but with exposed choir and solo passages.

KARG-ELERT, Sigfrid   **MARCHE TRIOMPHALE**   Warner
Arr. Ross Hastings   3:15

A glorious organ work (really a chorale-prelude, but martial in style), splendidly scored and very effective on concert programs. Technically modest (except for a few spots) but requires rich tone.

KIRCK, George T. (Arr.)   **RENAISSANCE TRIPTYCH**   Shawnee
6:00

An excellent alternative to the *EARLY MUSIC SET* previously listed, featuring a virelai by Machaut, a frottola by Mantuanos and an anonymous villancico. Technically modest (except for some intricate triplets in the virelai) but requiring a sense of the style and subtleties of nuance, rhythm and inflection.

KROEGER, Karl   **DIVERTIMENTO FOR BAND**   Boosey & Hawkes
An interesting, well-crafted work in five contrasting movements unified by a 4-note motive, with very effective variety of scoring and texture.

LIADOV, Anatol   **EIGHT RUSSIAN FOLK SONGS**   Belwin (Kalmus)
Arr. Richard Franko Goldman
Very engaging and attractive settings, technically modest in difficulty (except for two fast movements). Published in two parts of four songs each; has been out of print – however, Kalmus has recently reprinted Part I.

NIELSEN, Carl   **PRELUDE TO ACT II of "SAUL AND DAVID"**   G. Schirmer
Arr. John Boyd   4:30
A fine work with both contrapuntal interest and harmonic richness, superbly transcribed.

PERSICHETTI, Vincent   **O COOL IS THE VALLEY**   Elkan-Vogel
6:00

A lovely lyric and pastoral poem, with Persichetti's usual sensitive scoring and tasteful writing.

PURCELL, Henry   **CHACONNE AND RONDO**   Etling
Arr. Merle Isaac   5:35
A magnificent pair of excerpts from two different stage works. The scoring is rather heavy and unimaginative but the music is superb.

SCHUBERT, Franz   **FINALE, SYMPHONY NO. 5 IN B-FLAT**   Shawnee
Arr. Anthony Camillo   5:00
A real gem of classical style with romantic overtones. The transcription is a bit brass-heavy and thick in tutti passages, but is serviceable, and is worth working on for the sake of the musical value.

SHOSTAKOVICH, Dmitri   **HAMLET SUITE**   MCA
Arr. Benjamin Suchoff   6:00

An excellent transcription of three excerpts from Shostakovich's incidental music to "Hamlet". Somewhat challenging technically (in Presto section) and for endurance (brass in Funeral March), but worthy of performance.

STARER, Robert   **DIRGE FOR BAND**   MCA

An interesting and often powerful work, though somewhat contrived and constrained. Requires careful working out of dissonant harmonic formations and rhythmic intricacies.

STEVENS, Halsey   **FIVE PIECES FOR BAND**   Peer
Arr. Donald Bryce Thompson   10:40

These pieces show considerable imagination and creativity, though somewhat inconsistently. In fresh-sounding neo-classical idiom, technically not difficult – but use compound meters and bi-tonal harmony.

TICHELI, FRANK   **AN AMERICAN ELEGY**   Manhattan Beach

A very effective work projecting the feelings of tragic loss, pain and sorrow with accompanying hope and relief. Well-scored and proportioned.

TICHELI, FRANK   **SUN DANCE**   Manhattan Beach

An energetic rhythmically vital piece- very effective for a concert and valuable for developing rhythmic accuracy and ensemble precision.

WALTON, Sir William   **MINIATURES FOR WIND BAND**   Oxford
Arr. Bram Wiggins

Ten very attractive short pieces, technically modest, covering a wide variety of styles and moods. Scored with intelligence and taste.

WEINER, Lawrence   **TERTIAN SUTE**   Southern
   7:00

An effective work in moderately contemporary style, in three contrasting movements. Some technical challenges (clarinet articulation in 1st movement) and musical intricacies (brass entrances in 3rd movement), but eminently playable at this level.

WHITE, Donald   **RECITATIVE, AIR AND DANCE**   Belwin
   6:00

An interesting work, somewhat inconsistent in quality, but revealing both imagination and creativity in treatment.

• •

d'Albert, Eugene   THE IMPROVISATOR OVERTURE   Hindsley
Arr. Mark Hindsley   4:45

A wonderful neglected orchestral work, superbly transcribed. It begins with a lively and brilliant yet lilting theme (Very fast, E^b, 6/8), which is elaborated and developed. A short transition leads to a beautiful second theme in C major, legato in style, accompanied by the lilting rhythm of the beginning. The opening theme is then subjected to a short development; the recapitulation follows the original scheme closely, leading to a brilliant coda based upon the opening theme. Demands fluency of fingers and tongue (especially woodwinds), lightness, clarity, finesse, and good command of 6/8 and its dotted-rhythm subdivisions.

ARNOLD, Malcolm   ENGLISH DANCES   Belwin
Arr. Maurice Johnstone   8:00

A thoroughly ingratiating, imaginative and colorful treatment of four contrasting dance styles. (1) Andantino, B^b, 6/8 (dotted-quarter=50), gentle and rather languorous in character, requiring suave legato style and precise rhythmic placement of 8ths an 16ths. Mostly transparent or small-group scoring with several solo lines, but also balance problems in more fully-scored passages, with soloistic lines in moving notes against sustained chords. (2) Vivace, C, 2/4 - energetic and boisterous, demanding both fluency (legato 16ths) and brilliance (Brass fanfare-like figures). (3) Mesto, G minor, 4/4 - slow and poignant, featuring a lovely folk-like melody appearing in several voices (Bassoon, Horns, Piccolo). (4) Allegro risoluto, 3/4 - forceful and brilliant, with an emphatic theme decorated by rapid woodwind arpeggios and featuring cross-rhythms. (N.B. Tempo in this movement should be quarter=168, not 138).

BACH, J.S.   CHORALE PRELUDE   Witmark (Warner)
Arr. James Gillette   (We All Believe in God)   3:30

A magnificent work (Moderato ma energico, D Dorian, 2/4, quarter=60), full of great majesty, dignity and power, which has both contrapuntal intricacy and harmonic richness. Technically only moderately difficult, but requires fluency and tongue control on 16th-note passages, rhythmic solidity and independence, careful attention to balance for the sake of clarity, beauty and blend of tone, and phrasing and feel of line. The scoring is excellent, with considerable emphasis on woodwinds and low brass, and includes parts for English horn and soprano saxophone. Has been out of print for some time but is definitely worth seeking. Highly recommended.

BACH, J.S.   FANTASIA IN G MAJOR   Presser
Arr. R.F. Goldman, R. Leist   6:30

A glorious work for organ (Grave, G, 2/2, half=48) which sounds equally magnificent in this fine transcription. Though technically modest in difficulty, effective presentation requires beauty of tone, breadth of phrasing, careful listening for intonation and blend, attention to balance, and feeling of line and continuity. The key of concert G may cause initial problems but can be easily overcome. All wind players should be exposed to this work as a great musical experience.

BACH, J.S.   RICARCARE   Alfred
Arr. R.L. Moehlmann   5:00

A prime example of Bach's mature contrapuntal style, which treats an intricate theme in 6-part counterpoint with great rhythmic independence resulting in complex chromatic harmony. Requires a critical combination of rhythmic precision and flow of line; clarity of texture and balance of parts; and most of all an understanding of the musical style. The transcription is excellent, achieving an intelligent layout of the original 6-part texture. The optional introduction should be avoided.

BORODIN, Alexander   FIRST MOVEMENT from SECOND SYMPHONY   C. Fischer
Arr. Erik Leidzen   6:30

A serviceable arrangement of a 19th-century orchestral classic (Allegro moderato, C minor, 2/2,3/2). Though the doubling tends to be excessive, this version is faithful to the texture and text of the original. It is a work that is forceful and gentle by turns, with passages of legato, lyrical style alongside others that are marcato and staccato which demand precision and clarity. Technically somewhat demanding on bass instruments, with a few passages requiring flexibility of articulation in upper woodwinds.

BRAHMS, Johannes   **ACADEMIC FESTIVE OVERTURE**   Aeolus Music
Transc. Joseph Kreines   10:30

A wonderful transcription of this historical work that is very faithful to the original. It begins with a very soft and staccato march style (2/2, C minor) using the clarinet and bassoon as the dominant instruments. This continues to build both rhythmically and texturally with sweeps of eighth note (both duple and triple) interjections. A soft-lyrical section provides contrast to a quick return to the opening style. This leads to a tutti rhythmic theme (forte), which is answered quietly with greater reserve. A very noble and sostenuto theme is introduced by the trumpets supported by the horns and oboes (C major, Dolce). This is developed with accidentals and added sonorities. The march style returns containing tutti scoring (brass, clarinets and oboes providing the two measure melody) with all of the accompaniment parts playing the off beats. The very familiar processional ensues (Maestoso, ¾, new eighth note=old quarter note,) using dotted eighth sixteenth repeated rhythms in two measure phrases. This becomes very decorated with bursting woodwinds runs and tongued sixteenth notes (including tuba and euphonium parts). The chorus is repeated with overlapping rhythms using all the wind and percussion colors until the final three notes bring the work to an exhilarating conclusion. Highly recommended. Requires technically fluent woodwinds, French Horns with power and independence and brass who have endurance and complete control of tone in all registers. Well worth the effort! Reviewed by RH.

BRAHMS, Johannes   **A GERMAN REQUIEM: MOVEMENT I.**   Aeolus Music
Transc. Joseph Kreines   *SELIG SIND,DIE DA LEID TRAGEN*   10:40

A wonderful and authentic transcription for those who wish to perform the complete first movement of this Brahms masterwork. The opening material begins with the soft pulsating bass line, which introduces the expressive lyrical and repeated theme (4/4. F major, Rather slowly and with Expression). The choral parts are very ably scored for appropriate colors and are also cued in the woodwinds for a non-vocal performance. The sostenuto style is apparent throughout the work with clearly marked contrast indications and logical phrases. A smooth and brief shift to Db major, which takes the work through several chromatic and emotional peaks, eventually subsides to the opening mood back to F. After several instruments display a brief restatement of the opening theme, the style becomes increasingly agitated with echoing rhythms and punctuating fragments. This wanes into some of the most beautiful angelic-like qualities for winds. The work wistfully concludes pp on an F major triad. A very moving masterpiece. Although there are not advanced technical demands, maturity, in terms of style, pitch center and control of dynamics, is required of all wind players. This is exceptionally programmable for winds and choir. Reviewed by RH.

BRIGHT, Houston   **PRELUDE AND FUGUE IN F MINOR**   Shawnee
       6:30

An excellent original work. The opening Prelude consists of a dramatic, dissonant declamatory statement using an inverted rhythm (Poco lento e deleberato molto, 4/4), answered by a fast scherzo-like motive (Allegro scherzando, 4/4, quarter=140) using triplets, scored for woodwinds alone. The declamatory motive returns, abbreviated, closing softly. The scherzo reappears, stated first in trumpets, then with woodwinds, leading to a forceful series of dissonant brass chords which climax in a tutti bi-tonal formation. This leads to a final statement of the opening motive tutti, climaxing in a unison dominant C. The fugue now appears (Lento Moderato, half=72), beginning in trumpet - a noble, sustained, flowing yet majestic theme, with an effective counterpoint in 2nd trumpet. Succeeding statements follow in horns and baritone, trombones, flutes and oboes, clarinets, etc. – reaching a stretto climax followed by a B♭ pedal-point over which the theme is presented in parallel triads. A cadential line leading to an F pedal, with two last statements of the theme's opening, brings the work to a powerful dramatic conclusion.

CHANCE, John Barnes   **ELEGY**   Boosey & Hawkes
       6:00

A great original work which plumbs the depths of expression and meaningful content. Beginning with a simple flowing melodic line and its counterpoint, the music builds an elaborate, rich texture of interweaving lines, arriving at a climax which introduces a dramatic, agitated theme in faster tempo. A sudden interruption and the second theme is presented in a more reflective and nostalgic mood leading to a varied repetition of the opening, again building to an even more intense and powerful peak, only to be interrupted again. The opening mood returns and gradually becomes more and more subdued, with one last reminder of the second theme in English horn (alto sax) fading into a sustained chord in horns and low brass which trails into silence. While technical demands are modest (note values are mostly quarters and half-notes, except for the second theme and scale-runs for the flutes), this piece requires great musical sensitivity to phrase, nuance, feeling of line and continuity, as well as solid control of pitch, tone and blend. Strongly recommended for all groups capable of presenting its significant musical values.

CHANCE, John Barnes   **VARIATIONS ON A KOREAN FOLK SONG**   Boosey & Hawkes
7:00

An excellent, well-crafted work, with effective contrasts between its variations. The theme is stated by unison clarinets unaccompanied, followed by a harmonized version. Five variations follow: (1) *VIVACE*, featuring 16th-note figures of varying lengths, requiring fluency and facility in upper woodwinds, trumpets and percussion. (2) *LARGHETTO* – a lyric variation with the melody in solo oboe, then low flutes; accompanied by sustained chords. (3) *ALLEGRETTO* (6/8), featuring slurred-8th-note figures in various instruments. (4) *SOSTENUTO* (3/2), featuring solemn but rich-sounding chords. (5) *ISLANCIO* (3/4), featuring canonic entrances using the second phrase of the theme, leading to a coda with the theme in augmentation in the brass. Requires good clarinets, solo oboe, trumpet (solo and section), solid horn with both range and technique (2nd horn goes to low E^b in an exposed passage), facile and precise woodwinds, and intelligent and competent percussion (5 players).

COPLAND, Aaron   **THE PROMISE OF LIVING**   Boosey & Hawkes
Arr. Kenneth Singleton   5:40

A faithful and successful transcription of one of Copland's most poetic inspirations – the quintet from his opera "The Tender Land." Though it is not difficult technically, the work requires soloists with beautiful tone and musical sensitivity, and fluency and accuracy of rhythm in the accompaniment passages, as well as control of upper registers in trumpet and trombone. Recommended for the many musical qualities of the work and for development of ensemble proficiency.

COPLAND, Aaron   **VARIATIONS ON A SHAKER MELODY**   Boosey & Hawkes
6:00

An excerpt from one of Copland's best known works (*Appalachian Spring*), effectively transcribed by the composer. Has numerous passages of transparent solo and choir scoring, variations in Gb, technically demanding work for woodwinds in the fast section (16th-notes without any slurs indicated) and maturity and control of tone in brass.

DEBUSSY, Claude   **THE ENGULFED CATHEDRAL**   Barnhouse
Arr. Robert Longfield   6:10

A generally faithful transcription of a piano masterpiece which ranges in mood from mysterious to exultant to grimly tragic. Apart from some strange textural omissions and changes of register, this version is successful in capturing the mood and character of the original, and is generally slightly preferable to that of James Miller (pub. *Shawnee*). Requires players with good control of tonal and dynamic ranger, awareness of balance, refinement, blend, feeling of line and sensitivity to the musical subtleties of the Impressionist style.

DELIBES, Leo   **MARCH AND CORTEGE OF BACCHUS**   Alfred
Transc. Joseph Kreines   5:30

A very capable and exciting transcription of this wonderful French signature. A repeated soli trumpet fanfare opens the march (Eb major, 2/4, quarter note=104) and is answered by the tutti ensemble. A petite theme follows (requiring a short burst of tongued sixteenth notes) using unison rhythms and entwined with fragments of opening trumpet fanfare. This is contrasted with a warm, lyrical section (Ab major) containing volume and phrase swells and unison triple rhythms. A more noble section follows (G major) still containing triplet rhythms until another section appears (Ab major) using short sixteenth note patterns in the same style. These lead to more triple figures until a return to the opening material by the trumpets and tutti answers. A lively 6/8 section (dotted quarter note = 132, *Un Peu Plus Anime'*) is next containing unison eighth note rhythms that build in intensity until it reaches the majestic Largo chorus (2/2, half note = 66). This noble melody, using accented half note and triplet fragments in four measure phrases, is dressed with climbing eighth notes in the low winds. A rapid 6/8 section follows (Allegro vivace, dotted quarter note =160) for a thrilling yet magnificent ending. A great musical journey which merits strong consideration. Reviewed by RH.

DELLO JOIO, Norman   SCENES FROM "THE LOUVRE"   Marks (Belwin)

A fine work in five contrasting movements, using 16th and 17th century melodies as its basis. (1) *PORTALS* (Andante maestoso, 4/4) – sustained and eloquent, using choir scoring (trombones, woodwinds, trumpets, etc.), contrasted with a more flowing section (movendo) in 6/8. (2) *CHILDREN'S GALLERY* (Allegretto, 4/4), featuring a light, playful tune with woodwinds and brass in staccato articulation, contrasted with a slower legato variation of the tune in 6/8, featuring horns and trumpets, then upper woodwinds (including high oboe solo). (3) *THE KINGS OF FRANCE* (Allegro Moderato), opening with a noble, broad 4/4 with sweeping melodic lines, contrasted with a 3/4 section using imitation between voices and a succeeding 4/4 that is more marked and rhythmic in style. (4) *THE NATIVITY PAINTINGS* (Andante con tenerezza, 6/8), featuring the melody *"In Dulci Jubilo"* played by solo clarinet, with variants played by solo oboe and flutes, lightly scored. (5) *FINALE* (Allegro brilliante) – a festive, martial mood set by the opening timpani and brass motives, with effective contrasts provided by a lightly flowing woodwind figure. This work reveals all aspect of musicianship, with demands placed on both technical and stylistic areas. Highly recommended.

DVORAK, Antonin   TWO SLAVONIC DANCES   Shawnee
Arr. Andrew Balent   7:15

Dvorak's Slavonic dances have long been favorites on orchestra programs, but have not appeared often in complete form in adequate transcriptions. Here are two of the most popular ones , excellently arranged. The first (Allegro assai, C minor, 2/4) has considerable contrast in texture, dynamics and scoring, ranging from two solos with light accompaniment to fully-scored multi-textured passages. The second (Presto, G minor, 3/4 in 1), vigorous and delicate by turns, has similar contrasts and scoring variety. Major effort must be placed at keeping a light, dance-like touch, even in heavily-scored passages, and maintaining the flow of tempo and vitality of rhythm, while developing security in the exposed soli and lightly scored passages.

ELGAR, Sir Edward   THE SEVERN SUITE   Sam Fox
Arr. Alfred Reed   18:00

A fine work, originally written for brass band, that has been splendidly transcribed. In five movements: (1) *WORCESTER CASTLE* (Pomposo, B^b, 3/4) - a broad, noble prelude with two contrasting themes (marked and epic; gentle and lyric). (2) *TOURNAMENT* (Allegro molto, E^b, 2/2), fast, lithe and brilliant, demanding considerable technical facility (both slurred and tongued 8th-notes). A short transition in slower tempo leads into (3) *THE CATHEDRAL* (Andante molto, B^b minor, 4/4 in 8) a slow, solemn, rich-textured fugue. (4) *IN THE COMMANDERY* (Moderato con moto, E^b, 3/4), a gentle, amiable minuet with a faster, lilting trio with dotted-8th-16th rhythms. (5) *CODA* (B^b, 3/4), opening with a slow introduction leading to a varied restatement of the opening movement, brought to a nobly dignified yet stirring conclusion.

EWAZEN, Eric   CELTIC HYMNS AND DANCES   Southern Music
9:30

An interesting approach to recreating medieval and renaissance idioms with original melodic material and contemporary harmonic content. It opens with a moderately slow andante using short melodic fragments from which a majestic melody appears. This is brought to a tutti climax. The tempo suddenly changes to Allegro, using some of the andante ideas, including the majestic melody, which is now agitated and driving. A new section in 6/8 meter follows using variations of earlier material. The 4/4 allegro now reappears briefly, returning to the opening Andante. A fast 12/8 section follows, leading to a climactic statement of the majestic theme and a brilliant coda.

FAUCHET, Paul   **SYMPHONY IN B-FLAT**   Witmark (Warner)
Arr. F. Campbell- Watson & J. Gillette   30:00

An excellent original work in four movements, published separately. (1) *OVERTURE,* opening with a slow introduction featuring a noble fanfare-like figure in horns, then in trombones and trumpets. This idea is expanded and developed along with a dotted rhythm, leading to a lively allegro in 6/8, with the fanfare-figure transformed into a rhythmically well-marked and energetic theme. Two subordinate thematic ideas also appear, and are developed at some length, leading to a climactic coda using both introduction and allegro themes. (2) *NOCTURNE* (Lento, G minor, 3/4) - a very slow, poetic movement using two ideas – an opening unaccompanied horn solo and an English horn melody (cued trumpet). (3) *SCHERZO* (Vivo, B^b, 3/4, feeling in 1) – energetic yet lilting in character with contrasts between solo, small-group and tutti scoring, followed by a pastoral Trio in E^b, featuring a simple sostenuto idea in the horns, later expanded and developed in woodwinds and trumpets. (4) *FINALE* (Allegro vivace, B^b, 2/3) features a lively gallop-like main theme contrasted with a flowing secondary theme in E^b. After considerable development of both ideas, the two are effectively combined in an exciting and eloquent coda. This work offers players a rich musical experience along with substantial technical challenges.

FRANCK, Cesar   **PSYCHE AND EROS**   Kjos
Arr. A.A. Harding   5:30

A serviceable transcription of a 19th-century French orchestral classic that ranges in mood from a shadowy, mysterious opening to a lyrically songful main theme, reaching passionate eloquence at the climax and subsiding to a tender, gentle close. Technically moderate in demands (a few triplet-8th passages and intricacies in woodwinds), but requires great beauty of tone, subtleties of blend and nuance, well-focused intonation, careful attention to balance - and a conductor with the feeling for Romantic style and its expansive phrases with the ebb and flow of subtle rubato.

FRESCOBALDI, Girolamo   **TOCCATA**   Belwin
Arr. Earl Slocum   5:30

Although this work is not by Frescobaldi (it was composed for cello and piano by Gaspar Cassado), it is a repertory classic which makes both technical and musical demands. The slow, sustained introduction (Grave, C minor, 4/4) requires expressive legato, careful balancing of voices, and well-controlled intonation. The succeeding Allegro is lively and rhythmic; the horns state the main theme along with intricate 16th-note passages for woodwinds. Later the theme is taken up by trumpets and trombones, brought to a climax with a return of the opening section. A fantasia section follows featuring flutes and clarinets playing 32nd-note scales while the oboe (cued trumpet) plays a sustained ascending line. The work concludes with a final statement of the Allegro in full band scoring.

GLAZUNOV, Alexander   **AUTUMN FROM "THE SEASONS"**   Volkwein
Arr. Richard Bancroft   9:30

A wonderfully evocative ballet excerpt, effectively transcribed. The opening *BACCHANALE* (2/4, in 1) is fast, energetic and driving, with a more reflective and delicate subordinate section. The succeeding *ADAGIO* (4/4) is graceful and poetic, with beautiful flowing lines. The *FINALE* (6/8), a buoyant Allegro, uses a variation of the main Bacchanale theme, concluding with a broad coda. Demands good technical fluency (especially woodwind), sensitivity to balance, rhythmic accuracy and energy, and feeling for flowing line and phrase.

GLIERE, Reinhold   SYMPHONY NO. 3 (ILYA MUROMETZ) – 1ST MOVEMENT   EMS
Arr. Glenn Cliffe Bainum   7:30

An excellent transcription and abridgement of a Russian classic. It opens in a dark, somber mood (Andante sostenuto, C minor, 4/4) with low woodwinds and brass, followed by a majestic horn solo that is developed among various instruments to an intense climax. The succeeding Piu Mosso (2/2) is both lyric and dramatic in character, building to a powerful fanfare figure in the brass, which increases in intensity to a shattering outburst. This subsides into the return of the Piu Mosso theme which builds to an eloquently heroic coda. Technically not difficult, but requires musical and tonal maturity, with good horns, solid trumpets, low woodwinds and brass.

GOOSEC, Francois   CLASSIC OVERTURE IN C   Presser
Arr. R.F. Goldman and R. Smith   5:00

Another French Revolution original well scored for modern instrumentation. It opens with a majestic opening theme in full band followed by a passage of rhythmic syncopations and suspensions. These two ideas are extended, leading to a subordinate theme with descending melody and ascending bass. The second theme emerges, using imitation and a flowing 8th-note figure, leading to a closing theme featuring the syncopations and dotted rhythms introduced earlier. The development uses the 8th-note motive, leading to the customary recapitulation and a short coda restating the initial theme. This is a fine work that requires considerable technical facility and fluency in all parts as well as rhythmic precision, stylistic awareness and refinement of tone.

GRAINGER, Percy   COLONIAL SONG   C. Fischer
    6:15

One of the great works in the literature, requiring a high level of musicianship and artistry - beginning with the very opening, which requires a legato attack pp, continuing through the simple yet eloquently throbbing alto saxophone solo, the folk-like trumpet melody with its pizzicato-style woodwind accompaniment; its subsequent expansion with intricate yet graceful ornamentation and embroideries; the rich-textured horn and baritone lines – gradually subsiding into a final statement of the saxophone melody in solo trumpet at very slow tempo and a short coda with an intense dynamic swell fading into silence. As noted, musicianship is at a premium, and fine soloists (alto sax, oboe, trumpet, euphonium) and sections (horns, trumpets, clarinets) are required, as well as a conductor who demonstrates both sensitivity and technical control (for the slow tempos, subdivisions and metric and rhythmic intricacies). Strongly recommended.

GRAINGER, Percy   HANDEL IN THE STRAND (Clog Dance)   C.L. Barnhouse
Adopted by Sousa's Band and arranged by Brion and Schissel   4:00

A delightful work using original material with a Handelian flavor mixed with music-hall rhythms (hence the title). The opening (Fast and merry, 4/4, F major, quarter note =120-132, very lightly) features woodwinds, horns tuba and mallets, which requires light staccato style, rhythmic vitality and precision as the phrases swell and dip. Later, more sustained legato in melodic phrases are introduced simultaneously by the baritone. A brief section of shifting meters provides wonderful contrasts to previous sections before returning to the opening character. Several solos and sections are featured including oboe, baritone, clarinets, trumpets, trombones, piccolo, and xylophone - with both rhythmically intricate and melodically attractive parts. This arrangement is much more effective than previous settings of this masterful work.

GRAINGER, Percy   THE IMMOVABLE DO   G. Schirmer
    5:30

A rich-textured, hearty, warmly lyrical work, composed around an inverted pedal-point (high C in upper woodwinds) which sounds through the entire piece. The harmonies are elaborate, chromatic, intricate; while the melodic material is rather simple and straightforward. Requires beauty and blend of tone, good intonation, wide dynamic ranger, flowing legato style and solid, resonant bass voices.

GRAINGER, Percy   IRISH TUNE FROM COUNTY DERRY   C. Fischer
    3:40

A great band standard which demonstrates that "technically easy" pieces are often the most difficult. In the opening section, scored for brass, saxophones and low woodwinds, Grainger has placed the melody (played by trombones, baritone, 4th horn, baritone sax and alto clarinet) in the middle of the texture, surrounded by soprano, alto and bass voices, thus making balance difficult, especially at the prescribed soft dynamics of the accompaniment. The second section (scored for woodwinds, later with horn and trumpet) also demands great control of soft dynamics and great care in tuning and blend (all lines at the beginning are doubled except for the melody in flutes; on repetition melody is doubled by alto sax and 1st horn). The final section, for full band, demands beauty of tone (tends to be bright and overblown due to additional doublings) and balancing to permit clarity of contrapuntal texture. The last measures require great control of soft playing (e.g. low notes for tuba, oboe, bassoon; change of register for horns). Despite the challenges of Grainger's setting, all bands should be familiar with this magnificent work – a model combination of contrapuntal ingenuity, harmonic richness and emotional expression .

GRAINGER, Percy	**MOCK MORRIS**	Ludwig
Arr. J Kreines		3:30

A jaunty, rhythmically energetic work featuring original material in a "morris dance-like" style (hence the title). It opens with woodwinds alone (without flute, oboe and saxophone). The flutes join in on the melody for the last part of the phrase. The next statement features an oboe obbligato against saxophone choir. A new section features the brass choir, leading to another new melody in alto saxophone and horns which is repeated in flute and clarinet. A short oboe solo accompanied by mallet instruments leads to a return of the opening materials in varied treatments and featuring different solos (e.g. bass clarinet and euphonium).

GRAINGER, Percy	**TWO GRAINGER MELODIES**	Barnhouse
Arr. Joseph Kreines		5:30

Two more examples of the lyric Grainger output, with rich harmony, subtle counterpoint and imaginative approaches to the folk-melody material. Requires a number of soloists with musical sensitivity and tonal beauty; flute, oboe, euphonium, horn, trumpet, clarinet, soprano saxophone (cued various instruments in both pieces).

GUIRAUD, Ernest	**DANSE PERSANE**	Belwin
Arr. Herbert Fred		5:30

An exciting, vital and rhythmic work with appealing melodies. After a brief introduction, the main theme appears in upper woodwinds, accompanied by a rhythmic motive. A second section contrasts a sustained legato line with a counter-subject based on the rhythmic accompaniment. The succeeding middle section develops the opening theme with the rhythm, leading to a triumphant statement of the theme, gradually increasing in speed and energy to a brilliant conclusion. Requires both technical fluency and tonal finesse, with clean staccato tonguing from both upper winds and lower brass, particularly in the final pages.

GRIEG, Edvard	**HOMAGE MARCH from Sigurd Josalfar**	Boosey & Hawkes
Transcr. Joseph Kreines		9:50

A wonderful transcription of a lesser-known Grieg gem. The work begins with a rapid five-measure fanfare (Allegro molto, quarter note = 144, Bb major) then quickly proceeds to the processional in a somber and lyrical manner (*Allegretto Marziale*, quarter note=76). This builds using woodwind dominant sonorities with important contrasting brass interjections (which incidentally juxtaposes duple and triple cross rhythms at its peak.) A short "animato" section follows beginning with brass triplet figures and leads to a magnificent Maestoso using pervious material in a "FF" tutti setting. A quiet and simple march ensues (Eb major, quarter note=116) and ushers in a brief Allegro section (Bb major). This leads to a D.S. al coda back to the opening procession (Allegretto *Marziale*) and continues to the end of the Maestoso section. A very brief coda brings the work to an inspiring close in Bb major. Excellent scoring and faithful editing make this work a very worthy musical sojourn. Reviewed by RH.

HANDEL, G.F.	**THE GODS GO A-BEGGING**	Chappell
Arr. Sir Thomas Beecham		11:00
Trans. W.J. Duthoit and Erik Leidzen		

A fine suite of pieces excerpted from various Handel operas, tastefully arranged. The five movements are (1) *INTRODUCTION* (Moderato maestoso, G minor, 4/4), a grand epic opening with sweeping scales and rich chordal texture. (2) *ALLEGRO* (B^b, 4/4), a jaunty and light-hearted movement scored for smaller group, featuring oboes and bassoon. (3) *ENSEMBLE* (Presto, F, 4/4), a staccato, rhythmic movement with considerable unison and homophonic writing. (4) *MUSETTE* (Moderato, A^b, 3/4) a gently flowing lyric movement scored for smaller group. (5) *BOURREE* (Allegro, B^b, 2/2), a lively rhythmic movement with some intricacies of texture.

HANDEL, G.F.   **MUSIC FOR THE ROYAL FIREWORKS**   Hindsley
Arr. Mark Hindsley   17:30

An orchestral favorite for many years, this work has come into its own as an original wind work and has been skillfully transcribed for modern band by Hindsley. It is also available in a version by William Schaefer (Highland Music) and in the original wind scoring edited by Charles Mackerras and Anthony Baines (Oxford). Movements are (1) *OVERTURE* -a monumental, epic-style introduction using dotted-rhythm figures, followed by a lively, spirited Allegro using dotted-rhythm figures, followed by a lively, spirited Allegro using a fanfare figure, dotted rhythms and flowing 16ths. (2) *BOURREE* (2/2) -a staccato-style dance movement featuring terraced dynamics and scoring contrasts. (3) *LA PAIX* (Largo alla Siciliana, 12/8), a gently rocking slow movement. (4) *REJOUISSANCE* (Allegro, 4/4) - lively and energetic. (5) *MENUETS 1 & 2* - two contrasting pieces; one is epic, the other intimate.

HANDEL, G.F.   **PRELUDE AND FUGUE IN D MINOR**   Belwin
Arr. Hans Kindler, Trans. Herbert Hazelman   6:00

An effective and worthy transcription and elaboration of Handel's magnificent original (the opening movement of Concerto Grosso, Op. 3, #5). The opening Prelude is solemn yet intense (Largo appassionato, 3/4), with majestic chords interspersed with marcato triplets. The fugue (Allegro, 4/4) features a rhythmic theme with more sustained countersubject, developed and built to a powerful climax, when the opening Prelude returns. Requires good woodwinds (two solo oboes, cued flute and clarinet), intelligent brass playing with sensitivity to balance and blend, and well-placed intonation (considerable doubling throughout).

HANSON, Howard   **CHORALE AND ALLELUIA**   C. Fischer
                                                                                        5:30

A fine original, written for the American Bandmasters Association. It opens with a lush-sounding, richly harmonized *CHORALE* (Largamente, 4/4) stated in the brass, answered by a soft rhythmic motive in clarinets. These two phrases are restated and expanded; then, using the rhythmic motive as transition, leads in to the *ALLELUIA* without pause (3/4, quarter= 100), the theme of which is stated by horns and euphonium. The tempo gradually quickens and the energy and drive increases as both the Alleluia theme and the rhythmic motive are brought to a great climax which is suddenly interrupted by a massive statement of the Chorale in slow tempo again answered by the rhythmic motive. An exultant, driving coda using the rhythmic motive and Alleluia theme brings the work to a brilliant conclusion. Requires excellent horns, baritone and trumpets (6 parts), with power and endurance as well as control and beauty of tone; woodwinds with solid rhythm and clarity of tone; and good timpani (4 drums required).

HANSON, Howard   **DIES NATALIS**   C. Fischer
                                                                                        15:00

A major original work in theme-and-variations format, using an old Lutheran chorale. It opens with a slow, reflective introduction leading to the statement of the chorale, followed by five variations. (1) *Poco piu mosso*, using the opening segment of the melody with rich-textured harmonic and counter-melodic material. (2) *Molto Meno Mosso*, using an ostinato of quarter-notes against an augmented, octave-displaced statement of the melody. (3) *Andante calmo* - a chant-like variation with melody in woodwinds (solos: flute, oboe, bassoon, clarinet, bass clarinet, baritone, bass). (4) *Allegro feroce* - fast, brilliant, aggressive, with rapid 16th-note figures against motivic statements of the melody. (5) *Larghetto semplice* - solo woodwinds present canonic statements of the melody; leading without pause into the Finale (Maestoso), using elements of the previous variations, brought to a rich-textured, vibrant conclusion. Requires a group with well-grounded musical maturity; strong solos and sections, ability to sustain long phrases, endurance of brass, technical facility in rapid passages. Also demands beauty of tone throughout (much chorale-style and sustained-note writing).

HEARSHEN, Ira   **SYMPHONY ON THEMES OF JOHN PHILIP SOUSA:**   Ludwig
                          MOVEMENT II, AFTER "THE THUNDERER"   7:30

A powerful original based on the trio to the famous "The Thunderer" march by Sousa. This is the second movement from a much larger symphony from which all movements are based on Sousa marches. Opening in a *Mahleresque* manner (4/4, A^b, quarter note =48-52) the theme of the march becomes very apparent as performed in a somber manner by the woodwind choir with euphonium and tuba. A short transition leads to a "slightly faster" section (quarter note = 58-63) now in G. Using rhythmic and melodic variations this section quickly moves forward into short fragments in E^b that culminates into an agitated section (quarter note=112-120) containing more accidentals and brass effects. The motion slows back into the opening key but now with brass instruments containing the melody in rubato style. The texture thickens with embellishments including woodwind ornaments and builds to a tumultuous climax and then subsiding and building again to the final tutti "FFF" before a short subito-pianissimo Ab triad is finally performed by the low winds. Although there are few technical challenges, all winds must possess maturity of tonal and pitch focus, legato style and sensitivity to balance. The rubato style leaves much room for musical expression and expansion.

HOLST, Gustav   **FIRST SUITE IN E-FLAT**   Boosey & Hawkes
10:00

A band classic in three short movements, each of which is based on the same 4-note motive. (1) *CHACONNE* (Allegro moderato, E^b, 3/4) begins with an unaccompanied 8-bar theme presented in the bass voices, followed by various statements in different styles, textures and scorings, concluding with a magisterial coda. (2) *INTERMEZZO* (Vivace, C minor, 2/4), light, brisk, fleet in character – the melody derived from the motive is transformed into a flowing legato line (4/4) in the trio-like middle section. The 2/4 section returns - the coda (C major, 4/4) presents both ideas simultaneously. (3) *MARCH* (Tempo di Marcia, E^b-A^b-E^b, 2/2) opens with a spirited, vigorous theme in the brass, contrasted with an arch-like 32-bar theme in woodwinds. After an interesting and varied development, the two themes are combined to form a brilliant, exciting climax. Requires facility and fluency (legato and staccato), control of articulation in Vivace, beauty of tone in wide-ranging dynamics, good solo voices (flute, oboe, clarinet, alto sax, horn, trumpet, euphonium, bass), and overall musicianship and sensitivity.

HOLST, GUSTAV   **"SCHERZO" and "NOCTURNE" from "A MOORSIDE SUITE"**   Boosey & Hawkes
Arr. Gordon Jacob   Scherzo- 2:55, Nocturne- 7:10

The first and second movements from Holsts' suite for brass band superbly transcribed for wind band. The SCHERZO (B^b minor) is light and mostly delicate with robust moments, and a trio section in the parallel major featuring a lyrical theme played against the scherzo rhythm. The NOCTURNE (F minor) is very slow and sustained, requiring great control, finesse, and beauty of tone. A trio section in F Major is scored for full band, beginning pp with a crescendo to ff, only to recede into the opening material, transparently scored. This publication has been out of print for many years but is very much worth searching for.

HOLST, Gustav   **SECOND SUITE IN F**   Boosey & Hawkes
11:00

The companion to the preceding suite, also a classic, but in 4 movements, and based on folk material. The first, *MARCH* (Allegro, F major, 2/2) uses three contrasting tunes: a Morris dance in crisp staccato; a lyric legato melody first stated in solo baritone, then in full band; and a jig-like tune (B^b minor, 6/8). The second is a poignant, poetic setting of *"I'll Love my Love"* (Andante, F minor, 4/4). The third is a rousing, hearty setting of *"SONG OF THE BLACKSMITH"* (Moderato e maestoso, 4/4 – 3/4). The finale uses the *DARGASON,* a reel tune in 6/8, and *GREENSLEEVES*, in 3/4, and combines the two in brilliant contrapuntal fashion. Requires good solos: piccolo, oboe, clarinet, alto sax, trumpet, baritone, tuba; and finesse of tone, blend and balance, fluency and facility of tongue and fingers.

HUMPERDINCK, Engelbert   **PRAYER AND DREAM PANTOMIME**   Warner
Arr. Joseph Maddy   7:15

A magnificent work, generally well-transcribed. It opens with a simple prayer tune (Moderato, C major, 4/4) which is variously harmonized and given interesting counter-melodies. The Pantomime (A^b-E^b), which follows without pause, amounts to a great expansion and development of the tune and its counter-material, rising to great heights of eloquence and nobility. Requires great beauty of tone, good intonation and control of pitch, refinement and sensitivity to nuance, careful balancing of melody with accompaniment, and feeling for phrase and line. Solos and sections: Flutes, clarinets, oboe, alto and tenor sax, horns, trumpet, euphonium – and rich, resonant bass voices.

ISAAC, Heinrich   **A LA BATAGLIA**   **Medici**
Arr. Ronald Johnson   6:05

An excellent rendering of a Renaissance battle-piece – perhaps the earliest instrumental piece by a well-known composer. The opening section is scored for brass and percussion, then for woodwinds and percussion, followed by a contrasting triple-meter section for brass. The remainder of the work presents the two contrasting ideas in various sequences and scorings, and also includes two interludes for percussion alone. Highly recommended as a fine example of Renaissance music, well-presented and scored for band.

IVES, Charles   **THE ALCOTTS**   Associated
Arr. Richard Thurston   6:00

A superb transcription of a poetic, evocative piano work. It opens quietly with a motive based on Beethoven's 5th, leading into a short lyric melody in solo flute. After a further extension of the 5th motive and the lyric melody, the mood becomes more agitated, with dissonant harmony, building to a climactic statement of the 5th in full band, then subsiding into a quieter statement of both ideas. This leads to a new idea – a Scottish tune stated in alto saxes, answered with a cadence on "*Here Comes the Bride*" in horns. Yet another idea appears – an old hymn-tune in clarinet and sax. These two ideas are alternated; the closing segment of the hymn is used to build a powerful climax featuring the lyric melody of the first section and the 5th motive, gradually subsiding into a soft C triad. While technically most of the parts are not difficult (except for a rapid arpeggio figure in horns and baritone at the final climax), there are many musical challenges, including metric understanding (5/8, 7/8, 9/8) and intricate cross-rhythms and syncopations, tonal refinement and transparent scoring, stylistic awareness, solo and section talent (clarinets, trumpets, alto saxes, flutes) and a conductor who can unify the disparate elements described here into a musical whole.

JACOB, Gordon   **AN ORIGINAL SUITE**   Boosey & Hawkes
                                                                                                          10:15

A vital, fresh-sounding work composed entirely of original material (as distinct from so many earlier British works based on folk-material or transcriptions – hence the title). In three movements: (1) *MARCH* (Allegro, G natural minor, 4/4), using three contrasting themes – flowing melodic, staccato, and rhythmically energetic –with a lyric trio-like section in Bb. (2) INTERMEZZO (C Major – A minor, 3/4-4/4) featuring a reflective, nostalgic melody in a solo alto saxophone with sustained legato accompaniment, repeated and extended to a rich-textured climax. A segment of the tune is then developed and expanded to build another climax, leading to a return of the melody treated canonically, cadencing in A minor which becomes the basis of a short coda, using the first segment of the melody. (3) FINALE (Allegro con brio, Bb, 2/4-6/8), boisterous and aggressive in character, with both meters simultaneously at the beginning, featuring two main ideas –requiring both woodwind agility and trumpet tonguing. This piece requires fluent technique (both legato and staccato) in the first movement (especially solo clarinet and trumpet, both of which are given extended 16th-note legato passages near the end) and the finale; and beauty of tone, balance, blend, finesse and solo alto sax in Intermezzo.

JACOB, Gordon   **TRIBUTE TO CANTERBURY**   Boosey & Hawkes
                                                                                                          12:00

A fine work in three movements, which has been rather neglected. The opening movement is a broadly lyric chorale-prelude on "A Mighty Fortress is Our God", and uses several different approaches to the tune, including imitative counterpoint, embroidery and variation, reaching a massive climax stating the last phrase of the tune in full band. The second movement is a scherzo (3/4 in 1) – at first fast, light and delicate, featuring the woodwinds – later fuller, weightier, with the brass playing a variation of the chorale tune. A trio section features a smooth-flowing melody in clarinets, brought to a climax in full band. The scherzo then returns with some new elements (woodwind embroideries and horn syncopations), brought to a brilliant conclusion with both scherzo and trio ideas in full band. The finale, a march, begins with a percussion introduction, leading to the rhythmically vigorous first theme. A second idea is broader in character, answered by a light staccato phrase. A development section follows, featuring a return of the chorale tune. The recapitulation is varied, concluding with a powerful statement of the chorale at the coda. Requires strong players in all sections (including exposed oboe and bassoon in the second movement), and well-developed musicianship. Highly recommended.

JACOB, Gordon   **WILLIAM BYRD SUITE**   Boosey & Hawkes
                                                                                                          12:00

A band classic in 6 contrasting movements, each one of a free transcription of a keyboard work by the 16th-century English master. (1) *THE EARLE OF OXFORD'S MARCH* (Un poco pomposo, F major, 2/4) begins very softly with a stately dignified theme given free-variation treatment with increasing rhythmic and textural complexity, gradually building to an imposing climax. (2) *PAVANE* (Molto Lento, G minor, 4/4) - very slow and sustained, featuring solo and choir scoring, using imitative counterpoint and flowing counter-melodies. (3) *JOHN COME KISS ME NOW* (Allegro con grazia, F modal, 2/2) – pert, light and brilliant, again using variation technique, with considerable use of ornamental figuration and rhythmic counterpoint. Requires fluency and light articulation. (4) THE *MAYDEN'S SONG* (Moderato un poco lento, 3/4) features a sustained 16-bar theme in brass, used as a ground for a series of variations, beginning softly and rather subdued and building to a rich-textured, eloquent climax. (5) *WOLSEY'S WILDE* (Con Moto, B[b], 6/8), gently lilting, texturally intricate (16th-note passagework and cross-rhythms) and effective dynamic contrasts. (6) *THE BELLS*

(Moderato, B^b, 3/4), uses a great variety of melodic segments over a two-note bass ostinato to build a texturally complex but powerful climax. This is a superb work requiring mature musicianship and solo players in all sections (including an important E^b Clarinet, uncued). No baritone saxophone. Strongly recommended.

| **KALINNIKOV, Basil** | **FINALE from SYMPHONY NO. 1 in G MINOR** | EMS |
| Arr. Glenn Cliffe Bainum | | 8:30 |

A fine Russian Romantic classic with a winning combination of energy and sweep, epic breadth and lyric intimacy. In rather fast tempo through most of its length (Allegro risoluto, F major, 2/2), it requires considerable facility and fluency in all woodwinds (especially clarinets), solid brass with rich tone and endurance, and a feeling for the late 19th-century style. The opening section presents two contrasting themes – the first, animated and driving; the second more relaxed and gentle. The middle section develops and expands these two ideas, using more transparent scoring which requires good solo and small-group playing (including flute, oboe, clarinets, alto and tenor sax, bassoon, bass clarinet for short, rhythmic solos; and horns, saxes and baritone for lyric lines). The closing section, by contrast, calls for full band sonority, with brass intoning a chorale-like melody while upper woodwinds play a flowing 8th-note figure derived from the opening theme. The transcription, apart from the somewhat gimmicky device of antiphonal brass choirs at the close, is excellent.

| **KARG-ELERT, Sigfrid** | **SABBATH MUSIC** | Southern |
| Arr. William Rhoads | | 9:40 |

A rich-textured work comprised of three organ originals, written in an interesting combination of Baroque and Romantic styles. (1) *CHORALE* (Moderato molto sostenuto, G modal minor, 4/4), scored for brass alone, is a rather mournful and somber chorale-prelude with long, flowing legato lines and contrapuntal texture, requiring good control and endurance. (2) *INVOCATION* (Moderato, A^b, 4/8), for woodwinds, presents a simple lyric melody in flowing 8ths with chromatic legato accompaniment. (3) *PRAISE THE LORD WITH DRUMS AND CYMBALS* (Allegro Maestoso, C major, 4/4) for full band, is festive yet dignified, featuring fanfare-like figures for brass and percussion and 16th-noter lines for woodwinds (challenging in terms of articulation and precision) –reminiscent of Handel in its epic style and exuberant mood.

| **LAURIDSEN, Morton** | **O MAGNUM MYSTERIUM** | Peer International |
| Arr. H. Robert Reynolds | | 5:00 |

A beautiful hymn set simply, yet with imaginative use of suspensions and non-chord tones to produce a contemporary sound. The mood is largely lyric and reflective, but builds to an imposing climax. The final section returns to the mood and style of the opening. The band scoring is very effective, using chamber-style choirs and tutti passages to produce appropriate variety. Recommended for an excellent lyric work in contemporary style.

| **LO PRESTI, Ronald** | **ELEGY FOR A YOUNG AMERICAN** | Presser |
| | | 5:00 |

A poignant, deeply felt work that covers the gamut from muted sadness to angry frustration and back to serene resignation. It opens with a simple but striking motive in clarinets which is repeated and expanded to a tutti climax featuring a descending scalar motive, gradually subsiding into a cadence in trombones, using part of the clarinet motive. A new theme (actually a variant and expansion of the opening) now appears in clarinets, then in horns and upper winds, then in tutti, varied and in faster tempo. Next another version of the trombone cadence appears, while upper winds (beginning in flute) take up the clarinet theme in inversion. The pace gradually quickens as the theme is varied further, reaching an agitated, intense allegro using both elements and climaxing with a dissonant version of the cadence. This is suddenly interrupted by a return to the opening slow tempo using a climactic version of the clarinet theme, resolving into the descending line which then fades into a quiet coda. Technically not difficult (except for inordinately high E^b and 1st clarinet parts), but requires great sensitivity to tone quality, intonation, varying harmonic structures (from triads to minor 2^{nds} and 9^{ths}), feeling for sustained phrases and musical direction. Strongly recommended

MACDOWELL, Edward
Arr. Thomas Davis and Frederick Miller

SEA PIECES

Shawnee
7:00

An excellent transcription of 4 beautiful piano pieces in predominantly lyric vein. (1) *FROM A WANDERING ICEBERG* (Serenely, F, 4/4) is scored mostly in choirs, opening with upper woodwinds alone, gradually building to a rich, resonant climax, then fading into soft low brass at the end. (2) *STARLIGHT* (Tenderly, Bb, 4/4) is similar in mood and character, with occasional solo lines (baritone, clarinet, oboe) and sustained accompaniment. (3) *SONG* (Cheerily, F, 2/4) is rather lively and vigorous, with a passionate episode in the middle featuring horns and baritone, and a gentle, nostalgic close with solos for oboe and bassoon (cued trumpet, baritone). (4) *TO THE SEA* (Broadly, D^b, 4/4) is epic and sweeping in character, opening with full band using varying dynamics, succeeded by a more subdued, transparently scored section, then gradually building to a rich, powerful climax. Though technically this work is modest in its demands, the simplicity of material combined with richness of texture provides considerable challenges of intonation, blend, balance, and beauty of tone - as well as a feeling for long phrases and musical shape.

MAHLER, Gustav
Arr. Jimmie Reynolds

SYMPHONY NO. 3 –FINALE (EXCERPTS)

Shawnee
7:00

An intelligent abridgement of a great work that represents the summit of the late-Romantic style. In very slow tempo (quarter should = 44-48, rather than 60 as printed), requiring great control of pitch, tone and legato attack, and ability to play long phrases with great intensity and expression as well as beautiful tone. In addition, there are several exposed brass entrances (trumpet, horn, trombone) calling for soft playing in high registers near the end. Though there are several errors in the transcription (both notes and octave doublings), it is highly recommended for any band (and conductor) capable of handling its considerable musical demands.

MENNIN, Peter

CANZONA

C. Fischer
5:00

A great modern band classic in dissonant and polytonal style, in one continuous movement and tempo. It opens with a declarative statement in brass and saxes, then tutti, followed by a series of short contrasting statements. A more tranquil, lyric mood ensues, scored for solos (flute, oboe, piccolo, clarinet) with small groups accompanying (clarinets, horns, saxes, bass clarinet, bassoon). A varied recapitulation and climactic statement of the opening brings the work to a forceful conclusion. Requires good articulation in all sections (especially staccato rhythmic figures in horns, euphonium, and tuba), rhythmic precision and clarity, and solidity of solo and choir sonority. Strongly recommended.

MAILMAN, Martin

LITURGICAL MUSIC FOR BAND, OP. 33

Belwin
10:00

An imaginative and interesting attempt to set the different texts of the liturgical mass without the words. The opening INTROIT (Allegro moderato, C, changing meters) feature bell and chime sounds, imitated by woodwinds and brass, establishing the church atmosphere. The thematic material is chant-like in style, using melodic fragments of varying lengths. The KYRIE (Adagio, G, 3/4), solemn and subdued in character, features the woodwinds at the beginning and end, with soft brass as contrast in the middle. The succeeding GLORIA (Giocoso, F, 6/8), exuberant and joyous, elicits the rhythm of the word "Gloria" and expands on it, using varying combinations of 8ths and 16ths with some technical and rhythmic intricacy. The ALLELUIA (Allegro energico, C, 4/4) opens with an energetic theme in unaccompanied trumpets which is then treated fugally. Thematic elements from earlier movements are also brought back for contrast. The work concludes with a richly sonorous climax. Demands mature-sounding and technically secure brass, fluent upper woodwinds, lower woodwinds with good tonal focus and pitch, rhythmically solid percussion, and musically perceptive ensemble work.

MILHAUD, Darius

SUITE FRANCAISE

MCA
16:00

A band classic consisting of 5 movements, each of which uses a folk-tune from a different French province. (1) *NORMANDIE* (Anime, 6/8) uses a jolly, lilting melody and several attractive secondary tunes with effective canonic and contrapuntal writing. (2) *BRETAGNE* (Lent, 6/8 in 6), a rather poignant, nostalgic movement, with important parts for horns, bassoons and oboe, requiring great control of tone, pitch and musical finesse. (3) *ILE-DE-FRANCE* (Vif, 2/2, half=112), very rhythmic and energetic, with frequent repeated 8th-note patterns and two contrasting tunes. (4) *ALSACE-LORRAINE* (Lent, 2/4), a dirge-like slow march with melody in saxophones, a secondary melody in muted trumpets, rising to an affirmative climax using both melodies in full band. (5) *PROVENCE*

(Anime, 4/4), features a vigorous tune in upper woodwinds and a charming contrasting one in flutes and piccolo accompanied by drums (a hallmark of Provencal folk-music). This is a major work for band, with a variety of technical demands (some of which place the piece on a more advanced level) and musical maturity. Nonetheless, many less-advanced groups will be able to handle a sizeable portion of this work, and should become acquainted with it. Strongly recommended.

MOZART, W.A.   **ADAGIO AND FUGUE K.546**   Aeolus Music
Arr. J. Kreines   6:30

This is a very skilled transcription of a lesser-known yet magnificent work by Mozart. Beginning with full dark colors and mood (Adagio marcato, ¾, C minor) the section quickly develops using dotted eighth sixteenth patterns in various woodwind and brass alterations. The final measures of the Adagio are performed by the clarinet choir, which gradually fades into the closing on the dominant triad. The Fugue's subject (4/4, Allegro) begins loud with strong punctuations from the low woodwinds using both staccato and slurred notes. The scoring of the various wind groups, each presenting the subject, is very effective and reflect the intention of the string orchestra original. A very clever and lengthy development section exposed by the clarinet choir leads to several contrapuntal passages featuring brass, woodwind and mixed sonorities. The fugue becomes more technically challenging as required by light tongued and slurred sixteenth notes performed by all families using accidentals to augment the original tonal center. The final measures marked "molto marcato" bring the complete work to a convincing and fulfilling conclusion in C minor. Winds must possess rhythmic independence, ability to respond to balance and complete tonal control in all registers. A very worthwhile journey!

MOZART, W.A.   **THE IMPRESARIO OVERTURE**   Ludwig
Arr. Clifford Barnes   5:00

A sparkling and brilliant overture, one of Mozart's best. It opens with a theme in three sections, each of which has contrasting components of rhythm, dynamics and note-values, accompanied by a rapidly moving bass line in 8ths (Presto, B^b, 4/4 - should be conducted in 2). The second theme features a melodic fragment passed around to different instruments over a flowing 8th-note background, ending with an intricate articulated 8th-note passage in clarinets. The closing theme is more lyric in feeling, leading to the development section which concerns itself exclusively with the first theme-group but creates variety through the use of minor mode. The recapitulation follows the exposition closely, with a short climactic coda based on the first theme. Demands the utmost in musicianship and considerable technical facility, especially from woodwinds and bass instruments. Also requires delicacy, refinement and sensitivity to balance - but well-worth the effort required.

MOZART, W.A.   **ALLEGRO MOLTO**   Shawnee
Arr. Jack Snavely   8:00

The opening movement of Serenade No.10, K.361, from which the *MENUETTO AND RONDO* is taken (see previously under Medium). It opens with a spacious, expansive Largo introduction (B^b, 4/4 in 8), requiring careful working out of subdivisions (rhythms using 16^{ths} and 32^{nds}) yet maintaining linear flow. The Allegro utilizes the classical contrasts between loud and soft, lyric and epic, sustained and articulated, in a magnificent rich-textured movement. Requires good oboes and bassoons and an ensemble capable of contrasts between delicate and full sonority. The "enlargement" by Snavely is excellent. Highly recommended.

NELSON, Ron   **MEDIEVAL SUITE**   Boosey & Hawkes
                                                                                                                     15:40

A highly imaginative 3-movement suite that uses various stylistic characteristics of three medieval-era composers in contemporary language. The movements are published separately as follows: …

   (1) *HOMAGE TO LEONIN* – 5:00. An evocation of the chant-like style of Leonin's organa, in which the band members sing as well as play. Technically not difficult, but uses various contemporary compositional and notational devices, including ad lib unmeasured passages and spatial notation.
   (2) *HOMAGE TO PEROTIN* – 4:25. A driving, vital rhythmic movement (Joyously, C, 6/8), with frequent cross-rhythms, use of 8th-note ostinato figures and pedal points. Very exciting and dynamic with demanding mallet parts; also calls for piano.
   (3) *HOMAGE TO MACHAUT* – 6:15. Sustained and stately, yet flowing, with both rhythmic and melodic interest (Molto sostenuto, 6/4-3/2, quarter=54). Require beauty of tone, sensitivity to nuance and phrasing.

OFFENBACH, Jacques   THE DRUMMAJOR'S DAUGHTER OVERTURE   Kjos
Arr. Lawrence Odom   6:40

One of the best of all 19th-century operetta overtures, with a wealth of good tunes, rhythmic energy and lyric grace. It opens with a lively introduction (Allegro, D major, 6/8), suddenly interrupted by a mysterious, subdued transition in B^b, leading to a waltz (F, 3/4 in one), with a graceful melody in flutes and more animated material in tutti scoring, developed and expanded to a climax, then modulating up a half-step to a lyric Andante (A^b, ¾), featuring a beautiful melody in oboe (later with flute). Another short transition leads to an abbreviated return of the waltz, interrupted by a soft maestoso brass fanfare, gradually building intensity and excitement to a brilliant Vivace (D^b, 2/4) with a rhythmically active melody in clarinets. This leads to the final Presto which provides an exhilarating conclusion. Requires considerable facility, fluency, and clarity of articulation from woodwinds, lightness and delicacy in brass with good tone and solidity in climactic movements.

ORFF, Carl   CARMINA BURANA   Schott
Arr. John Krance

A contemporary choral-orchestral classic in 25 sections, 13 of which have been brilliantly transcribed by Krance. Many different styles and moods are represented: poetic, serene, mysterious, menacing, forceful, raucous, joyous, triumphant. Requires both flowing legato and clean articulation from woodwinds, good sustained tone and forceful marcato from brass, and skilled, intelligent percussion. Several movements require proficient soloists (flute, oboe, baritone), frequent use of unusual meters (3/2, 4/2, 5/2, 6/2) as well as compound metrics (4/4-3/8; 4/4-6/8, etc.).

PAULSON, John   EPINCION   Kjos
6:00

The title refers to a victory song sung by the ancient Greeks as they walked through a battlefield sorting the wounded from the dead. It is in contemporary idiom and notation, with passages of aleatoric writing, multiple tempos and indeterminate pitches. A very powerful, emotionally intense work that repays attention, and a valuable experience for players and conductor. Requires some extended pitch and dynamic ranges, intelligent percussion, and willingness to explore new musical approaches. Highly recommended.

PERSICHETTI, Vincent   BAGATELLES   (Kalmus) Elkan-Vogel
6:00

A set of four short, tightly-knit pieces. (1) Vivace (quarter=160), utilizing 8th-note rhythmic figures (legato, staccato, tenuto – in various combinations, and rapid 16th passages. (2) Allegretto (quarter=92) contrasting a legato idea (mostly in woodwinds) and an accompanying staccato 16th-note figure. (3) Andante sostenuto (quarter=58), slow and sustained legato with both contrapuntal and homophonic texture. (4) Allegro con *spirito* (dotted-quarter=120) - fast, light, delicate, with use of a repeated 8th-note pattern and a lilting melodic figure, later building to an energetic, driving climax, with very effective and imaginative percussion writing. This piece requires good players in all sections, with both technical fluency for rapid and intricate passage work and well-controlled and refined tone for soloistic and small-choir writing. Also demands an ear for the bi-tonal and extended triad harmony that is the basis of Persichetti's style.

PERSICHETTI, Vincent   PAGEANT   C. Fischer
7:00

An accessible and appealing work in two contrasting sections, played without pause and each using contrasts and overlaps of choir scoring. The opening is slow, sustained and legato throughout, with long, flowing lines richly harmonized. The second section is fast, vital and rhythmic, with both staccato and marcato style contrasted with short slurred figures. Demands good intonation, blend and balance in the slow section; clean, well-defined articulation and rhythmic precision in the fast.

PROKOFIEFF, Serge   THE MONTAGUES AND THE CAPULETS   Highland
Arr. William Schaefer   from "ROMEO AND JULIET"   5:00

A magnificent excerpt from the famous full-length ballet, containing intensity, power, majesty and lyricism. It opens with a depiction of the bitter family feud by means of a slowly-building dissonant chord; answered by a soft, mysterious progression. This is followed by a striding theme stated in flutes and clarinets with a pesante accompaniment. A subordinate theme more forceful in character, then appears in the brass. These are contrasted with a gentle, lyric section featuring solo flute, later embroidered by alto sax and bells. The first section then makes an abbreviated return, bringing the work to an emphatic conclusion. Technically modest in requirement, but demands considerable musical maturity and sensitivity.

PURCELL, Henry   **SYMPHONY from "THE FAIRY QUEEN"**   Kendor
Arr. Frank Cipolla   6:30

A wonderful one-movement work in several contrasting sections. It opens with a majestic introduction using dotted rhythms, leading to a *CANZONA* in moderate tempo using imitative counterpoint and effective use of choir and tutti scoring. This is followed by a soft, sustained *LARGO* in 3/2 meter using scoring contrasts between sections. The work concludes with a lively *ALLEGRO* (6/8), interrupted by a brief but highly expressive *ADAGIO* (4/4). Technically not difficult, but requires musical and stylistic sensitivity (especially in slow sections) and rhythmic precision and continuity in the Allegro.

REED, Alfred   **RUSSIAN CHRISTMAS MUSIC**   Sam Fox
12:00

A large-scale, rich-textured work, utilizing folk-material, liturgical motives and original themes woven together into an elaborate structure. The opening, very slow and solemn, provides an appropriately religious tone. This is followed by an emphatic declarative section with chant motives stated in brass accompanied by intricate woodwind figuration. A more reflective passage ensues, using variations of earlier material, featuring an important English horn solo (cued alto sax). The long closing section features a fanfare-like proclamation in juxtaposition with a climactic statement of the main liturgical melody. The coda is appropriately epic, sumptuous and brilliantly sonorous. Requires mature woodwinds with both fluency and tonal beauty, strong brass with both richness and endurance, and intelligent percussion with important parts for chimes, bells, and xylophone.

RHODES, Philip   **THREE PIECES FOR BAND**   Belwin
4:40

An interesting and imaginative work using 12-tone technique. (1) INTRADA (Briskly, quarter=96) - a declarative piece featuring three contrasting motives, ending with a slow, soft coda. (2) PASSACAGLIA (Moderately, 2/4) uses a short 8-note theme accompanied by a 4-note chord and several counter-subjects, including material stated in the Intrada. (3) VARIATIONS (Brisk and Steady, 2/4), really a rondo using a ritornello that is stated at the beginning and after each variation. Technically not too difficult, but challenging to the ear due to the dissonant and complex harmonic content. Also requires great concentration on rhythmic precision (many entrances occur after short-value rests and linear continuity is established from one instrument or group to another). Scoring is colorful and varied, with interesting parts for all players including percussion.

RIEGGER, Wallingford   **DANCE RHYTHMS**   Associated
7:00

A very appealing and energetic work whose simple, straightforward character belies its rhythmic and technical intricacies. The main thematic material is syncopated and accented in style, contrasted with short legato motives. Percussion parts are important, especially mallets; and both brass and woodwinds are challenged by range problems, accidentals and rhythmic subtleties. This may account for its neglect, but it deserves attention and is very effective on concert programs.

RIMSKY-KORSAKOV, Nikolai   **PROCESSION OF THE NOBLES from "MLADA"**   C. Fischer
Arr. Erik Leidzen   4:30

A brilliant and exciting orchestral showpiece in a generally excellent transcription. (Allegro moderato e maestoso, E^b, 3/4, quarter=108). It opens with an arresting fanfare featuring trumpets and horns, leading to a proud, stately melody in horns, saxophones, baritone and clarinets, later doubled by trumpets. After a brief subordinate section based on the fanfare motive, featuring solo trumpet and woodwinds, the opening fanfare returns and builds to an impressive tutti climax with the fanfare figure in timpani. The key changes to A^b and the mood becomes more lyrical as the woodwinds dominate (but rhythmic precision is still essential due to the syncopated nature of the material). Elements of the fanfare material are then juxtaposed with the lyric theme, suddenly interrupted by the return of the introduction. A recapitulation follows with a short coda based on the lyric theme, concluding with the timpani stating the fanfare. This work is technically rather demanding, requiring trumpets, horns and baritones with clean articulation, accuracy, precision and endurance; fluent and precise woodwinds, and well-focused pitch and ensemble sonority. It also requires an awareness of both epic and lyric stylistic elements, and feeling for phrase and line in the middle section. (N.B. – major error in score and parts: in melodic voices, 6th measure of #10, 3rd beat quarter-note should be concert D, not E^b).

ROSSINI, Gioacchino	**BALLET MUSIC from "WILLIAM TELL" (PAS DE SIX)**	Ludwig
Arr. Eric Hanson		6:00

A delightful and charming work given an effective arrangement that allows the lightness and delicacy of much of the material to be well delineated. It requires considerable technical facility and fluency in woodwinds (numerous tongued repeated notes and staccato passages; triplet 16th figures), clarity and precision in brass, with frequent sudden dynamic contrasts between pp and ff. The closing section rises to a boisterous, brilliant climax requiring good control of tone and balance.

ROSSINI, Gioacchino	**LA CENERENTOLA SELECTIONS**	Daehn
Arr. Larry Daehn		4:50

A brilliant showcase for the mature ensembles. Opening with hunting-like calls in the French horns soli (6/8, dotted quarter note = 126 in E^b) this work quickly moves to soft tutti passages inspired by the opening material. Many swells and subito-dynamic contrasts give the opening segment excitement and rhythmic drive. A short accelerando segue in duple time leads to even more melodic motion (Vivace quarter note =178). This becomes more developed into a very thrilling finale. This work requires strong wind players (especially French horns) with rhythmic independence and ability to tongue repeated rhythms over a number of measures. Very well-orchestrated, this is a welcome addition to the viable transcriptions for winds. Percussion is reserved for basic battery of four players typical of this time period.

ROSSINI, Gioacchino	**TANCREDI OVERTURE**	Kjos
Arr. Leonard Falcone		6:20

A wonderful little-known overture in an idiomatic and intelligent transcription. It opens with a majestic, spacious introduction with exposed passages for oboes, horns (cued alto saxes), flute and clarinet. This is followed by a sparkling, vibrant allegro, with a bouncy theme in staccato dotted and triplet-rhythm played by clarinets. A rhythmically energetic transition leads to the secondary section featuring a lithe melody in upper woodwinds and a short legato phrase building to an exciting tutti climax. The recapitulation follows the usual pattern, leading to a brilliant coda in fast tempo. Requires fluent woodwinds with control of light-tongue articulation (especially clarinets) and brass that are flexible and sensitive to balance and blend.

RUSSELL, Armand	***THEME AND FANTASIA***	Marks
		9:00

A superb original work with strong dramatic and emotional content, in somewhat chromatic, dissonant style. It opens with a tranquil statement of the theme in three four-note groups, then develops its various aspects: (1) Expressive – melody in solo trumpet with undulating 8th-note triplets in accompaniment. (2) Theme divided between bass and treble instruments with 8th-note ostinato chords. (3) Chordal treatment using small groups with cross-rhythm ostinato (2 against 3) in woodwinds, then percussion. A further thinning of texture leads to (4) Aggressively – a variation of the theme in an intricate ornamental clarinet line, punctuated by dissonant chords and expanding trumpet line. (5) Rhythmic variations using duplet and triplet figures. (6) Lightly – in transparent, delicate scoring. (7) Vigorously – using a combination of a rhythmic 8th-note motive and undulating triplets to build a powerful climax. (8) Chordal statement in muted brass, using extreme dynamic contrasts. (9) Expressively – using previously introduced elements (the clarinet variation and flowing triplets) with an insistent staccato 8th-note figure, leading to (10) Very Broadly – using the first 4-note melodic segment to build to the climactic chorale-like statement in full band with the theme harmonized in tonal triads. An intense, sustained coda states the theme over a pedal Bb. Requires fluency, flexibility and technical accuracy in all sections (particularly clarinets), full control of playing range (delicate to powerful) in brass; intelligent, musical percussion (5 players); and a conductor with both intellectual and emotional grasp of the work's considerable content.

SCHUMAN, William   **NEW ENGLAND TRIPTYCH**   Presser
                                                                                    18:00

A three-movement suite based on tunes by the American Revolutionary master William Billings, published separately. This is a major work which should be played by all bands capable of mastering its musical and technical challenges. Highly recommended.

I. *BE GLAD THEN, AMERICA* (7:00) – a highly rhythmic, vital and exuberant work (12/8, dotted –quarter=126-132). It opens with an unaccompanied, soft timpani solo providing the chief motive of the first section, the melody of which appears in baritone and tenor and baritone saxes in a somewhat intricate statement. It is then presented in parallel thirds, then full triads, building in intensity to a new section (Allegro vivo, 2/4) which states Billings' melody in a fast, driving setting, using a dotted-8th-16th rhythm antiphonally and canonically between choirs and registers, gradually subsiding into sustained soft brass chords while the timpani continues the various rhythmic figures (dotted and triplet motives). This leads to another variation using several rhythms. The texture becomes more contrapuntal, then antiphonal, with numerous rhythmic variations (including a lilting 6/8 passage), building to an emphatic and forceful coda using the dotted rhythm, cadencing in F major while percussion closes with the final phrase. Requires an excellent timpanist, brass that are rhythmically and tonally solid, woodwinds with fluency and precision, and intelligent percussion.

II. *WHEN JESUS WEPT* (5:00) – a beautiful, elegiac slow movement (3/2, half=60), opening with a field drum solo which leads to the first phrase of the melody in unaccompanied solo euphonium. The second phrase is taken by solo cornet while the euphonium continues with a countermelody, closing with a contrapuntal dialog in which both voices use melodic elements. The changes (Piu Mosso, half=72) as the band enters, with upper woodwind and saxes playing the melody, harmonized with sustained chords. The last phrase is stated in unison, leading to a variation of the melody stated by upper voices in unison. The next section features an expansion of contrapuntal treatment, richly harmonized. The closing phrase (descending line) leads to a varied version of the cornet-baritone dialog over sustained chords, with the closing phrase stated over field drum alone, then with a sustained clarinet chord. The dialog fades into a coda using elements of the melody, cadencing in G minor as the field drum states the opening rhythm one last time. Requires excellent cornet and euphonium soloists, with beautiful tone, capacity to play sustained legato and rhythmic accuracy; a musically sensitive field drum; and band ensemble with beauty and blend of tone and well-defined intonation.

III. *CHESTER* (6:00) – an imaginative and stirring work which, though nominally an overture, is actually more like a theme and variations. It opens with a rich-textured legato chorale setting (Religioso, 4/4, quarter=72) – first with woodwind choir (tonality G), then brass (tonality E♭), then closing with woodwinds. The tempo abruptly changes (Allegro vivo, 2/4, quarter=160), with cluster chords punctuating a lively march-like version of the melody. Soon fragments of the tune are broken off and developed, with much antiphonal writing between woodwinds and brass. A new variation appears, rhythmic and staccato, chordal and dissonant, with the tag of the phrase extended, leading to another variation (Flowing , 4/4), this time legato, with the melody in parallel triads scored in woodwinds while the low brass and horns play sustained chords. The style again returns to staccato and 2/4 meter, using more variants of thematic fragments. A final variation uses both the tag and opening of the melody in different rhythmic patterns and note-values, leading to a coda which states the theme richly harmonized, legato style, with militantly rhythmic snare drum accompaniment. The opening and closing phrases are then elaborated and brought to a triumphant conclusion. Requires a combination of technical facility and fluency (rapid rhythmic figures in woodwinds and trumpets), legato tone and intonation (slow section and chorale passages), tempo control (sustained passages in fast sections), rhythmic precision (rapid unison and syncopated figures), and solid, musical percussion.

SCLATER, James   **PRELUDE AND VARIATIONS ON "GONE IS MY MISTRIS"**   Powers
                                                                             12:30

An interesting, well-crafted original work in chromatic harmonic style, with excellent contrasts of mood and character. It opens with a fantasy-like lyrical Prelude for woodwind alone (Moderately Fast, 4/4, quarter=104-108), using elements of the theme. The succeeding Allegro (quarter=132-138) is agitated, rhythmic, tense, with effective contrasts between choir and tutti scoring, and making use of compound meters (5/8, 7/8) and irregular note-groupings. This is followed by a solemn, elegiac slow variation (3/4, quarter=84), opening with low brass followed by a clarinet line which is joined by other instruments and worked up to an eloquent climax, subsiding to a soft, tranquil close. The final variation uses several motives from earlier variations in a rhythmically driving setting, arriving at a chorale-like statement of the opening segment of the theme chromatically harmonized, gradually fading into the coda which states the original theme in tonal harmonization for the first time, ending with a last echo of the prelude and a final G triad in low brass. Requires woodwinds with legato tone and rhythmically defined articulation; brass with richness and resonance as well as precision; intelligent percussion; and ability to aurally focus on dissonant harmonic structures.

SEIBER, Matyas   **AN IRISH TRILOGY**   Daehn
Arr. Larry Daehn   5:00

A skillful and effective treatment of three contrasting Irish melodies – reel, ayre and jig. The opening REEL requires fluency and flexibility of tonguing and interval accuracy. The AYRE is lyrically expansive, with solos for alto saxophone and euphonium, while the JIG is a lively 6/8 with the melody appearing first in solo oboe, then trumpet, flute, and clarinets. The key then changes to the parallel major and features a new reel tune and demanding lightness and precision.

SPARKE, Philip   **DANCE MOVEMENTS**   Studiomusic
       21:00

A very clever and dance-inspired work in four contrasting but connected movements. The first movement, Ritmico (multi meters, quarter note =138) opens tutti with a punctuated theme stated in the horns and saxophones. A contrasting theme soon follows featuring a variety of instruments (including bells and harp). This is further developed with echoes of the opening theme by meter, texture and melodic contrast. A final recapitulation of the opening theme that is quickly fragmented brings the movement to a close. Without pause, the second movement begins, Molto vivo, which features the woodwind families (2/2, half note = 134). A charming and syncopated dance tune appears with increases of 3/4 interruptions. This is eventually answered in the tutti clarinet section with rapid-tongued-articulated patterns. Additional woodwind echoes follow in a succession of highly developed contrasts. This subsides into a perpetual motion of thinning eighth notes and trills culminating with a solo bass clarinet as the connecting bridge to the third movement, Lento (for the Brass, 4/4 quarter note = 60). After a quiet opening with muted trumpets, interjections by the trombone and French horn alternate statements until a chorale-like section evolves. This reaches a climax with a return of previous material. Gradually, the muted trumpets reappear with their opening pyramids as the movement closes tutti "ppp." This starkness is boldly interrupted by a burst of accented layers of percussion colors in the final movement, Molto Ritmico, (4/4, quarter note = 144). The winds eventually consume the texture with hints of syncopated fragments from the opening movement. The underlying percussion material provides the color thread that binds this extensive development section. A short accelerando leads to a final and furious Molto vivace (4/4, half note =104), tutti with full brass sonorities decorated by woodwind runs, percussion colors, and dynamic contrasts. A very full and punctuated final statement brings the work to a curt finish.

STRAUSS, R.   **PRESENTATION OF THE SILVER ROSE**   Masters
Arr. Alfred Reed   **FROM "DER ROSENKAVALIER"**   5:30

A generally faithful and effective version of Strauss at his most poetic, romantic and eloquent. The scoring closely follows the original orchestration, thus requiring strong solo players and sections – including oboe, clarinets and horns. There are also important solo parts for piano (celesta and harp in the original). Recommended as one of the few Strauss transcriptions that provide a close representation of the original.

SWEELINCK, Jan Pieterszoon   **BALLO DEL GRANDUCA**   E.C. Schirmer
Arr. Michael Walters   8:00

A fine late-16th century organ work in theme and variations format, superbly scored. It opens with a fully scored phrase followed by a series of contrasting choir statements. Succeeding variations are: (1) Flute, oboe, and English horn figurations (cued clarinets) with brass choir stating the theme. (2) Theme in upper woodwinds and trumpets with ostinato-like 8th-note line in low brass and woodwind. (3) Theme first in clarinets and horns, then low brass, with obbligato 16th-note line first in flute then in oboes and clarinets, with the closing segment featuring horns and English horn (cued alto sax) on embroidery; and the theme in brass, then low woodwinds. (4) Theme in low brass, 8th-note counterpoint in horns succeeded by trumpets, upper winds, saxophones; closing segment fully scored. The work concludes with the opening thematic statement slightly altered in ornamentation, scored folly. This is a fine work which … has great musical value, requiring technical fluency and pitch control in upper woodwinds and all brass, as well as sense of style, tonal refinement, awareness of phrase and feeling of line. Scoring includes 3 oboes and English horn (exposed passages are cued) and omits baritone saxophone and percussion. Highly recommended.

TCHAIKOVSKY, P.I. **FOUR CHARACTERISTIC DANCES FROM SWAN LAKE** Ludwig
Arr. John R. Bourgeois 13:17

A magnificently scored arrangement of four diverse dances from Act three of "Swan Lake." The work begins with The Hungarian Dance (Maestoso, 4/4, quarter note = 76). After a brief introduction (centering around D major) the dance proceeds in G minor using ornamented and light woodwinds statements. The melody is developed by varied rhythms, dynamics and articulation. A subito-vivace section follows (2/4, quarter note = 144, G major) containing sixteenth note passages with many woodwind exchanges. This is punctuated with brass and percussion which grow with harmonic intensity into the final last note. Spanish Dance (3/4, quarter note = 120, F minor) uses the familiar bolero-style rhythm to accompany the melody in the flutes and oboes. A shift to F major, beginning with a more optimistic melody in the clarinets, gradually builds with both woodwind and brass sonorities (including repeated dotted sixteenth and thirty-second-note figures) that brings the movement to a close. Danse Napolitane (4/4, quarter note = 106, E^b major) is in two parts. After a brief introduction, the dance proceeds featuring a brilliant trumpet solo accompanied by woodwind choir. A short accelerando introduces a lively *Tarantella* (6/8, dotted quarter note = 190) containing idiomatic eighth note figures, swells in volume and accented passages. This continues to drive forward into the exciting last note. The final dance, Mazurka (3/4, quarter note = 144, F major) also begins with a brief introduction and quickly moves to the tutti sonorities using dotted eighth sixteenth and triplets as its rhythmic source. Several repeated sections occur while shifting tonality using various accidentals. A quiet contrast (in B^b major) ensues featuring two solo clarinets and later reassigned to flutes and oboes. This ushers in a skillful contrasting section (back to F) using simpler rhythms and chromatic accompaniment. This builds until a return to the opening material and tutti textures. The final piu mosso coda brings the entire work to an electrifying finish.

TCHEREPNIN, Alexander **FIVE BAGATELLES** MCA
Arr. William Rhoads 6:00

A highly enjoyable, fresh-sounding set of five piano pieces, sensitively transcribed. (1) Allegro Marziale (C minor, 4/2) – highly rhythmic, marked, well-articulated, demanding precision and clean tonguing. (2) Vivo (3/8 in one, D^b) – light, fast, brilliant, also requiring light and fluent tonguing – also demands solo talent and choirs (flute, piccolo, oboe, clarinet). (3) Dolce (A^b, 4/4) a gently lyric, flowing, slow movement featuring woodwinds. (4) Allegro marcia (A^b, 12/8) – contrasting light staccato and heavier marcato styles as well as legato lines. (5) Presto (2/4 in one, C minor) – very fast and brilliant, demanding fluency and lightness.

TURINA, Joaquin **FIVE MINIATURES** Associated
Arr. John Krance 8:00

A real gem that deserves to be better known –superb transcriptions of five short piano pieces. (1) *DAWN* (Andante, 3/4) – a slow, atmospheric portrait, beginning softly in transparent scoring and building to a brilliant climax in full band. (2) *THE SLEEPING VILLAGE* (Lento, 4/4-3/4-4/4) – features a lovely folk-like melody in woodwinds, followed by solo trumpet, then clarinet and sax and upper woodwinds leading to a brilliant, short flute cadenza, concluding with upper woodwinds. (3) *PROMENADE* (Andantino, 2/4) – a moderate-tempo piece featuring a staccato motive, rhythmic in character, contrasted with a more sustained outburst in the middle, closing as it began. (4) *THE APPROACHING SOLDIERS* (Allegro alla marcia, 2/4) – opening with martial but soft percussion alone followed by a trumpet call, gradually building to tutti climax, closing with a short coda based on the call. (5) *FIESTA* (Allegro vivo, 6/8) – lively and rhythmic, with excellent scoring and textural contrasts. This is a very colorful, brilliant work with a wide variety of moods, styles and textures, requiring strong solo and section talent throughout the ensemble. Highly recommended.

VAUGHAN WILLIAMS, Ralph **FOLK SONG SUITE** Boosey & Hawkes
10:00

A band classic using several fine English folk-tunes in imaginative and creative ways. (1) *MARCH* (Allegro) begins with a short 4-bar introduction which goes from f to pp, leading to a light staccato setting of "*I'm Seventeen Come Sunday*" (F minor, 2/4), followed by a fully scored version. This is succeeded by "*Pretty Caroline*" (A^b), presented as a lovely, legato melody in solo clarinet and trumpet with light accompaniment that has both rhythmic and sustained elements. The last tune, "*Dives and Lazarus*" (F minor, 2/4-6/8) is presented in broad ff marcato strokes in low brass, while upper woodwinds play a strongly marked reel-like dotted-rhythm line in 6/8. (2) *INTERMEZZO "My Bonny Boy"* (Andantino, F minor, 3/4) is a hauntingly beautiful melody scored for both solo oboe and trumpet (probably meant for either rather than both) with chordal accompaniment. It then appears in clarinets and baritone with counter-melodic material. A short transition in solo clarinet leads to a trio-like Poco Allegro (Scherzando) which features the lilting "*Green Bushes*" (should be conducted in one), with melody in piccolo, oboe, and E^b clarinet and chords in horns and clarinets; succeeded by a setting with oboe, alto sax, trumpet and baritone accompanied by clarinets and flutes playing legato-8ths in succession, dovetailing to make one flowing line. The tag of the melody leads to a varied recapitulation of the opening section. (3) *FOLK SONGS FROM SOMERSET* (Allegro, B^b, 2/4), in march style using four contrasting tunes. The first, "*Blow Away the Morning Dew*" is set in light-staccato style (p, later a boisterous ff), followed by "*High Germany*" with melody in trombones, baritones and alto sax ff, accompanied by mf 8th-notes – a very rhythmic and vital marcato setting. This is followed by a return of the first tune. A short transition leads to the *Trio* (C minor, 6/8) featuring two contrasting tunes - one in soft upper woodwinds, lightly accompanied; the second, hefty and heroic, in low brass and woodwinds with a fanfare-like figure in upper winds, trumpets and horns. While the technical demands are not great, this work is musically quite challenging, with a wide variety of styles (from very short staccato through marcato, tenuto and legato), abrupt changes of dynamics covering a wide range, mastery of dotted and triplet rhythmic figures, feeling of phrase, beauty and control of tone and well-focused pitch center; as well as care in working out details of balance, clarity and blend.

VON SUPPE, Franz	**LIGHT CAVALRY OVERTURE**	Boosey & Hawkes
Trans. Joseph Kreines		7:00

A superb transcription of one of the most popular overtures from the Romantic period. The opening begins with the familiar trumpet fanfare (*Maestoso*, 4/4 in B^b major) and is repeated and answered by the tutti ensemble. This leads to a delicate section with extreme volume and color contrasts and eventually to a tutti section with the theme presented in all brass while decorated with woodwinds. A very vibrant section ensues (*Allegro*, half note = 96, B^b minor) featuring various woodwind colors and articulative contrasts. Without interruption the clever "cavalry" theme is introduced (6/8, *Allegretto brilliante*, dotted quarter note= 116, B^b major) using brass sonorities (requiring both slurred and intricately tongued sixteenth notes) and later joined by the woodwinds. A short clarinet cadenza introduces a solemn lyrical section (4/4, Adantino con moto, B^b minor) containing unison dotted eighth-sixteenth and triple rhythms. After a return to the "cavalry" theme (Allegretto brilliante, B^b major, 6/8) a very stirring coda follows using all of the wind and appropriate percussion sonorities to render a brilliant and traditional conclusion. Highly recommended for advanced ensembles with excellent solo woodwinds, brass with endurance and advanced tonguing skills and a musical percussion section that understands their role in this Romantic composition. Reviewed by RH

WAGNER, Richard	**DIE MEISTERSINGER VON NUREMBURG PRELUDE TO ACT III**	Aeolus Music
Transc. Joseph Kreines		9:30

A much more authentic alternative to other transcriptions of this work. After a very heroic opening (4/4, C major, Very Strong) the work climbs through several tonal centers using alternating motion in the outermost voices. This subsides into a thinner texture featuring various and appropriate solo and tutti woodwind colors. A brilliant brass fanfare enters, decorated by sweeping woodwinds, which uses accidentals and texture contrasts for additional support. A lyrical and tonally complex section transitions into a slightly slower and thinner section (In moderately warm tones, Chromatic in E major) exposing several solo woodwind colors. This quickly modulates into numerous new key centers and isolated textures containing more complex rhythms (duple and triple cross rhythms and thirty second notes) as the technical demands (including double sharps, tongued sixteenth notes and tenor clef) continue to increase as the soaring material develops. This leads to the opening key of C major and a restatement of the opening theme but this time in thinner brass ornamented with woodwinds. The trumpets and upper woodwinds are later juxtaposed using both themes. After several textural contrasts a new section appears (Very Heavy) containing more punctuated articulations and further exposition of the second theme by the brass. This functions, as a coda in which the material builds in rhythmic and harmonic intensity into the final quarter note comprised of a C major triad. A powerful composition worthy of those ensembles and conductors who wish to perform this great work of art, which is tremendously faithful to the original. Reviewed by RH.

WAGNER, Richard	**DIE MEISTERSINGER ACT II: PRELUDE;**	Aeolus Music
Transc. Joseph Kreines	**DANCE OF THE APPRENTICES; ENTRY OF THE MEISTERSINGERS**	15:30

This transcription provides a very authentic representation of parts of Wagner's most famous pages. The Prelude begins with a dark and mysterious opening (4/4, Bb major, *Etwas Gedehnt*) containing unison and overlapping phrases and shifting tonality. A lush brass choir ushers in a newer section (G major) using similar direction and style. Very expressive statements (dolce) ensue using woodwind sonorities but generally at the softer levels. This leads to additional material presented by the low wind sonorities. A sudden shift

(*Sehr Beit*) to tutti forte colors and various tonal centers continue the expressive lines. These begin to thin and the Prelude concludes pianissimo on a unison G. Note: this is a practical option for performances that exclude the remainder of the selection. The Dance begins very fast and festive (*Lebhaft*, 3/4, F major) with trills and layered textures that build and soar in an ornamental-like style. This becomes more rhythmically consistent until another tonal change to C major, which begins with soft trills similar to the previous setting. A duple section results (4/4, *Massig*) containing march rhythms performed by woodwind and brass sonorities. This is further developed technically (slurred and tongued sixteenth notes) as the textures and volume contrast in quicker motion. A seemingly endless burst of unison woodwind patterns introduces the gallant brass fanfare (ben tenuto). This is repeated with additional woodwind embellishments until the tutti sonorities present the opening rhythmic material of the Prelude but in a more robust setting. The fanfare figures quicken as the lush textures become more forceful until the timpani roll reinforces the final thundering notes in C. A very assessable effort that provides advanced winds an opportunity to perform Wagner's most familiar music in a faithful and expert setting. Reviewed by RH.

WAGNER, Richard	**ELSA'S PROCESSION TO THE CATHEDRAL**	Warner
Arr. Lucien Cailliet		5:00

This is one of the great standard-repertory works that should be in all upper-level libraries. It opens with a beautiful, serene and soft legato phrase. (Slowly, solemnly, E^b, 4/4, quarter=60) in solo woodwinds (two flutes, oboe, English horn, two solo clarinets – difficult to maintain pitch). This is answered by a more fully scored second idea consisting of two melodic lines (ascending and descending). This leads to an expressive, beautifully arched oboe solo, continued in solo clarinet, with soft woodwinds and horns accompanying. A modulatory transition leads to the key of E major with a restatement of the oboe melody in flutes and 1st clarinet while the brass plays the rich-textured chorus part. A subtle modulation returns to E^b, with a transitory expressive phrase in upper woodwinds answered by brass. This leads to the return of the opening phrase ore fully scored, with brass continuing to provide the important choral texture. This is followed by the second idea, extended and brought to a magnificent climax which expands on the descending line carried by trombones and horns. This work contains all the hallmarks of the Wagner style, with its long, melodically eloquent phrases, rich contrapuntal texture and elaborate harmony. Demand the utmost in musical maturity, including tonal beauty, intonation, phrasing, balance and blend . also requires solid soloists (flute, oboe, English horn, clarinet, bass clarinet, bassoon) and sections (clarinets, horns, trombones) as well as brass choir unity.

WAGNER, Richard	**GOOD FRIDAY SPELL from "PARSIFAL"**	Chappell
Arr. Dan Godfrey		9:00

One of the great orchestral excerpts from opera, well transcribed. Slow, sustained, mostly lyric and poetic in character with a few more emphatic and climactic moments, it requires above all beauty of tone, blend, intonation and poetic feeling, with soloists (oboe, flute, trumpet, clarinet, horn, alto sax) that can carry long, flowing lines with control of phrasing and nuance. Highly recommended, and preferable to the version by Earl Slocum (Belwin) which is, however, more readily available.

WAGNER, Richard	**LIEBESTOD FROM "TRISTAN AND ISOLDE"**	Auelos Music
Transc. Joseph Kreines		7:30

A magnificent newer transcription of this Wagner classic. The work begins slow and dark (4/4, *Sehr Massig beginnend*) with the trumpet assuming the solo role. Moving chromatically, yet seamlessly, the music climbs from pp to f and quickly into the key of B^b major (Etwas Bewegter). This increases with intensity and textures and slowly continues to move chromatically while increasing the rhythmic ornaments. As the rhythmic activity, tension and harmonic direction begin to slow, an elaborate harp part becomes more apparent with sixteenth note arpeggiated figures. The volume becomes quieter and the music swells and diminishes into the final Bb major triad. Highly recommended for conductors and ensembles that can maintain long phrases, perform consistently in a lyrical style with focused pitch and tone and ability to build tension into cadences as appropriate. Reviewed by RH.

WAGNER, Richard	**TRAUERMUSIK (WWV73)**	Ludwig
Arr. Votta/Boyd		6:00

A magnificent work, filled with noble eloquence and lyric beauty, in slow, measured tempo using themes from Weber's opera "Euryanthe" in tribute to that composer (the piece was composed for the torchlight ceremony at Weber's re-burial in Germany). This setting is much more faithful and effective than previous arrangements. It opens with a mysterious introduction (Adagio, 4/4, quarter note =52, Bb minor), which leads to the main body of the work in Bb major, using several lovely lyric melodies, and a brief but affecting coda based on the introduction. This work is one of the most difficult to perform satisfactorily because, although the individual parts are technically easy (note-values are mostly quarter, half and whole-notes in comfortable ranges), it requires perfection of intonation, blend of tone, beauty of sonority and feeling of legato line and long phrase. However, all wind players should become familiar with this work. Strongly Recommended.

WARD, Robert   **PRAIRIE OVERTURE**   Galaxy

6:15

An enjoyable and effective original work with attractive tunes in folk and Western style, using syncopated and rhythmically energetic motives as well as a simple flowing line; effective developmental passages with imitation and canonic textures, and exciting buildup (a long accelerando requiring good control) leading to a brilliant coda (Vivace, 3/4 in one). Demands considerable fluency from woodwinds (especially in the coda which requires rapid 8th-note tonguing), secure trumpets with flexibility and clarity of articulation, horns with extensive range (from bass clef notes to high A), well-focused low brass and sensitive percussion.

WHITE, Donald   **AMBROSIAN HYMN VARIANTS**   Elkan-Vogel

6:00

A fine original using an authentic church chant as the theme (Slowly, changing meters, quarter=66-76). The first phrase is in brass, the second in woodwinds, third in brass finishing in full band - all linked by percussion rolls (suspended cymbal and gong). Three contrasting variations follow: (1) Moderately fast (2/4, quarter=108), using imitative writing, featuring a rhythmic staccato statement using contrasts between choirs. (2) Slowly (quarter=66-76, changing meters like the beginning), very sustained and legato, similar to the theme in style and character. (3) Fast (6/8, dotted-quarter note=144), opening with a driving snare-drum solo punctuated by irregular entrances in brass and woodwinds, with interesting use of duplet and triplet groupings, climaxing in a powerful coda which presents the theme in unison trombones. Technically not difficult, but requires rhythmic precision, well-defined articulation which clarifies the difference between slurred and staccato groupings, beautiful brass sonority and solid, precise percussion. (N.B. Requires a minimum of five trumpets to cover three cornet and two trumpet parts which are frequently independent of each other.)

WHITE, Donald   **MINIATURE SET**   Shawnee

11:00

An attractive work with many imaginative touches in this composer's usual bi-tonal neo-classical style. In five contrasting movements: (1) Prelude (Fast and lively) using a rhythmic theme in upper woodwinds punctuated with brass chords; contrasted with a more extended phrase in woodwinds with an ostinato bass accompaniment. These two sections are developed and brought to a vigorous climax. (2) Monologue (Slow, 4/4), featuring various instruments stating short lyric phrases against a flowing 8th-note figure. (3) Interlude (Fast, 2/2) contrasting a light and bouncy theme against a flowing 8th-note figure. (4) Dialogue (Slow, 4/4) opening with a portentous brass-chord introduction leading to a dirge-like quarter-note accompaniment under a lovely melody (solo trumpet, then horn), reaching a climax using the introduction and the melodic motive and closing with a short coda restating the same softly. (5) Postlude (Fast, 2/4), which is a variation of the opening Prelude, providing a brilliant and exciting conclusion.

WILLAN, Healey   **ROYCE HALL SUITE**   Associated

Arr. William Teague   9:00

A fine piece in three contrasting movements: (1) PRELUDE AND FUGUE – featuring a slow, sustained introduction (4/4 in 8), fully scored, followed by a lively fugue (Allegro, 4/4) in neo-baroque style, scored in concerto-grosso manner with small groups contrasted with larger ones and tuttis (includes exposed passages for oboes, English horn and bassoons). (2) MINUET (Allegretto grazioso, 3/4), scored for 14 solo instruments –smooth, supple and graceful. (3) RONDO (Alla Marcia, 2/2), in vigorous march style, again using concerto-grosso devices. The opening section features a boisterous, energetic tune in tutti scoring, contrasted with the second section featuring oboes, bassoons and clarinets. The third section uses solo trumpet and baritone with woodwind accompaniment. After a final statement of the opening, the work concludes with a brilliant coda.

WOOD, Haydn   **MANNIN VEEN**   Boosey & Hawkes

10:00

A band classic using four contrasting Manx folk-tunes. It opens with a rather nostalgic melody in clarinets (Moderato, 4/4, D minor), followed by a tutti statement which is extended, building to a resonant climax. This subsides into a transition which leads to a fiddler's

84

reel-tune (Allegro moderato, 2/4, F major) featuring clarinets with light staccato accompaniment, which is developed and expanded. A more lyric legato section follows (C major) featuring solo cornet. After further development of this and the reel-motive, the mood gradually becomes more sustained, leading to a beautiful hymn (G major, 4/4) emphasizing woodwind sonority, with horn and baritone doubling. A recapitulation follows leading to a climactic coda, which presents the hymn tune in full brass choir embroidered by 16th-note clarinet figuration. Requires good clarinets, flutes, solo oboe, cornet and baritone; ensemble sonority and care in balancing solo and melodic voices against accompaniment. Highly recommended.

WOOD, Haydn **A MANX OVERTURE** Boosey & Hawkes
Arr. T. Conway Brown 8:30
A beautiful work using original themes in the style and character of Manx folk melodies. It opens with a majestic introduction (Poco Maestoso, 3/4), leading to a broadly flowing melody in upper woodwinds which is restated and extended, building to a new section (Allegro moderato, 2/4, C major), rather lively and animated in character, featuring a woodwind line in legato 16ths. A second subject is broad and noble in character with rich chromatic harmony. This leads to a beautiful lyric theme in solo oboe, which is then restated in upper winds and cornet. A quickening of tempo leads to the development of the 16th-note woodwind line followed by a fugal treatment of the oboe melody – first in unaccompanied horns, then baritone and lower winds; clarinets; bass instruments – and a rhythmically active counter-subject. The two subjects are developed further, along with a segment of the allegro theme, leading to a recapitulation following the exposition sequence. A brilliant coda using the allegro theme concludes the work. Requires technically facile players in all sections, especially woodwinds, tonal beauty, well-focused pitch center and sent of both epic and lyric styles.

ZDECHLIK, John **CHORALE AND SHAKER DANCE** Kjos
9:00
A highly effective and imaginative work using an original chorale and the Shaker tune *"The Gift to be Simple"* as its basis. It opens with the chorale in woodwinds (difficult to tune due to unusual voicings), followed by segments of the tune in solo trumpet, flutes, and clarinets, interrupted by parts of the chorale in brasses. The mood changes abruptly with a timpani roll and a fast-tempo statement of the Shaker tune in solo alto sax and flute, while part of the chorale is transformed into a rhythmic figure which becomes the basis of the entire first section. Various contrapuntal devices are used on the material, including canon, augmentation and combination, eventually subsiding into a slower tempo using fragments of both chorale and tune in various guises. This leads to a varied recapitulation of the Shaker-dance section, followed by a brilliant, exciting coda using both tunes in contrasting manners. Technically not difficult, but requires musical maturity - including rhythmic precision, control of articulation (many styles and combinations), focus of ensemble pitch, solo solidity (trumpet, alto sax, trombone, oboe, flute) and section strength (horns - which must play stopped notes - clarinets, brass choir); intelligent and musical percussion (some rhythmic and articulative intricacies in snare drum part in closing section); details of balance and blend; and maintenance of tempo (both speed and steadiness in fast sections.

85

MEDIUM ADVANCED SUPPLEMENT

ARNOLD, Malcolm   **PRELUDE, SICILIANO AND RONDO**   C. Fischer
Arr. John Paynter   5:00

An enjoyable and attractive work with a good combination of technical brilliance and melodic appeal.

BACH, J.S.   **IN DULCI JUBILO**   G. Schirmer
Arr. Richard Franko Goldman   2:15

A beautiful piece, combining epic majesty and rhythmic energy, simple chorale statements and intricate melodic embroideries – very well scored.

BACH, J.S.   **CHACONNE**   Bourne
Arr. Frank Erickson   11:00

An interesting and generally successful realization of the great solo violin original. Erickson has made reasonable abridgements and thoughtful harmonic elaborations and accompanying voices. Worth investigating - though it requires depth of solo and section talent throughout ensemble (except percussion).

BENSON, Warren   **THE MASK OF NIGHT**   C. Fischer
                                                                                           10:30

A highly expressive work in very slow tempo, technically not difficult but requiring great control of ranges (both upper and lower), dynamics and attacks, particularly in brass. Trumpet parts are in C, and opening baritone solo is challenging (starting on low E and ranging up to high B^b).

DEL BORGO, Elliot   **MUSIC FOR WINDS AND PERCUSSION**   Shawnee
                                                                                           6:45

A generally effective work, with good interplay of percussion with choirs and tuttis. Somewhat contrived in content and treatment, but does provide musical and technical challenges.

GLIERE, Reinhold   **RUSSIAN SAILORS' DANCE**   C. Fischer
Arr. Erik Leidzen   3:40

An exciting and brilliant work, technically rather demanding – excellently arranged.

GROSS, Charles   **IRISH SUITE**   Shawnee
                                                                                           7:30

An interesting work using original material with an Irish style and character, in three well-contrasted movements. Technically not difficult but does require good facility, rhythmic awareness and security in sharp keys (1st & 3rd movements) passages.

HALVORSEN, JOHAN   **IN MEMORIAM OPUS 30**   Wingert-Jones
Arr. John Bourgeois   5:40

A somber funeral march (C minor; 4/4) with an eloquent main theme and a more lyric secondary subject. The return of the first theme is brought to a noble, powerful climax, leading to a concluding section in the parallel major, with the first 8 bars to be sung by the band members in 4-part harmony. An effective and worthwhile work for a concert or ceremonial occasion.

HANDEL, G.F.   **CONCERTO GROSSO IN C MAJOR**   Warner
Arr. Don Malin   12:45

A wonderful work, well transcribed, using a concertino group of 2 flutes and clarinet (rather intricate technically, but idiomatic for the instruments).

HARTLEY, Walter   **SINFONIA NO. 4**   MCA
                                                                                           11:00

An attractive, well-written work for wind ensemble, technically not too demanding but requiring solidity and security of soloists and sections (much of the scoring is transparent and choir-style).

HOLST, Gustav	**CAPRICCIO**	G. Schirmer
Arr. John Boyd		6:00

An interesting and unusual work using two contrasting ideas – a rather haunting, nostalgic legato melody and a rhythmic, well-marked motive. Not entirely successful, but intriguing and worth exploring.

HOLST, Gustav	**A SOMERSET RHAPSODY**	Boosey & Hawkes
Arr. Clare Grundman		8:30

A lovely work using three beautiful folk-songs, skillfully woven together. The transcription is generally very good, though balance is a problem in several sections. However, the music is superb and worth the effort required.

MC KAY, Neil	**EVOCATIONS**	Shawnee
		8:00

A colorful and imaginative work in two contrasting movements. The first, slow and delicate, attempts to evoke the spirit of ancient Japan; the second is fast, bustling, rhythmic, depicting modern Japan. Requires both sensitivity and facility and uses contemporary sonorities and rhythmic character.

MUSGRAVE, Thea	**SCOTTISH DANCE SUITE**	G. Schirmer
		10:00

An imaginative, fresh-sounding treatment of traditional Scottish airs and dances in four contrasting movements.

NICOLAI, Otto	**THE MERRY WIVES OF WINDSOR OVERTURE**	Kalmus
Arr. L. Laurendeau		8:40

A delightful and appealing work with both melodic charm and rhythmic vitality. The transcription is faulty in several places, but can be made to work, and the music is worth the effort.

OFFENBACH, Jacques	**ORPHEUS IN THE UNDERWORLD OVERTURE**	Kjos
Arr. Lawrence Odom		9:00

A classic operetta overture full of tunes that are still well-known (including the famous *Can-can*). Requires good technical facility in woodwinds and solo voices (including baritone). This transcription supersedes all others in both faithfulness and effectiveness.

RIMSKY-KORSAKOV, Nicolai	**POLONAISE from "CHRISTMAS EVE"**	Kjos
Arr. Leigh Steiger		4:10

A brilliant, lively work with infectious rhythms and vitality. Technically rather demanding, especially for staccato articulation and rhythmic precision, and in a challenging key (concert D).

SAINT-SAENS, Camille	**DANSE BACCHANALE (from "SAMSON ET DALILA")**	Kjos
Arr. Leigh Steiger		7:45

An excellent transcription of an orchestral standard. Requires both technical facility and delicate refinement, as well as rhythmic precision and sweep of phrase.

SWEELINCK, Jan Pieterszoon	**VARIATIONS ON "MEIN JUNGES LEBEN HAT EIN END"**	G. Schirmer
Arr. Ramon Ricker		5:00

A beautiful organ work, sensitively transcribed for wind ensemble (no saxes except for soprano). Requires good talent throughout ensemble, since scoring is in small groups and solos, with good rhythmic control (many intricate 16th-note passages).

TCHAIKOVSKY, P.I.	**MARCHE SLAV**	C. Fischer
Arr. M.L. Lake		8:30

An exciting orchestral standard, very well transcribed. Requires a mature sounding group with facile woodwinds and resonant brass.

TULL, Fisher   **PRELUDE AND DOUBLE FUGUE**   Boosey & Hawkes

9:00

A well-crafted work which makes effective use of the fugue form in clearly defined manner. Requires rhythmic independence and solidity in all sections, especially woodwinds.

VAUGHAN WILLIAMS, Ralph   **NORFOLK RHAPSODY**   Oxford
Arr. Robert O'Brien   10:00

A lovely orchestral work, sensitively transcribed. Technically not too difficult, but requires security in sharp keys, fluency in legato passages, rhythmic accuracy, sensitivity to dynamics and shadings. Also requires a number of good soloists (flutes, oboe, clarinet, alto sax, trumpet, horn, harp, piano).

VAUGHAN WILLIAMS, Ralph   **PRELUDE ON THREE WELSH HYMN TUNES**   Jenson
Arr. Jim Curnow   7:20

A rich-textured contrapuntal work, originally for brass band, well scored by Curnow. Requires solid players in all sections with both ensemble precision and rhythmic independence, as well as beautiful, rich sonority.

VERDI, Giuseppe   **NABUCCO OVERTURE**   Dehaske
Arr. Franco Cesarini   8:30

A very well-scored arrangement of this Verdi classic. Much more accessible than previous arrangements, this setting allows for modern instrumentation that is both characteristic and more faithful to the original.

WAGNER, Richard   **PROCESSION OF THE KNIGHTS OF THE HOLY GRAIL**   C. Fischer
Arr. Bruce Houseknecht   8:00

A solemn, noble work with rich harmony and expressive power, well arranged and scored. Somewhat repetitious but musically worthwhile, requiring beauty of tone and feeling for the expansive style and stretched phrases.

WARD, Robert   **FOUR ABSTRACTIONS**   Galaxy

A very interesting set of pieces, each one dealing with a concept in abstract painting and related to musical style. Demands good players in all sections (considerable use of choir and small-group scoring), strong sense of rhythmic independence, general musical maturity.

WHEAR, Paul   **WYCLIFFE VARIATIONS**   Ludwig

9:30

An imaginative and well-crafted work, using an old hymn-tune as its basis, with considerable variety of style, character, texture and scoring. Interesting writing in all parts. Some challenging passages (e.g. Variation 1) but technically not difficult.

• •

ALBENIZ, Isaac FETE-DIEU A SEVILLE SamFox
Arr. Lucien Cailliet 9:00

A generally brilliant transcription of a Spanish masterpiece that depicts the spectacular Corpus Christi festivities in Seville. It opens softly and mysteriously (Allegro gracioso, F minor, 2/4) but with great rhythmic energy, gradually building to an enormous climax (F major, 4/4) featuring a broad, noble and passionate theme in the brass. This subsides to a more tranquil mood with the brass theme transformed into a more sensuous, lyric character (melody in horn, then oboe, English horn, clarinet and alto sax). The first section returns, again building to the brass theme, but this time followed by a technically intricate scherzando version of the opening motive (difficult for woodwinds). This leads to a brilliant climactic variation of the first theme (3/8 in one) building to a moment of great tension, only to be cut off abruptly and followed by a very slow, reflective coda, transparently and delicately scored. Despite a short passage of some twelve bars that does not follow the piano original and Arbos orchestral version closely, this is a generally faithful transcription that provides bands with one of the great authentic Spanish works. Requires considerable technical facility, secure and musical soloists and sensitivity to the sound and style.

ARNOLD, Malcolm FOUR SCOTTISH DANCES C. Fischer
Arr. John Paynter 8:30

A brilliantly effective and enjoyable set in four contrasting movements. The opening dance (Pesante, 4/4) begins with a rather slow strathspey conveying both dignity and energy and utilizing the characteristic "snap" inverted rhythm. The Piu Mosso section which follows requires some technical facility in brass (triple-tonguing in trumpets and trombones; horn glissando to high notes) and brilliant woodwind figuration. The second dance (Vivace, 4/4, quarter=160), a lively reel, is highly virtuosic, requiring rapid tonguing and fluent finger work from woodwinds and comfort in widely different keys (modulating by half-steps from E^b to E, F, G^b, and G). An important bassoon solo (cued bass clarinet and baritone sax) presents a somewhat tipsy version of the reel tune at reduced tempo. The movement closes as it began with the tune pp. The third, a slow and expressive song (Allegretto, F-A-D^b, 3/4) presents a lovely tune in solo oboe which later appears in more fully scored form return to the lightly accompanied oboe for the last two statements. The finale, a brilliant fling (Con Brio, 2/4) contains many problems of fluency, articulation and precision while creating a mood of exuberance, abandon and excitement, leading to a breathtaking Presto conclusion.

BACH, J.S. FANTASIA AND FUGUE IN G MINOR Ludwig
Arr. John Boyd 8:30

One of the great masterpieces in a superb transcription which is idiomatic for all players. The opening *FANTASIA* features a highly elaborate line in flowing 16th-notes scored for the woodwinds and supported by brass chords, followed by a more reflective chromatic contrapuntal passage requiring strong woodwind soloists. These two ideas are worked over and varied, with considerable use of chromatic voice leading, resulting in extraordinary harmonic progressions which are brought to a monumental and eloquent conclusion. The *FUGUE* is rhythmically quite intricate and texturally complex, requiring careful working out for ensemble, precision, balancing of voices and musical continuity, with all instruments sharing in the technically challenging theme, including low brass. The closing pages are among the most imposing and magisterial in all of Bach's output. No percussion except for a supportive timpani part. Highly recommended for mature groups with the technical facility and musical understanding necessary to project its great musical content.

BACH, J.S. FUGUE A LA GIGUE Boosey & Hawkes
Arr. Gustav Holst, Ed. Geoffrey Brand 4:00

One of the best of all transcriptions of Bach's organ music, this little gem scored by Holst was out of print for many years, but has been re-issued with a full score and newly edited parts. As the title (not by Bach) suggests, it is a lively, dance-like work that requires considerable facility and lightness of tonguing as well as accuracy of interval leaps. Strongly recommended as an excellent resource for learning the Bach dance style, and for developing fluent technique.

BACH, J.S. PASSACAGLIA AND FUGUE IN C MINOR Southern
Arr. Nicholas Falcone 12:30

A magnificent work expertly transcribed for symphonic band (as differentiated from the equally valid wind ensemble version made by Donald Hunsberger, published by G. Schirmer). The *PASSACAGLIA* uses a bass line theme as the foundation for a wide ranging series of variations, from simple melodic embroidery to rapidly flowing ornamental lines and intricate contrapuntal texture. This theme becomes the basis for a monumental *FUGUE* which builds in power to a massive rich-textured climax. Requires technical fluency and facility in all sections (many 16th-note passages and intricate rhythmic configurations with suspensions and note-rest patterns), well-focused tonal and pitch center (virtually all voices doubled in both transparent and tutti passages) and considerable musical understanding with a command of the ebb and flow of phrases for continuity of line, and careful balancing of voices in complex passages.

BACH, J.S.   **ST. ANNE'S FUGUE**   Southern
Arr. William Rhoads   6:00

Another great organ masterpiece, expertly transcribed. This work is really three fugues, succeeding each other without pause. The opening one is smoothly flowing and noble (Andante moderato, E^b, 4/2), requiring blend and beauty of tone and smooth legato style. The second (Allegro moderato, 6/4 in 2) has an undulating, rhythmically more active theme requiring excellent technical fluency (evenness of 8th-notes, including lower woodwinds), rhythmic control and precision. The final fugue (Maestoso, 12/8) is more marked and articulated in style, which demands clean, fluent tonguing and rhythmic evenness, as well as richness and beauty of tone in the resonant climactic pages. Highly recommended.

BASSETT, Leslie   **DESIGNS, IMAGES AND TEXTURES**   Peters
                                                                               11:00

A highly imaginative and creative work that attempts to relate to five types of modern art through musical expression. (1) *OIL PAINTING* (Fast, 4/4) opens with brilliant flowing lines rhythmically overlapping, followed by cluster chords and several short motives. (2) *WATER COLOR* (Moderate, 2/2) - a slow, quiet piece using cluster chords and two short melodic ideas, both of which use overlapping. (3) *PEN AND INK DRAWING* (Slow, 4/4), composed of numerous rhythmically independent lines, scored in small-group and choir settings. (4) *MOBILE* (Moderately fast, 3/4) uses breathy sounds (flutes, low-register elements) and rustling sounds (suspended cymbal, fingers on piano strings, muted brass trills), gradually focusing on several distinct musical ideas, only to return to the rustling sound of the opening. (5) *BRONZE SCULPTURE* (Fast, 4/4) – a brilliant many-faceted movement with great rhythmic complexity (e.g. irregular entrances after 16th rests, syncopations of varying lengths, etc.) A difficult and challenging work, both technically and musically, requiring aural sophistication through its use of dissonance, clusters and serial techniques - but worth exploring by advanced groups.

BASSETT, Leslie   **SOUNDS, SHAPES, AND SYMBOLS**   Peters Corporation
                                                                               13:00

A very creative work, in four contrasting movements, using the element of color as its primary source. The piece opens with a succession of flourishes (4/4, quarter note = 138) containing isolated triple fragments, parallel woodwind runs and rhythmical and textural contrasts. Pyramiding sonorities close the movement in a quiet and yearning manner. The second movement (4/4, quarter note =42) begins with a soft and dissonant brass choir (sans trumpets) that quickly surrenders to the clarinet. This pattern continues to alternate in a melancholy mood while growing in rhythmic intensity. Again the movement closes quietly but this time with waning sounds of just the solo horn, flutes, tuba and suspended cymbal. The third movement begins unmetered optimizing overlapping woodwind colors. This is followed by a succession of contrasting episodes including marked brass figures and quick, lyrical and sustained tutti sonorities. The movement ends with quiet percussion improvising while slowly withdrawing into silence. The fourth movement is more rhythmically clear. Beginning with interrupted surges of highlighted sixteenth patterns (multi meters, quarter note =144) the movement quickly develops into a repetitive structure with intriguing alternating characters (including blurred tonality and shifting musical directions.) A final section (Faster, 3/4, quarter note = 152) emerges using trills in all winds and pyramiding effects with several interventions of time. This continues using multi meters and overlapping (and in some cases tongued) sixteenth patterns until sustained qualities are once again interrupted in time. The final measure calls for some percussion to improvise while sustained tutti wind sounds crescendo into the last "FF". Requires rhythmic independence of all players and sensitivity to unusual and hazy tonalities as well as a complete understanding of the desired colors.

BEETHOVEN, Ludwig Van   **ALLEGRO CON BRIO**   Boosey & Hawkes
Trans. Joseph Kreines   **(1ˢᵗ MOVEMENT FROM SYMPHONY NO. 5 IN C MINOR OP. 67)**   6:30

A remarkably first-rate and successful transcription of the most recognizable composition of all the literature. Opening in the authentic key of C minor (2/2, half note = 108) the three-note motif begins with tutti ensemble and quickly fragments into various note groupings. This is contrasted by a lyrical second theme (E^b major) using woodwind colors while the underpinning motif continues its presence. A very well-scored development section ensues exploring several key centers and containing very dramatic shifts of volume, color and moods. This leads to the closing of the exposition using the opening motif. A thrilling coda brings the movement to a faithful and very convincing conclusion. Many wind parts are identical to the orchestral original. Highly recommended for advanced ensembles with strong French horns, skilled oboe soloist and technically proficient wind players. Reviewed by RH.

BENNETT, Robert Russell   **SUITE OF OLD AMERICAN DANCES**   Chappell
                                                                                              15:30

A delightful original work evoking the style and character of five different dances. (1) *CAKEWALK* (Moderato, 2/4, B^b) with constant use of the characteristic inverted rhythm (16ᵗʰ-8ᵗʰ-16ᵗʰ), requiring precision and clarity of articulation; effective syncopations, and a lovely ballad against which the cakewalk rhythms are played. (2) *SCHOTTISCHE* (Moderato, G minor, fast 4 or easy 2) – using the dotted-8ᵗʰ-16ᵗʰ and triplet-8ᵗʰ rhythms in both accompaniment and melody. (3) *WESTERN ONE STEP* (Lively, 2/4, C) – vigorous and energetic, with use of detached 8ᵗʰ-notes contrasted with a nostalgic legato tune in the middle section. (4) *WALLFLOWER WALTZ* (Allegretto, 3/4) – languorous and lazy in mood yet using syncopations, featuring flutes (doubled in English horn) and muted brass. (5) *RAG* (Lively – easy 2/2) uses intricate rhythm and rest patterns and irregular articulation in grouping of 8ᵗʰ-notes against the beat, which helps to produce the "rag" feeling. Requires careful working out to produce the necessary rhythmic effect. While it is technically not demanding, this piece is deceptive due to its many rhythmic and textural intricacies, and does demand good control of attack, focus of articulation and steadiness of rhythm and tempo. A full score edited by Edward Higgins is now published.

BENSON, Warren   **THE LEAVES ARE FALLING**   Marks
                                                                                              11:00

A very poetic and atmospheric work, technically not difficult yet requiring great control of very slow tempo (half=32-34) with sustained playing and ability to subdivide accurately (quarter-note triplet and suspension figures against half-note beat). It opens with soft chimes solo, gradually adding instruments and filling in texture, increasing in both harmonic and rhythmic complexity, with a powerful bi-tonal climax. A short three-note melodic motive gradually grows into the chorale *"A Mighty Fortress"* which is stated in several versions, including a powerful triumphant unison trumpet statement at the end, only to fade into solo clarinet playing the final note of the melody. Very challenging for both players and conductor due to the slow tempo and the necessity to control sustained playing – (The composer indicates that the two-beat pulse per measure should be preserved with a minimum of subdivision) – but well worth any effort required.

BENSON, Warren   **THE PASSING BELL**   E. C. Schirmer
                                                                                              11:00

A powerful, intense, dramatic work making use of contemporary compositional and instrumental technique along with two old chorale melodies. Harmonically and rhythmically rather complex, and musically advanced in its multi-layered textures, technically demanding percussion and control of wide dynamic range. Requires highly intelligent and sensitive music-making from both conductor and players, with many intricacies that must be worked out for effective musical results; but can create an overwhelming impression in performance.

BERLIOZ, Hector   **ROMAN CARNIVAL OVERTURE**   Aeolus Music
Transc. Joseph Kreines   9:00

A brilliant showcase for advanced ensembles that is amazingly loyal to the original. The short and quick opening burst of sound (6/8 and 2/4, dotted quarter note = 156, *Allegro assai con fuoco*, Bb major) leads to a charming and expressive English horn solo (3/4, quarter note = 56, *Andante Sostenuto*, Db Major) accompanied by clarinet choir. A short answer (F major) by woodwind sonorities guides back to the English horn solo. A contrasting section ensues (Bb major) with the melody contained in the upper woodwinds and energetic accompaniment figures in the brass and percussion. This is interrupted by a *poco animato* section and a return to tempo I

(6/8, allegro vivace) beginning with fragments of the opening material thinly scored in the woodwinds. This lengthy section becomes exceedingly well developed using various textures, articulations, extreme dynamics, accidentals and elaborate brass combinations. A seamless two-measure duple section provides a new transition for the previous 6/8 section but this time it begins pp using unison legato woodwind articulations and rhythms. This builds in both intensity and volume with clever contrasts of dynamics and meter into one of the most thrilling conclusions of all the literature. Highly recommended for those ensembles possessing outstanding wind players with exceptional tonal focus, advanced tonguing techniques, and endurance. Reviewed by RH.

BERLIOZ, Hector	**LE CORSAIRE OVERTURE**	Shawnee
Arr. Walter Beeler		8:00

An exciting and brilliant orchestra showpiece, superbly transcribed, requiring the utmost in facility and virtuosity in the fast sections (problems of rhythmic precision and execution of articulation patterns at indicated tempo of half=152) and sustained legato, tonal beauty and phrasing in the slow section that occurs near the beginning. Despite the difficulties, this is a wonderful work that is deserving of more frequent performance by musically and technically mature groups.

BERNSTEIN, Leonard	**CANDIDE SUITE**	Boosey & Hawkes
Arr. Clare Gundman		12:00

An excellent selection of five numbers from the Bernstein musical. The opening *"BEST OF ALL POSSIBLE WORLDS"* is bright, sparkling, and witty. The next section *"WESTPHALIAN CHORALE AND BATTLE SCENE"* opens with a sustained introduction followed by a boisterous and energetic section. The *"AUTO-DA-FE"* comes next – another rhythmic, brilliant number. *"GLITTER AND BE GAY"* is in the style of an Italian opera aria – a slow, nostalgic melody in the minor key followed by a brilliant "cabaletta". The closing number *"MAKE OUR GARDEN GROW"* is effusively lyrical, reaching a noble climax.

BRAHMS, Johannes	**TRAGIC OVERTURE OP. 81**	Aeolus Music
Transc. Joseph Kreines		13:30

A highly valuable transcription of this epic overture which remains very faithful to the original. The beginning is marked by a pounding two-note exclamation (2/2, Allegro non troppo, D minor) signaling the tragic character. This is quickly contrasted by a *subito* piano section before the reoccurring bounce theme (dotted eighth sixteenth notes and eighth note sixteenth variances) is presented. Extreme shifts of fortissimo accented colors ensue with gleaming sonorities, unusual phrase entrances, and lingering expressive soli passages. A recapitulation of the opening measure gestures a new section that is lyrical and drapes repeating oboe solos. This is developed using extreme volume and color contrast as well as overlapping layers of phrases. It begins to build chromatically until a release is interjected but this time using the double dotted quarter and sixteenth note. A very marcato section follows using similar rhythms, contrapuntal textures, accents and many shifts of tonality until energy completely stops as signaled by the two-note theme. This is contrasted by a soft- lyrical section that precedes a return to the repeated rhythmic and marcato material (dolce), which is now in 4/4. Exchanges of tonal centers and meter follow which include similar contrasts of marcato and lyrical statements short interjections of previously presented material. Rich soli brass sections are grouped with woodwind suspensions that build into a satisfying release into the swelling and fading woodwind choirs. A chromatic transition into F major follows again using the unison rhythm as its catalysis. This is fully developed using eighth note staccato patterns and eventually contrasted legato fragments using triple accompaniment figures (un poco sostenuto). This becomes very quiet and thin until a subito statement (In time) brings the work to a domineering close in D minor. Highly recommended for advanced ensembles with musicians capable of executing extreme contrasts, technically proficient woodwinds (including oboe), and brass with endurance and clear tonal focus in all registers. Reviewed by RH.

BROOKS, Jeffrey	**DREADNAUGHT**	Boosey & Hawkes
		9:00

An energetic and unusual work using creative phrase patterns, color combinations and irregular meters as its source of inspiration. The short solo snare drum sets the mood (2/4, multi meters, quarter note =90) and is quickly joined by overlapping and syncopated sixteenth notes in the brass. This builds with layers of textures until a sustained sound in the solo trombone interrupts these repeated patterns. This is re-stated with color variants but each time using a different syncopated thread. The energy slows (quarter note =72, with inconsistent shifts of duple and triple meters) but the syncopated patterns continue. A short trumpet transition (canonic, using metric modulation) leads to a return of the opening tempo but this time using the second thread as its opening source. Alternating rhythmic colors followed by tutti sections leads to a FFF climax. This is followed by a silent 2/4 measure and then layers of syncopated patterns in the woodwinds and percussion. Sustained sounds ensue but are now combined with the syncopated patterns, which grow in both volume and color into the final release of energy in the last measure. The work requires endurance, winds with advanced tonguing technique, a clear understanding of meters (including 11/16) and a percussion section that can maintain the tempi through the various phrase patterns.

CATEL, Charles Simon	OVERTURE IN C	Mercury
Arr. R.F. Goldman and R. Smith		5:30

A fine original from the French Revolutionary period, well-adapted for modern instrumentation. It opens with a slow, solemn introduction (Larghetto, C minor, 4/4) featuring contrasts of small-group and tutti scoring and terraced dynamics. This is followed by a brilliant and vital Allegro Vivace (C major, 2/2) comprising three theme-groups. The first consists of a soft chromatic legato line followed by a light staccato rhythmic figure, which is repeated in tutti scoring after a short transitional section. A subordinate phrase consisting of a syncopated figure and a turn motive leads to a repetition of the first phrase. Another transition using an 8th-note rhythm motive and quarter-note chords leads to the second theme-group, featuring a graceful oboe solo with light articulated accompaniment in woodwinds and horns, repeated with fuller scoring. A closing group which elaborates on the dominant, and also uses the staccato figure from the first theme, brings the exposition to an end. The development section utilizes all the previous elements (including some of the transitional material) to great effect, while the recapitulation follows the exposition closely (except for an extension of the first transition and an abridged and varied closing section) coming to a vibrant and heroic conclusion. Requires woodwinds with considerable articulative technique, brass with good control of tone, octave tuning (many in horns and trumpets), precision and facility, and a good sense of the classical style.

CHANCE, James Barnes	BLUE LAKE	Boosey & Hawkes
		5:30

A dynamic and spirited work in modified ABA form. The opening section is very rhythmic, using irregular groupings of 8ths (3+3+2; 3+2+3, etc.) as well as their subdivisions. (The original manuscript was barred using 5/8, 7/8 and 8/8 meters, later changed to 4/4 at the request of the publisher.) These various rhythmic configurations are contrasted with a lovely legato line in oboe and horn, leading to an intricate fugato section which is brought to a sweeping climax. This is interrupted by a dramatic change of mood with the introduction of a graceful waltz, the melody of which is a variation of the opening motive. This is brought to a powerful tutti climax, suddenly becoming soft and delicate as the waltz section closes. The recapitulation begins as abruptly as the exposition ended, with some variation from the original pattern, including a climactic statement of the lyric legato line in the brass while the rhythmic motive is presented in woodwinds. A final explosion of the opening motive brings the work to an exciting conclusion. Requires great rhythmic precision and control, good understanding of rhythmic groupings, technical facility in all instruments (especially horns and low woodwinds) and musicality of phrasing in the waltz section. Highly recommended.

CHANCE, James Barnes	SYMPHONY NO. 2	Boosey & Hawkes
		17:00

A powerful, intense, deeply-felt work in three movements which are all built on the same four-note motive. (1) *SUSSURANDO – ENERGICO* (3/4-4/4). A slow, mysterious introduction presenting the motive in four different settings leads to a dramatic fast section which states the motive in powerfully accented brass, answered by a rapidly-flowing ascending woodwind version in 16th-notes. This is followed by further variations of the motive in both ostinato and syncopated rhythms. The second section uses a rhythmically syncopated chord progression as accompaniment to a long legato-line statement of the motive in horns, closing with a flute version of the 16th-note statement. These various statements are all developed, reaching a climax with the horn motive in brass and woodwinds reiterating 16th-notes. The closing flute idea is now stated is solo oboe, followed by a coda which begins with the rhythmic ostinatos and rhythmic figure. (2) *ELEVATO* (quarter=60, 4/4) – a slow, chorale-textured movement, elegiac in mood, using the motive and various expansions of it (both harmonic and melodic), reaching a deeply affecting climax with trumpets stating a permutation of the motive. The mood abruptly returns to that of the opening, with final statements by clarinet, flute, and piccolo. This leads without pause to (3) *SLANCIO* (6/8, dotted-quarter=168) using the motive both rhythmically and melodically, with frequent use of ostinatos throughout, maintaining intense drive and forward momentum to the galvanic conclusion. This is a major work that has come to be regarded as a classic masterpiece in some quarters, while others find its repetition of motives, rhythmic figures and chord progressions tends to wear thin. However there is no denying its considerable impact in performance. Requires total control of rhythmic subdivision in 6/8 (where the constant stream of 8th-notes in rapid tempo is divided among groups of instruments); fluency and facility (e.g. 16th-note figurations in 1st movement), control of attack and pitch (pedal B^b for trombones in 2nd mvt; horn statements in 1st mvt); solo and section talent (flute, piccolo, oboe, clarinet, horns, timpani, saxophone and low woodwind sections, etc.) and a conductor who can meld the technical and rhythmic details into a large architectural and emotional whole.

COPLAND, Aaron	**EL SALON MEXICO**	Boosey & Hawkes
Arr. Mark Hindsley		11:20

A standard orchestral work, brilliantly transcribed, this piece evokes the spirit of a popular dance hall in Mexico with both languorous and lively tunes, filled with exciting rhythms and frequent meter changes. It opens with a short, fast introduction presenting a syncopated rhythm and a bouncy tune. This is succeeded by a slow section introduced by several cadenzas in trumpet and clarinet, accompanied by a relaxed syncopation. A new tune emerges in bassoon and tenor sax, succeeded by a cross-rhythm passage (6/8=3/4). The tune is restated leading to a return of the opening music, expanded and elaborated along with the cross-rhythm which reaches an energetic climax, leading to a new section first stating a rather romantic tune, then a more lively one. The romantic one returns with a syncopated figure at the end, which becomes the basis for a new section – rhythmically rather intricate and syncopated in both tunes and accompaniment. This is developed at some length, eventually leading to the recurrence of the opening material and other ideas, increasing in metric complexity and rhythmic energy, concluding with a climactic statement of the opening. Requires great rhythmic and metric skill from both conductor and players, solo talent and feeling for the diverse styles and moods.

COPLAND, Aaron	**EMBLEMS**	Boosey & Hawkes
		11:10

One of the great original band works, with all the hallmarks of Copland's mature style. It opens with a bold declarative statement, epic in character, followed by a nervous dotted-rhythm passage and a more lyric, legato chorale-like section, with accompanying 16th-note scale passages. A varied statement of the opening leads to a new lyric and sustained idea, expanded upon at some length, which leads to a quote of "*Amazing Grace*" (fitting the previously stated harmonic and phrase layout of the lyric section). A short return of the opening idea leads into the second section of the work (Quite Fast, quarter=126). This opens with an unaccompanied percussion statement of much of the ensuing rhythmic material, which is perky, lively and marked in character (stated in solo piano, cued upper woodwinds). The rhythmic motives are then elaborated and expanded, arriving at a more melodic idea in upper woodwinds and bassoon accompanied by one of the rhythmic motives, then restated in varied form by trumpets, expanded further and combined with earlier fast motives and brought to a breathless climax – then suddenly interrupted by music from the first section, which is then restated in varied form. A majestic coda using the declarative music brings the work to a powerful and eloquent conclusion. Demands a first-class ensemble with strong players and solo talent in all sections, including a technically accomplished pianist (though, the exposed parts are cued, the cues are not very successful). Strongly recommended for all upper-level groups.

CRESTON, Paul	**CELEBRATION OVERTURE**	Shawnee
		7:30

An exuberant, vital and colorful work in three contrasting sections (fast-slow-fast). The first (Con Spirito, 3/4, quarter=104) opens with a rhythmically marked fanfare-like figure leading to a syncopated rhythm using varying combinations of 8ths and 16ths which accompanied the first theme – a flowing legato line first stated in clarinets, then trumpets, then low brass, reaching a climactic statement of both melody and rhythm. Fragments of both are used for the transition to the slow section (Andante, 6/8, dotted-quarter=58), which starts with a gently undulating accompaniment figure in clarinets, under a sustained, singing melody which first appears in solo oboe, then later in baritone and upper woodwinds. Meanwhile, a new rhythmic accompaniment figure appears, supporting part of the theme in a climactic statement by low brass. The undulating figure suddenly returns to accompany the oboe, as at the opening of the section. This leads to the final section (Allegro giusto, 4/4, quarter=108), which introduces another rhythmic figure in trumpets, accompanying an energetic melody in tubas. These ideas are worked out and varied with a number of different scorings, leading to a climactic statement of the tuba melody in augmentation in low brass, while a variation of the trumpet rhythm appears in upper woodwinds. Requires excellent players in all sections due to many passages of choir and section scoring (clarinets, saxophones, trumpets, as well as the indicated solos. Also requires strong rhythmic sense, ensemble sonority, precision, balancing of parts (much complex chordal texture with complete 5- and 6-part chords) and balancing lead voices with accompaniment.

DAHL, Ingolf   **SINFONIETTA**   Alex Broude
                                                                       17:00

A great masterpiece in three contrasting movements that are a model of imagination, craftsmanship and musical content. (1) INTRODUCTION AND RONDO. The introduction opens with a brief phrase that contains the elemental motivic structures that bind the entire piece together. This is followed by fanfare for three off-stage trumpets which further establishes the tonal framework. This leads to the Rondo – a brilliant, lively, exuberant movement which presents a rhythmic, lithe melody that is restated after each succeeding idea is introduced. Along the way, a wide variety of textures, rhythmic configurations and musical highlights occur, including a brilliant cadenza-like passage for the clarinet section, a reprise of the trumpet fanfare as a coda, and a percussion roll-off to finish! (2) PASTORAL NOCTURNE (Andantino con moto, 12/8), opens with an introductory lyrical idea in unaccompanied clarinets that is transformed into several other ideas, including the succeeding high alto saxophone solo and the main theme in solo bassoon (accompanied by a waltz-like rhythm). The middle section (Quasi Gavotte, 4/4) serves as the focal point of the movement, clearly contrasted rhythmically and metrically (using duplet groupings rather than the triple of the 12/8). A short transition for solo English horn leads to the return of the 12/8 section which is developed and elaborated further. A short coda parallels the opening introduction, with the clarinet line transformed into an alto clarinet solo, closing with a final echo of the waltz rhythm. (3) DANCE VARIATIONS (Vivacissimo, 3/4) opens with an emphatic, energetic unison theme in accented quarters (answered by staccato 8ths) which is the basis of the entire movement, emphasizing rhythm and the expansion and variation of the intervals and melodic shapes. As in the first movement, there are numerous contrasting elements held together by thematic and intervallic unity. A coda which uses the 1st-movement fanfare as its basis brings the work to a quiet conclusion. (The alternative ending that is supplied, which ends 'climactically' should be avoided.) Requires a high degree of technical and musical skills from the ensemble, and solos in all sections, including a wide-ranging, colorful, intricately scored and detailed percussion.

DAUGHERTY, Michael   **BELLS FOR STOKOWSKI**   Peermusic
                                                                       14:00

A very creative, powerful and complex work containing layering textures, several canons, polyrhythms and multiple exchanges of chamber choirs and tutti colors. Additionally the score calls for extended instrumentation including a large and essential percussion battery, 2 harps, acoustic amplified guitar, 2 contra basses and optional pipe organ. Beginning with measured free time in the percussion, the work quickly introduces the theme with saxophone choir in a baroque-like style. The texture changes from chamber to tutti using a variety of techniques and styles. Moods are developed and varied from the seemingly simple and thin sonorities to the very complex and highly technical requirements. Near the end of the composition a transcription of Bach's "C major Prelude for the Well-Tempered Clavier" is introduced to evoke the "Stokowski sound." Highly recommended for very advanced ensembles with virtuosic musicians in all sections and a musical conductor who can control the various moods, meters, codes and colors required of this important work.

DAUGHERTY, Michael   **NIAGARA FALLS**   Peermusic
                                                                       10:00

An extremely creative band original inspired by the mystical properties of the Niagara River. Opening with a menacing harmonic succession of syncopated exchanges, the work continues using a four note chromatic phrase as its primary thread (4/4, quarter note = 56). Several blues-like interruptions provide additional interest to this progression (including unaccompanied solo harp using arpeggiated figures) as the motion gradually increases. Numerous canonic ideas accompanied by the unrelenting rhythmic impression in the timpani and lower brass decorate the second motive presented first in the upper brass. Later the saxophones and clarinets layer additional counterpoint, in a 'bluesy riff' style. This continues to build in intensity and rhythmic unity containing Native-American-like motifs bringing the work to a roaring close with just the sustaining winds. A very worthwhile musical journey for advanced ensembles with a strong harpist and pipe organ, mature winds, seven expert percussionists performing on many instruments and a musical conductor who can combine these elements into a musical product.

DAUGHERTY, Michael RED CAPE TANGO Peermusic
(FROM METROPOLIS SYMPHONY) 13:30

A very innovative movement extracted and rescored from a larger work by the composer. The transcription begins with a mysterious French horn soli primer (Rubato, 3/4, quarter note =60) before the Tango dance commences. An ingenious bassoon solo, using hints of the *Dies irae* chant (4/4, quarter note = 92 G minor) is featured with string bass and percussion accompaniments. Afterwards, the soprano saxophone, flutes and piccolo join the dance. This continues to build and vary in meter, rhythm, texture, tension and tempi (including very adept percussion colors) into a very marked and quicker section (quarter note = 160). This section contains syncopated presentations of the theme along with flutter tonguing, glissandi and continued percussion interjections. A slower section follows (quarter note = 60) using double-tongued variants in trumpets and more ornamentation of the theme. This tango death dance continues to transform itself into many moods applying many contrasts including alternating sections of legato and staccato choices. These range from the most simple, thin segments to the highly technical and thick sectors. The closing episode (3/4, quarter note = 152) begins with rapid soli trumpet alternatives and piano and woodwind accompaniment. Sweeping chromatic runs convert the theme into a 4/4 section that alters the perception of the meter as well as the ornate syncopation of the accompaniments. This builds and recedes, in both density and motion, until the theme is finally spun out to the anticipated final note! This is a superb work for advanced ensembles with excellent solo winds (including bassoons) trumpets that can double tongue and six mature percussionists that are able to perform on all the percussion instrument families.

DAUGHERTY, Michael **ROSA PARKS BOULEVARD** Peermusic
11:30

A brilliant concertante for three trombones and extended wind ensemble in a tribute to the life of civil rights champion Rosa Parks. The opening measures (Maestoso, multi meters, quarter note = 72) include woodwind and harp glissandos and pyramiding figures from the solo trombones (positioned within the ensemble, standing). This quickly is echoed by additional winds using forward motion (quarter note =96, 3/4). Beginning in the vibraphone and joined by the bass trombone solo, a short canon ensues, using much slower motion (quarter note =56) over sustained textures. This leads to a solo trombone 1 feature in a blues-like manner accompanied by a gentle canon (quarter note =66). Using rhythmic hints of the canon material, solo trombone 2 is exposed in a slightly slower setting, accompanied by chromatic runs and glissandi figures as solo bass trombone and tenor sax are subsequently featured in a similar style. This leads to a transitional accelerando by all three solos into a very energetic section (quarter note = 152, in C#). Highly technical woodwind and brass fragments are exchanged with colorful percussion interruptions. This is further developed using syncopation as well as tempi, style, tonal and texture contrasts. A beautiful slow setting for bells, harp and English horn appears (quarter note = 56) using fragments of the canonic material. Additional color such as saxophone choir and percussion further develop this idea. A contrasting 5/8 transition is next (eighth note = 86) and gradually doubling the tempo to quarter note =86 in 4/4. This new idea features the trombone section with horns accompanied by echoes of the canon theme. A chamber section follows beginning with solo flute and vibraphone. This is varied in texture and eventually exposes the concertante solo trombones. A tutti Maestoso, using syncopated ostinato fragments, leads to a powerful "FFFF" climax. In a slow cadenza-like passage, each of the soloists have the option of playing a brief parting before the tutti ensemble joins the final 2 measures, "pp to FFF!"

DEBUSSY, Claude FETES Belwin
Arr. William Schaefer 7:00

A well-known orchestral masterpiece, remarkably well-transcribed. The opening section (Animated, very rhythmic, 12/8), featuring a flowing 8th-note figure, requires fluency of articulation and evenness of fingers in woodwinds, with many passages of tongued 8ths, while the subsidiary section (15/8, 9/8) demands even more articulative staccato skill and is also in the key of A major! This is brought to a forceful, energetic climax, suddenly interrupted by a distant processional featuring muted trumpets, then taken up by a woodwinds and becoming progressively louder, to a powerful tutti presenting both the processional and legato woodwind motives together. Suddenly the opening section, varied, returns, fading into a shadowy echo of the earlier exuberant mood with fragments of the processional. A coda using part of the first theme and the rhythmic accompaniment of the subordinate section brings the work to hushed close. Requires both technical facility and musical sensitivity, especially with regard to delicacy of color, dynamics, lightness and awareness of style. Highly recommended for advanced groups.

DEBUSSY, Claude   **MARCHE ECOSSAISE**   Shawnee
Arr. William Schaefer   6:15

A relatively unknown but wonderful work, superbly transcribed. It opens with a gentle but spirited tune in the flutes (Allegretto, 2/4), featuring dotted-rhythms, which is developed and expanded on by numerous other soli and small groups. A subordinate section follows which features some of the same rhythmic intricacies in new melodic guises. This is succeeded by a return of the first theme, leading to a trio-like section in slower tempo featuring English horn (cued oboe) and flute soli. The opening idea returns, but in 6/8 meter, gathering speed and galloping to a brilliant conclusion. Requires adept and sensitive soloists and considerable technical facility and rhythmic accuracy and control. Recommended for mature, advanced groups with the requisite solo talent.

DEBUSSY, Claude   **DANSE**   Ludwig
Arr. John Boyd   6:00

Another less-known but fine work, expertly arranged. Technically not too difficult, but provides a major rhythm and ensemble challenge, in that the music constantly shifts between 3/4 and 6/8, and sometimes both occur simultaneously. The middle section, by contrast, is lyric and poetic.

DELLO JOIO, Norman   **FANTASIES ON A THEME OF HAYDN**   Marks
14:20

A fine original in four sections – the theme and three contrasting fantasies. It opens with an introduction (Allegro scherzando, 2/4) which uses fragments of the theme divided between short motives in woodwinds and brass. This leads to the theme, taken from a short piano piece. The first phrase is stated in flute, bass clarinet and bassoon, then clarinet, trumpet and low brass. The second phrase is divided between different instruments, while the third phrase is in upper winds and trumpets. The closing phrase is again divided, and the theme section closes with a humorous "pun" on the opening two notes. *FANTASY I* (L'istesso tempo. 4/4), which follows without pause, uses a short basso ostinato figure over which various elements of the theme are stated. Then the basso ostinato becomes melodic, with imitative passages among and between sections. The rest of the fantasy uses elements of each thematic phrase, closing with the scalar shape of the theme's opening. A low C in flute held over leads into *FANTASY II* (Adagio), an intensely lyric section, using the various segments of the theme as the basis for rhapsodic elaboration, rising to an intense, rather anguished climax, then gradually subsiding into the material of the opening. The final A, in timpani and string bass, becomes the jumping-off place for *FANTASY III* (Allegro molto spiritoso) which returns to a mood similar to Fantasy I, with its use of staccato 8ths and rhythmic and energetic treatment of motives, but with interesting control (especially cornet and trumpet accuracy in staccato leaps) finesse, precision, flexibility and musical nuance in slow section, delicacy in lightly scored passages.

DELLO JOIO, Norman   **VARIANTS ON A MEDIEVAL TUNE**   Marks
11:40

An excellent work using "In Dulci Jubilo" as the basis for five contrasting variations preceded by an introduction featuring a fanfare-like rhythmic figure in trumpets, (Andante Moderato, 6/8, dotted quarter=52) and the theme (in piccolo and bass clarinet, then oboe, bassoon and clarinet). *VARIATION I* (Allegro deciso, 4/4) – rhythmic, staccato, brilliant, with 16th-note staccato figuration and fragmentary motivic outlines of segments of the theme. *VARIATION II* (Lento, Pesante) – broad, epic, rather grim in character, using elements of the introductory fanfare accompanying the melodic outline and motives, followed by a more tranquil legato statement of the melody's second phrase. *VARIATION III* (Allegro spumante) is, as indicated, sparkling and effervescent – using staccato 16ths outlining and accompanying thematic motives. (Difficult to play with the required lightness and delicacy). *VARIATION IV* (Andante) – broadly lyric and flowing, opening with a recitative-like phrase in low woodwinds, building to a noble climactic phrase, then returning to the opening phrase and ending serenely. *VARIATION V* (Allegro giocoso, 3/4 in one) – opening with a joyous outburst, with a wide variety of stylistic aspects covered in the middle section (legato, staccato, marcato), climaxing in a canonic treatment of the theme and sweeping to a triumphant conclusion. Requires mastery of staccato articulation, precision, rhythmic accuracy, in addition to richness and resonance of tone, depth of solo talent, control of stylistic spectrum.

DOHNANYI, Ernest von   **ANDANTE AND RONDO (from SUITE, OP.19)**   TRN
Arr. A.A. Harding   10:00

A wonderful work that is a prime example of late 19th-century orchestral style, splendidly arranged for band. The opening Andante (G minor, 2/4), which is actually the introduction to the first movement of the suite, is in the singing legato style, with a lovely tune simple in shape but with rich-textured harmony and accompaniment. The succeeding Rondo (Allegro vivace, B^b, 2/2), which is the finale of the suite, is lively and energetic in character, but also contains a wide range of moods and characters – tender, passionate, majestic, triumphant – and demands considerable technical facility for both staccato articulation and fluent legato, especially in woodwinds, as well as rich resonant sonority in climactic moments for the brass.

ELGAR, Sir Edward   **ENIGMA VARIATIONS**   Shawnee
Arr. Earl Slocum   15:30

Slocum has transcribed about half of the great orchestral classic, and has produced a respectable arrangement. *THEME* (Andante, G minor, 3/4) - somewhat sad in mood, though noble and tender, requiring legato style and tonal beauty. *VARIATION 1* (Andante, 4/4) - a gentle, expansive, romantic statement with interesting decorative voices, rising to an impassioned climax, only to subside into the opening gentle mood. *VARIATION 2* (Allegro di molto, G minor, 3/4 in one) – boisterous and energetic in character – very rhythmic and well-marked in style. *VARIATION 3* (Moderato, 12/8 – 4/4) a variation in two moods - serious and reflective contrasted with sunny and cheerful. (The legato opening phrase in woodwinds vs. the staccato, delicate idea in woodwinds and horns), closing with the serious mood. *VARIATION 4* (Allegro di molto, 2/2) – fast, headlong, brilliant 16th-notes and staccato 8ths in both loud and soft dynamics frame the heroic statement of the theme in the middle. *VARIATION 5* (Adagio, E^b, 3/4). The sublime eloquence and beauty of this variation are equal to any music in profundity and intensity of expression, beginning with a simple, noble statement which gradually builds to an intense and passionate climax, only to suddenly fade into a tranquil serenity. *VARIATION 6* (Finale, Allegro, A^b, 2/2) a heroic statement with a reflection back to Variation 1, concluding in a thrilling triumphant climax. Requires all aspects of musicianship, with great musical demands in Variation 5 and technical facility and fluency required in the finale.

ELLERBY, Martin   **PARIS SKETCHES**   Maecenas Music
                                                          14:00

An Attractive, well-scored suite of four movements, each of which relates to a different locale in Paris. The first, "St. Germain-de-Pre," is tranquil yet flowing in character, with numerous contrasts of choirs and textures. The next, "Pigalle," is brilliant and energetic but with much chamber-like scoring. Movement 3 "Pere La Chaise" is in the style of Satie's Gymnopodie, with a lilting accompaniment supporting flowing melodies. The finale, "Les Halles," is fast and driving – technically brilliant and demanding, apart from a brief slower passage.

GANDOLFI, Michael   **VIENTOS Y TANGOS**   Boosey & Hawkes
                                                            11:00

A remarkable composition incorporating impressions of the various styles of the Tango. Opening with a succession of overlapping and short solo woodwind declarations (4/4, quarter note =100) the work proceeds with similar patterns using longer phrases and accompanied by a tango rhythmic and melodic progression. The tango begins to acquire different moods ("like the sound of a *bandoneon, melanconico, Presago, mysterioso, and Festoso*") each with its own diverse character. A long accelerando leads to new section (quarter note =210), which is very marked with syncopated and unison rhythms trailed by gusts of alternating sixteenth patterns (including tuba). This continues until another succession of tango moods are introduced (*Tango virile),* which is followed by three variations. A return to the opening rhythmic declarations ensues but this time in the low brass with altered meter and tempo (6/8, dotted quarter note =80). This is developed with solo clarinet (using a duple shape) followed by another long accelerando (in 5/4) that leads to "*El Ultimo Tango en…Cinco* " (The Last Tango in Five, quarter note =210). After a tutti presentation of a clear melodic phrase (introduced by the flutes, clarinets and trumpets) the activity subsides into a quiet, slower and more lightly scored ending with only the clarinet choir echoing the opening declarations into pp. Must have strong solo winds, musical patience and facility in the brass and a percussion section capable of understanding its role throughout the various tango presentations.

GIANNINI, Vittorio   **SYMPHONY NO. 3**   Belwin
                                                                            23:20

A band classic of full symphony proportions, in four well-contrasted movements. (1) *Allegro energico* – opening with a broad heroic theme in upper woodwinds, comprised of several motives which are expanded and developed. A rhythmically active transition in rapid 8th-notes using materials from the opening theme lead to a flowingly lyric second theme (in baritone, accompanied by harmony in trombones) which rises to an intense climax, closed by a motive augmented from the first theme. The development section takes up the transition material in fugato manner (difficult clarinet passages for all three parts), along with motives from the opening theme, which build to a climactic statement using the opening theme intervals. This leads to the recapitulation which follows the exposition fairly closely. An energetic coda based on the transition and the opening theme ends the first movement in affirmative fashion. (2) *Adagio* – a highly romantic and poetic movement, opening with a beautiful introductory oboe solo (using intervals from the 1st movement opening) accompanied by trombone quartet, followed by a lovely flute theme with woodwind accompaniment. After repetition of this theme (along with a rich-textured horn quartet passage), a second section, more agitated in character, appears rising to an eloquent climax which subsides to a return of the flute theme, extended into a broadly lyric coda that also uses the second theme. (3) *Allegretto* – a sparkling scherzo movement presenting a rhythmically intricate theme using both 3/4 and 6/8 meters, along with a constant stream of 8th-notes that shift in accentuation between the two. A contrasting trio section features a long-lined melody while the flowing 8th-note pattern continues. The two ideas are then combined, leading to a final statement of the opening material, ending softly. (N.B. – should be conducted in 2 throughout the movement – metronome marking of 112-116 refer to dotted-quarter, not quarter). (4) *Allegro con brio* (4/4, quarter=176, conducted in 2) – an exultant and brilliant movement with a rhythmically energetic first theme comprised of three distinct ideas; a more lyrically flowing second theme with a rhythmic tag; and a heroic closing theme. The development uses the second and closing themes, leading to a slightly varied recapitulation. The coda, using the opening material, brings the work to an exciting conclusion. This work calls for a fully mature group, demanding considerable technique in both woodwinds and brass (especially clarinets and horns), and uses much small-choir and soloistic scoring, while requiring a high level of musicianship, sensitivity and command of both tonal beauty and power. Highly recommended.

GIANNINI, Vittorio   **VARIATIONS AND FUGUE**   Belwin
                                                                            15:00

A great work that covers the gamut of emotional expression within the framework of a highly disciplined formal organization. The "theme" on which the variations are based is really two chromatic lines (ascending and descending) and the implied harmonic progressions that result from their combination. There are 14 succeeding variations that are increasingly complex and intricate (with many problems of rhythmic continuity and precision) arriving at a climactic outburst of passionate intensity in Variation 10, gradually subsiding into a profoundly expressive Lento section which comprise the last 4 variations .The succeeding Fugue theme is in a "wedge" shape (the intervals grow out from minor 2nd to major 7th) which parallels the shape of the original theme. This fugue is very intricate rhythmically and technically due to its chromatic nature, and utilizes all the devices common to fugal treatment (including inversion and stretto), arriving at a climactic statement which is interrupted by a second fugue whose theme is stated by the brass, accompanied by the rhythmic outline of the first fugue theme in percussion. After the second fugue is presented, the two fugue themes are stated together and developed further, arriving at an intense climax, at which point the opening theme of the work returns for a final powerful statement. This work requires everything in terms of technical command, tonal spectrum, musicianship and expressive power, as well as solos and sectional talent covering the entire ensemble. Strongly recommended for all upper-level groups who have the musical and technical resources required.

GILLINGHAM, David   **HEROES, LOST AND FALLEN**   Composer Editions
                                                                           11:15

A dramatic, frequently powerful, technically and musically challenging tone poem created as a Vietnam War memorial. It opens with mysterious, haunting music featuring the piano (an important soloistic part) and mallet percussion. A chorale-like statement follows, alternating with fanfare-like figuration in woodwinds and percussion. The main body of the work follows – fast, driving, harsh, dissonant rhythmic and intense – and is extensively developed. A faster 6/8 section then appears. The driving mood gradually subsides and the work closes with a combination of the chorale and fanfare materials. Requires strong technical and musical playing from the entire band.

GORB, Adam **DANCES FROM CRETE** Maecenas Music
20.00

This powerful and highly technical four-movement work uses dance material inspired by Greek mythology. *Syrtos,* opens the collection with a snarling fanfare in F major. This quickly moves to a fast dance (quarter note=144) introduced by the percussion followed by uneven note groupings and mixed meters in the tutti response. Many solo and soli voices develop and trade the theme until the return of the opening material. A short coda employing rhythmic percussion colors brings the movement to a dramatic close. *Tik,* the second movement, is a challenging dance beginning in 5/8, eighth note = 280. The multi meter movement is scored very thinly in places with single wind instruments accompanied by solo percussion at times. Off stage trumpets segue into movement III, Sanmarie Gorge, without a pause. This movement begins in 7/4 (quarter note = 100), featuring the English horn (cued in alto saxophone). After some extensive development at this tempo a short flurry of fast brass calls accompanied by wind runs lead back to off stage trumpets in a call and answer setting. An Andante section ensues, now using upper woodwinds with both tremolos and rhythmic echoes. The final movement, Syrtaki begins as an extension to the trumpet calls but in G major, 4/4 *Moderato Pasante,* (quarter note = 88). Off stage trumpets take their place on stage while continuing to play a new theme accompanied by low brass and percussion. The rhythmic theme begins to accelerate until the tempo reaches *Presto* (quarter note = 176) in 2/4. Rapid woodwind patterns are exchanged as well as brass and percussion punctuation arcs. This section transitions to a half pulse (eighth note =previous quarter note) element that eventually accelerates back to the Presto tempo, which acts as a coda section. Very demanding in all areas including solo winds (including E-flat clarinet and E-flat trumpet) percussion virtuosity and brass with endurance. Highly recommended for those ensembles with advanced players and a conductor who can communicate all of the multi meter sections with logical and creative phrasings as well as clarity.

GOULD, Morton **SYMPHONY FOR BAND** Chappell
16:00

A superb work in two contrasting but related movements (1) *EPITAPHS* (Slow flowing movement) opens with a tranquil, poignant section scored mostly for small groups and choirs and featuring numerous solos. This leads to a ghostly march section featuring repeated 16th-note figures in antiphonal muted trumpets with a basso ostinato around which various martial figures are presented, building to a powerful climax, interrupted by a sudden return of music from the first section. A slow, mournful coda (with one last echo of the march) concludes the movement. There are important passages for all woodwinds including 2 oboes and English horn; E^b Clarinet), trumpets divided into 6 parts, solo horn and baritone. (2) *MARCHES* (Brisk March tempo, 2/4, quarter=132) a series of widely-varied march tunes, beginning very softly and delicately, requiring fluency and flexibility of tonguing in both woodwinds and brass. This section is followed by a more subdued legato tune (like a trio melody) which gradually becomes more heroic and martial, finally appearing in a triumphant tutti outburst, which leads to an elaborate coda (beginning in 6/8, then returning to 2/4) which varies the opening tunes, increasing in speed and intensity to a frenetic and exuberant conclusion. This work requires depth of solo and section talent in all areas. Many passages are scored for 3 or 4 instruments (oboes, bassoons, saxophones etc.) with no cues, as well as divisi parts (2 solo clarinets, 2 baritones, 2 snare drums and 2 bass drums, etc.). Technically challenging, particularly with regard to tonguing, but not rhythmically or harmonically complex. Highly recommended.

GRAHAM, Peter **HARRISON'S DREAM** Alfred
14:00

An explosive and original composition inspired by the fate of several British ships in 1707 that were trapped in rocks off the shore of Sicily before the chronometer was invented. Opening with a bustle of percussion thirty-second notes, woodwind trills and rapid articulated passages (ferocious, but with clarity, 4/8 eighth note =168), this episode uses energy and texture as its structure. Following accented brass lines, which add expansion to the draped-syncopated accompaniment, the energy recedes into a thin and calmer section (4/2 and, 5/2 half note = 60) featuring solo material for double reeds, French horn and flute (this is briefly accompanied by important bass and cello parts!). A return to the opening tempo and character ensues but this time using rapidly tongued low brass colors to expose the shift of energy. This is well developed using texture and occasional meter contrasts (including 11/16, 6/16 and 7/16) and judicious syncopation. A exposed and haunting oboe solo evolves into a Largo section (quarter note = 60) and is later joined by flutes and surrendered to the brass choir and solo horn and clarinet. A slightly slower chorale section is presented (Serene and tenderly) which ends with the ensemble members performing structured but unmeasured hand bells (signifying the 'Eight Bells signal aboard ship') into a long percussion crescendo. A recapitulation of the opening material ensues building in intensity and complexity until the luminous chorale reappears (4/2 and 5/2 half note = 84). This time, however, it uses the full power of the tutti texture with running eighth note passages and thick brass scoring. A thinning of the texture follows using cross rhythms, color exchanges and overlapping dynamics, which result in an extensive and sustained final crescendo into the last staccato resonance. An excellent musical journey for ensembles with superior musicians (including double bass, optional cello, harp and extensive percussion) and a conductor who can negotiate the various meters, rhythms, phrases and moods required of this exceptional product.

| **GRAINGER, Percy** | **HILL SONG NO. 2** | MCA |
| | | 5:45 |

A fresh sounding, unusual work using entirely original material, scored for 23 solo winds and brass and 1 percussion, but provided with additional parts for full band. Inspired by Grainger's long hikes through Northern England and Scotland in the early 1900's (it was completed in 1907) and evocative of the rugged hills and outdoor spirit (hence the title), it is in one continuous movement, with several melodic ideas that are developed, expanded and varied in an intricate contrapuntal and harmonic web. While it is not very difficult technically (except for use of upper ranges for clarinets and some intricate passages for low woodwinds), there are considerable subtleties of texture, rhythmic intricacy and independence of voices, balancing of parts, and overlapping phrase structures requiring mature, knowledgeable players, all of whom have melodic parts.

| **GRAINGER, Percy** | **LINCOLNSHIRE POSY** | Ludwig |
| | | 15:00 |

A band masterpiece in six short but highly expressive movements, each of which is based on a different folk-song. (1) *LISBON* (Brisk, 6/8) - a lilting, jaunty sea-chanty, first stated in detached style in muted trumpets and horn, then in woodwinds with a staccato rhythmic figure. The next setting is legato in clarinets with gliding chromatic harmony, while horns, saxes and baritone state "*The Duke of Marlborough*" as a counter-melody. The final setting returns to simple harmony with a flowing counter-melody in low woodwinds, closing with a short coda using the last 2 bars of the tune. Requires rhythmic precision, clarity of articulation, balancing of voices, tonal blend and feeling of lilt. (2) *HORKSTOW GRANGE* (Slowly flowing, changing meters) in a richly-harmonized series of settings, beginning with a fairly straightforward one (melody in horns and baritone) with counter-melody in lower woodwinds. The next setting is fully scored with different harmonic progressions. Solo cornet presents the melody in the third setting, with sustained chords in woodwinds, leading to a climactic setting in upper woodwinds and 1st cornet supported by highly chromatic and dissonant harmony, fading into a tonally indeterminate chord. Requires beauty of tone and blend of phrase and lines. (3) *RUFFORD PARK POACHERS* (Flowingly, eighth= 132, changing 8th-meters), the most complex and lengthy of the movements, stating the tune in canon at the beginning (Piccolo and Clarinet answered by E♭ Clarinet and Bass Clarinet), in solo flugelhorn (or cornet); full band with intricate backgrounds; horns and baritone with gliding chromatic harmony and intricate textures; finally, a return to canonic treatment but with each pair of voices a 5th apart (Piccolo & E♭ Clarinet; Oboe & Bassoon). Requires considerable care in working out ensemble in canonic passages, comfort with changing meters and rhythmic subdivisions, textural clarity and balance, and musical flow and continuity. Some controversy still exists with regard to tempo indication of this movement (the printed indication is quarter= 132); based on internal evidence which gives the 2nd speed (Somewhat faster) as quarter=80 as well as a recording of Grainger playing the opening, it seems clear that the unit indication of quarter is an error and should be an eighth. (4) *THE BRISK YOUNG SAILOR* (Sprightly, 3/4) is a charming, breezy tune first set for clarinet choir and bassoons, then upper woodwinds with staccato rhythmic accompaniment; solo baritone with rapidly rippling woodwind figurations (difficult for precision and fluency); canonic version between oboe and soprano sax accompanied by baritone sax and bassoon; upper woodwinds with rhythmic background like the 2nd setting but in brass, extended by re-setting the last segment of the melody three different ways; and closing with a short coda using the first segment of the tune ending on a bi-tonal chord. (5) *LORD MELBORNE* (Heavy, fierce) - the first half of this powerful war song is stated in massive brass chords in free time (no meter, each chord dictated by conductor); the second half is stated in solo cornet and horn accompaniment with changing meters; then in full brass back in free time. Succeeding settings use various scoring combinations using changing meters, free time and rhythmic and harmonic variations, culminating in a climactic statement for full band using free time, changing meters, irregular rhythmic shapes leading to a powerful, intense closing cadence. (6) *THE LOST LADY FOUND* (Fast, sturdily, 3/4 in 1) – a strongly rhythmic and well-marked dance-song using widely varied settings from unison to parallel triads to octaves with sweeping counter-melody; to the climactic statement in full band with bell-tone accompaniment. This work demands high levels of musical and technical ability from all players and repays the effort required with a profoundly satisfying musical experience and substantive understanding. The new edition prepared by Frederick Fennell, with its correction of the hundreds of errors and discrepancies in the original publication, is indispensable for satisfactory presentation.

GRAINGER, Percy   **MOLLY ON THE SHORE**   C. Fischer
                                                                                        3:50

A brilliant virtuoso work full of energy and drive (Presto, A^b, 2/2, half=112-126) with contrasting episodes calling for a light, delicate touch. Technically quite demanding, requiring rapid 8th-note staccato articulation in all instruments (especially woodwinds) and demanding precision (for lining up rapid 8th notes in doubled passages) and maintenance of tempo (tendency to slow down in tuttis). Many details of balance and clarity also need to be worked out in texturally complex passages (e.g. where the two tunes *Molly on the Shore*" and "*Temple Hill*" are combined with background material). Requires an exceptional solo clarinet (who must play long staccato 8th passages), facility and fluency of low woodwind and bass voices, control and focus of staccato accompaniment figures (especially horns).

GRANTHAM, Donald   **KENTUCKY HARMONY**   Piquant Press
                                                                                        10:00

An interesting and effective three movement suite comprising five contrasting hymn-tunes. (1) *ROCK BRIDGE/LENOX*: A march-like movement opening with rhythmically active woodwind and percussion contrasting with brass in chorale style. A second setting features trumpets playing 8th-note figurations. A varied version of the opening then fades into a quiet ending. (2) *HIDING PLACE*: a sorrowful, lyrical movement n woodwinds with a solo euphonium line. Beautiful writing in rich texture and contrapuntal style (3) *ENTFIELD / DUBLIN*: A lively march opening with percussion followed by woodwinds, then brass. The second section features chorale-style in both woodwinds and brass. The two styles are then brought together.

GRANTHAM, Donald   **J'AI ÉTÉ AU BAL**   Piquant Press
                                                                                        10:00

A significant and flamboyant work using some of the popular Cajun folk music sources of Louisiana. Literally meaning "I went to the dance," much of the music is inspired by two traditional Cajun dances. The first dance, *"Allons danser, Colinda"* ('Let's go dancing, Colinda') is marked by counterpoint, several solo instruments and irregular subdivisions of the meter. *"Les flames d'enfer"* ('The flames of hell'), the second dance is ushered in by fiddle-like tunes but faster and lighter than its tradition. A solo tuba introduces the brass band style of New Orleans, followed by a duet with the euphonium. This builds until the tutti scoring is complete with this color bringing back shades of the opening dance. Requires strong solo wind players, flexible percussionists and a conductor who can navigate the meter/subdivisions and various colors required of this work.

GRANTHAM, Donald   **SOUTHERN HARMONY**   Piquant Press

A suite of four contrasting movements, an excellent, consistently interesting work ,with good contrasts of texture, rhythm, and scoring. (1) *THE MIDNIGHT CITY*: several settings of the tune with a variety of textures and accompaniment figures. The woodwinds have a number of intricate technical passages. (2) *WONDROUS LOVE*: a very slow movement in nostalgic mood. After a woodwind introduction, the melody is stated in euphonium. (3) *EXHILARATION*: rhythmic hand-clapping by the brass punctuates the lively, energetic woodwinds. The horns make two brief appearances playing the first phrase of the melody. (4) *THE SOLDIER'S RETURN*: this is the most complex and difficult movement in a fast 6/8, with a number of intricate technical passages for both woodwind and brass.

GRIFFES, Charles   **THE WHITE PEACOCK**   G. Schirmer
Arr. Frank Erickson   6:00

A beautiful, poetic Impressionist masterpiece, expertly transcribed. It opens with a languorous oboe line followed by a graceful flute motive and a decorous clarinet phrase. These three ideas are then expanded and developed, with increasingly lush harmonic content and intricate textural background, to an intense peak. This is followed by a return to the flute idea which is given a brief sequential development, reaching an eloquent climax, then gradually subsiding into the final section featuring the flute and clarinet ideas, closing with the beginning oboe solo over an unresolved chord. Requires good musical sensitivity, tonal beauty, fluidity of phrase and nuance, capacity to play softly yet securely, and quality woodwinds.

HESKETH, Kenneth   **DIAGHILEV DANCES**   Fiber Music
17:00

A wonderfully creative and original work inspired by the great ballet music of the early twentieth century. The structure consists of an Introduction, three dances with three intermezzos. The Introduction theme opens with a virtuosic and somewhat lyrical bass clarinet solo accompanied by low winds (including divisi euphoniums), piano, harp and solo clarinet (4/4, quarter note = 72). The bass clarinet and Bb clarinet become a dialogue as the texture slowly becomes more complex. Additional woodwind solos are spun off along with piano, percussion and harp exclamations. This leads to the first intermezzo, which uses more pointed articulations and multiple meters. Dance I (*Allgremente*, 2/4 half note = 45 or quarter note =90) opens with a flute solo (accelerando) echoed by flute 2 and later joined by clarinet. The tempo gradually quickens as the texture and mood becomes more energetic. This wends its way back to a slower tempo and ending with reminiscence of the opening bass clarinet solo accompanied by piano and harp. Intermezzo II contains a livelier mood (quarter note=100) with similar woodwind-dominant textures ornamented with various solos. Dance II (Soave, ¾ quarter note =86) begins with thirty-second note fragments in the clarinets that continue throughout the dance in varied forms and textures. This is eventually augmented by tempo, meter and style contrasts while the solo instruments continue to prevail into the slow (quarter note = 60) and sustained close. The third Intermezzo provides the most contrast to the previous ones. It opens with a double reed soli triplet pattern (2/4 and 4/4 quarter note = 148) into marked and ornamented woodwind colors. Trumpets provide technically echoing color contrasts as this energetic segment flows smoothly into Dance III (2/4, quarter note = 156, *Vivace Scherzando*). Tongued sixteenth note passages followed but uneven thirty-second note runs in the woodwinds open this dance. Limited but accented brass scoring gives this dance a syncopated yet march-like feel. A continued shift of tonality and texture using several soli passages, with flurries of woodwinds, gives the dance much forward motion. Tutti textures near the end, this time with full brass power, bring this work to a commanding close. An exceptional and worthy challenge for ensembles with technically fluent winds, musical and sensitive percussion and an excellent pianist and harpist. Highly recommended.

HILL, William H.   **DANSES SACRED AND PROFANE**   Barnhouse
11:00

An imaginative and powerful work in three movements. (1) *MAY DANSE* – opens with an explosive statement in brass and percussion with woodwind punctuation, followed by a slower rhythmic vamp interrupted by a solo flute cadenza which leads to a fast section featuring the flute with the vamp. Another contrasting slow section follows, and the movement concludes with the climactic development of the last music with vamp. (2) *DANSE MACABRE* begins with slow, dissonant chords followed by a soft statement of the "melody of death", which is expanded, then interrupted by a clarinet cadenza. A faster section using an ostinato under the death-melody follows, gradually increasing in speed and volume to a powerful cluster chord, closing with a soft and mysterious return of the opening. (3) *ESTAMPIE* states a 14th-century melody in trumpet which undergoes numerous transformations of rhythm, tempo, and meter, followed by a coda in slow tempo using harp and xylophone accompanied by string bass. This work requires considerable technical and musical maturity, including solid brass with good range and power, fluent and flexible woodwinds and adept, musical percussion as well as expert flute and clarinet soloists and proficient bassoon and bass clarinet.

HINDEMITH, Paul   **MARCH from "SYMPHONIC METAMORPHOSIS"**   Schott
Arr. Keith Wilson   4:40

An excellent transcription of an exciting orchestral standard, made at the suggestion of Hindemith himself, it is strongly marked and rhythmically energetic (2/2, half=80) opening with a horn introductory fanfare figure leading to the first theme in oboe accompanied by a crisp dotted rhythm, repeated and expanded. This leads to a heroic theme in horns accompanied by chattering staccato triplets in woodwinds, later the horn theme is taken by upper woodwinds while brass play the triplets. A development section follows using the opening fanfare figure and the first theme, climaxing in a bold statement of the horn theme in full brass choir with triplet accompaniment, followed by a final statement in horns and baritone. A coda using the opening fanfare theme and triplet accompaniment brings the work to an affirmative conclusion. Requires considerable tonguing facility and technical fluency in both woodwinds and brass, strong horns with solid upper range, and rhythmic precision and control of dotted-8th-16th rhythms in the rapid tempo indicated. (In fact, maintenance of tempo is a frequent problem in performances of this work).

HINDEMEITH, Paul **SYMPHONY IN B-FLAT** Schott
18:00

A major masterpiece by one of the most important 20th-century composers, in three amply-proportioned movements. (1) *MODERATELY FAST, WITH VIGOR* (2/2, half=88-92) – featuring three themes. The first is epic and majestic, played by trumpets with an intricate woodwind background. The second is more lyric and graceful, played by solo oboe followed by tenor sax, then woodwinds. The third consists of two ideas simultaneously – an ostinato flowing line in woodwinds, first alone and then accompanying the theme itself stated by horns. The development presents a rhythmic motive (dotted 8th-16th figures closed off with a triplet 8th) treated in fugato fashion and expanded into various m configurations, built to a powerful climax at which the second theme is presented in augmentation, resolving into the recapitulation which combines both first and second themes, climaxing with the third theme brought to a triumphant conclusion. (2) *ANDANTINO GRAZIOSO* (2/2, half=56) opens with a lyric dialog between cornet and alto sax soli with a light rhythmic background, then stated by alto and tenor sax together. A short transition using the rhythmic background lead to the middle section, a brilliant scherzo (Fast and Gay, 12/8, dotted quarter=112), featuring a lithe, fluent, spirited melody of 8ths and 16ths in clarinets which then appears throughout the woodwinds accompanied by staccato 8ths. The clarinet figure is expanded and developed, reaching a climax stated in augmentation by trombones and horns, then fading into recapitulation which combines both the lyric theme and the scherzo, concluding with the transition phrase and ending softly. (3) *FUGUE* (Rather broad 2/2; Fast). After a brief introduction (itself based on the theme), the theme is stated by cornets and trumpets, succeeded by horns and baritone, oboes, flutes, etc. and worked out. A second theme (espressivo), appearing in bass clarinet and bassoon, is then treated fugally and developed at some length, with varying background material adding to the opening theme of the first movement is triumphantly stated in trumpets and trombones,. A large-scale coda which develops both the opening and tag of the first theme brings the work to a magnificent conclusion. Technically challenging with important parts for all players (except for modest percussion), this work remains above all a musical challenge that repays years of study and re-study. Strongly recommended for all upper-level libraries.

HOLST, Gustav **HAMMERSMITH (Prelude and Scherzo)** Boosey and Hawkes
12:30

One of the great works for band, containing a wide range of musical and emotional content. The Prelude opens mysteriously (Poco Adagio, F minor, 4/2) with an ostinato line in tubas and baritones which becomes an accompaniment to a long-lined legato melody in horns, later taken by woodwinds and extended. A whimsical scherzando phrase intrudes in solo piccolo; reiterated by trumpets it becomes aggressive and angry. The ostinato and melody continue as the tempo increases, leading to the Scherzo (Poco Vivace). The first motive (in 2/4) is in staccato style, stated in flutes which continue with legato 16ths as the motive appears in clarinet. The continuation leads to a lilting 6/8 tune a the 2/4 material continues (challenging subdivision distinction). Meanwhile another staccato idea appears as counterpoint to the first motive. All these are worked out and developed in various configurations along with the scherzando motive from the prelude, culminating in a climactic section where both 2/4 and 6./8 motives are stated together with dissonant harmonic content, gradually subsiding into a more tranquil mood, with the 6/8 motive transformed into an expressive alto sax solo in 3/4. A brief interruption by the 2/4 scherzo motive leads to a Lento section (3/2), featuring a poignant melody in solo clarinet in long note values (taken up successively by flute, oboe, tenor sax, brass choir) with elements of the 6/8 scherzo as counterpoint (Difficult to relate the two ideas rhythmically and maintain precision of ensemble). The scherzo section returns varied and abbreviated, again building to a powerful climax using the scherzo 6/8 augmented to 3/4, the dissonant contrapuntal motives and the scherzando motive from the Prelude. All the activity is suddenly interrupted by the reappearance of the initial Adagio, complete with bass ostinato, scherzando and scherzo motives in various voices (difficult to put together), gradually becoming more subdued with only the initial sustained ideas remaining, fading into the mysterious mood of the opening. In many ways, this work provides the greatest challenges of all the great literature, with its awesome combination of musical profundity, emotional range, technical and rhythmic problems, solo requirements and a conductor who has a true command of the musical conception. It is, however, worth any effort required to perform a work as magnificent and deeply moving as this one, which will provide an overwhelming musical experience for players and listeners alike. Strongly recommended – at least in terms of serious study.

HOLST, Gustav   **"MARS" from "THE PLANETS"**   Boosey & Hawkes
Arr. Unknown   6:30

An intense, powerful and dramatic work with relentless drive and energy, in quintuple meter (5/4, 5/2) throughout (Except for a brief excursion into 3/4) with an ostinato rhythm and three elemental thematic ideas – the first, a three-note motive which is expanded and later harmonized; the second, a dotted rhythm; the third, a brass call. The second becomes the basis of the middle section (5/2, difficult to maintain precision). Requires good control of rhythm, precise well-defined articulation, rich and resonate sonority (especially in brass), wide dynamic range and maintenance of tempo and forward momentum.

HOLST, Gustav   **"JUPITER" from "THE PLANETS"**   Boosey & Hawkes
Arr. Unknown   7:20

A great contrast with the above, this movement exhibits exuberant vitality, hearty vigor and warmth, and energetic brilliance. The opening section is highly rhythmic in nature, with all the tunes being strongly marked and articulated. The middle section features a broadly lyric melody which rises to eloquent heights, leading to a varied return of the opening and a coda that begins massively in slow tempo and erupts in a brilliant Presto flourish. Requires great technical facility from woodwinds (articulation and fluency in tongued and slurred fast notes), brass (intricate counter-subject in trombones, interval leaps in trumpets), resonance and richness of tone (horn melodies), feeling of phrase and line (middle section) and rhythmic precision (intricate figures using dotted rhythms, ties and 16th-notes).

HUSA, Karel   **APOTHEOSIS OF THIS EARTH**   Associated
       25:30

An epic work of enormous expressive and emotional range and variety, in three highly dramatic movements. (1) *APOTHEOSIS* – begins with a "point of light" (glockenspiel, then solo clarinet) gradually building in density of texture, volume and rhythmic and harmonic complexity to a majestic, expressive phrase, leading to a brilliant cadenza-like passage featuring solo xylophone with brass clusters and woodwind chatterings, then gradually fading into a simple line as at the beginning. (2) *TRAGEDY OF DESTRUCTION* is explosive, aggressive, agitated, frenetic in mood, dominated by percussion and brass eruptions of rapid-fire rhythmic figures, along with dense clusters, trombone glissandos, trills spread over wide ranges gradually focusing on an obsessive rhythmic figure which appears throughout the ensemble, against which fragmentary motives (chords, short melodic ideas, rhythms etc.) appear. This leads to a free-time episode during which all instruments repeat short rhythmic fragments at different times. Brass and saxophone clusters lead to an ad lib xylophone solo (only lower and upper notes indicated). This is followed by a painfully anguished climactic section during which all the preceding devices are brought together to a final explosion and expiration. (3) *POSTSCRIPT* – remains at a soft dynamic level throughout, describing the aftermath of destruction, using subdued chord clusters, brief melodic and rhythmic motives, and the text "This beautiful earth" spoken by the band in specified rhythm, gradually diminishing in density to just one spoken voice and a final "point of light" played by solo xylophone. This work requires great technical virtuosity and rhythmic skill from the entire ensemble especially brass and percussion, and a conductor who has the epic concept of the work in hand. A powerful work which should be experienced by all mature wind and percussion players.

HUSA, Karel   **CONCERTO FOR PERCUSSION AND WIND ENSEMBLE**   Associated
       18:00

A major contribution to the literature; certainly the finest work featuring the percussion as a solo concertante group. In three movements: (1) Maestoso – featuring the metallic percussion. (2) Moderato molto – featuring marimba, vibraphone and timpani. (3) Allegro ma non troppo – using all the percussion in various combinations. Technically and musically extremely demanding and difficult for the percussion, as well as challenging the ensemble with rhythmically and technically intricate passagework.

HUSA, Karel   **MUSIC FOR PRAGUE 1968**   Associated
       18:30

This has become an established band classic and deserves its elevated place as one of the great works composed in any medium in the past 50 years. In four movements: (10 *INTRODUCTION AND FANFARE,* opens with a s low, mysterious statement of many of the main motivic and harmonic ideas (Adagio), which include a Hussite war chant stated first in timpani, and a flute solo supported by dissonant chords. This leads to the Fanfare (Allegro) stated by trumpets, the motives of which are worked over throughout the ensemble, built up to an intense climax on the note D, at which point the music gradually subsides in volume and tempo while the timpani motive is reiterated, arriving at the opening Adagio tempo with the chime-note D and concluding with a varied statement of the flute solo. (2) *ARIA* (Moderato molto), featuring a long, soulful recitative-like phrase in saxophones, accompanied by bell sounds in marimba and vibraphone. The recitative line is gradually built up in volume and intensity, with increasing elaboration of texture, reaching an anguished, almost painful climax then gradually diminishes into a few fragmentary notes, while the bell sounds continue. (3) *INTERLUDE* for percussion alone (Misterioso, eighth=63-66), requiring 3 sets of antique cymbals, triangles, suspended cymbals and gong, each set using different sizes, in addition to snare drum and vibraphone. Rhythmically very complex, with intricate subdivisions into 32nd-notes, rests and ties and with the parts closely inter-related – but provides an important link to the succeeding movement and thus must be carefully worked out. All players must have considerable rhythmic understanding. A long snare drum solo concludes the movement   leading without pause into (4) TOCCATA (Vivace, 6/8) beginning with a highly energetic, agitated unison rhythmic statement which provides the basis of the entire movement. (the 8th-note rhythm-rest patterns provide melodic formations as well as ostinato figures). This idea and its off-shoots are elaborated and expanded, later using themes from the 1st movement, gradually building to the climactic section where the fanfare motive reappears. The intensity continues to increase, arriving at the unison rhythmic statement which began the movement, interrupted by the chime note D which becomes the basis of the succeeding Adagio and the return of the timpani motive. This is succeeded by its unison statement in brass, answered by the toccata rhythm. An ad lib measure using toccata, aria and fanfare figures is gradually overwhelmed by a powerful snare-drum march rhythm which is then inundated by the timpani motive stated in full band but not completed. As with the other Husa works listed above, this piece requires great technical and musical skill in all sections but repays the considerable effort needed with esthetic and musical reward many times over.

IANNACONE, Anthony	SEA DRIFT	Ludwig
		18:00

An imaginative and complex work in three contrasting movements: (1) *OUT OF THE CRADLE ENDLESSLY ROCKING*: mostly poetic and lyrical in character, with many passages of transparent and soloistic scoring – contrasted with dramatic, vehement and turbulent outbursts, building to a powerful and intense climax; then subsiding into the tranquil mood of the opening. (2) *ON THE BEACH AT NIGHT*: a very slow, dream-like section with rhythmic arabesques in woodwinds and percussion. A faster, more agitated mood featuring the opening materials provides effective contrast. The movement concludes in quiet reflection. (3) *SONG FOR ALL SEAS, ALL SHIPS*: a driving, energetic movement with much technically intricate passagework. The final pages are exciting and dramatic.

IVES, Charles	FINALE from SYMPHONY NO. 2	Peer
Arr. Jonathan Elkus		11:00

A delightful, amusing and spirited work that is archetypically American, filled with quotations of popular and folk tunes and fragments that resemble other tunes – yet somehow manages to hold together. Rather difficult, requiring technical fluency, precision of articulation, good solo flute and clarinet, and woodwind choir and trumpet section – but very enjoyable to work on. With its rousing surprise ending, it is also a successful audience pleaser.

JACOB, Gordon	FLAG OF STARS	Boosey & Hawkes
		10:00

A fine original in overture format. The opening introduction features an epic trumpet fanfare contrasted with a slow, mysterious lyric melody. The main Allegro, in 5/8, features a restless agitated, highly rhythmic idea with intricate 16th-note subdivisions. This is developed and expanded at some length, leading to a 3/4 section featuring an anthem-like melody. The allegro material is developed further, followed by a return of the slow section, varied in scoring and shape. The work concludes with a recapitulation and a coda combining the fanfare and 3/4 anthem. Requires a well-developed control of 5/8 meter and its subdivisions, excellent trumpets, flutes, clarinet, E^{b} Clarinet (important and not cued), saxophones (exposed 5/8 passage for the section), baritone and tubas(important for rhythmic stability in many passages), as well as overall ensemble and choir sonority.

JACOB, Gordon   **MUSIC FOR A FESTIVAL**   Boosey & Hawkes
                                                                                                   30:00

A major work of elaborate dimension, in eleven movements, featuring a brass choir (4 trumpets, 3 trombones, preferably doubled, with timpani) and band, both separately and together. (1) *INTRADA*, for Brass (Grave e Maestoso – Allegro) opens with a sustained but well-marked chordal statement in noble, majestic style, followed by a joyous, rhythmic marcato section. (2) *OVERTURE*, for Band (Allegro vivace, B^b, 3/4) – lively, energetic and rhythmic, with contrasts of choir scoring, consisting of three themes developed and elaborated, with a short emphatic coda. (3) *ROUND OF 7 PARTS* (Brass) – a short 4-bar phrase is treated in strict round manner, beginning softly with a gradual crescendo to a strong ff statement. A 3-bar pp transition leads to (4) *AIR* (Band) (Adagio, F major, 3/4 in 6, 8th= 58) – a lovely, legato movement with a flowing line in solo cornet, later solo clarinet, then fully scored, reaching a rich-textured conclusion. (5) *INTERLUDE* (Brass) (Adagio, 4/4) – using the opening motive of the Intrada stated softly and legato in trombones, answered by chords in trumpets. (6) *MARCH* (Band) (Vivace, C minor, 2/4) –states a perky staccato idea in upper woodwinds leading to the main theme in cornet and answering motive in clarinets. The second strain features a syncopated melody for full band followed by a varied return of the opening idea. The Trio (in A^b,) is legato and lyric with detached bass line. After a restatement of the 2nd strain idea, the March opening returns to C minor combined with the trio melody, concluding with a last statement of the 2nd-strain idea and a short coda using the opening motive. (7) *SARABANDE* (Brass)(Lento, G minor, 3/2) – very slow, expressive, sustained legato, written mostly in half-notes. (8) *SCHERZO* (Band)(Molto Allegro e brilliante, E^b, 2./4) – a fleet, breathless 3-note motive in upper woodwinds accompanied by staccato 8ths sets the tone, scored transparently and delicately with intricate interplay among voices using the 3-note motive. A solemn trio (C minor in much slower tempo, cantabile and legato in style, offers substantial contrast. The Scherzo returns D.C. (9) *MADRIGAL* (Brass)(Allegro, Ab, 2/2) – a hearty, warm, spirited piece in the style of the 16th-century English composers whom Jacob greatly admired, using both homophonic and contrapuntal textures and terraced dynamics. (10) *MINUET AND TRIO* (Band)(E b, 3/4) – a charming, gentle movement with flowing legato lines, contrasted with a trio that contains staccato and marcato passages and more emphatic moments. (11) *FINALE* (Brass and Band)(Grave e Maestoso, 4/4) – a fitting climax to the entire work, opening with the Brass in a fanfare-like statement which also uses the Intrada motive. The band enters with an answering phrase, followed by the brass, then both together. This is followed by a full-length fugue scored in choir fashion, using stretto and augmentation, climaxing in a return of the Grave introduction and a powerful unison sonority, closing with a rich Bb, epilog. Though technically this work is not very demanding (except for the Scherzo), it requires a mature sound with sensitive and intelligent musicianship in all sections (except for modest percussion).

JADIN, Hyacinthe   **OVERTURE IN F (1795)**   Belwin
Arr. Douglas Townsend   6:00

An original work from the French Revolution, written in the classical overture form – slow introduction and lively allegro. This piece is technically rather difficult and demanding, particularly for clarinets and trumpets, who are frequently playing in the upper register. Low woodwind and tuba have rapid tongued passages which also cover a wide range. However, it is decidedly worthwhile to work on and perform, as an excellent example of a classical original wind work.

JENKINS, Joseph Wilcox   **AMERICAN OVERTURE**   Presser
                                                                                                   5:00

An energetic, vital and exuberant work in lively tempo throughout, with effective contrasts of dynamics and scoring, vigorous rhythms and attractive folk-like tunes. Requires considerable technical fluency, including rapid staccato tonguing, strong, mature horns (the section is used as a soloistic concertante throughout), solid precise brass and rhythmically accurate and facile woodwinds. A highly successful piece for concert programs. The new edition is now published with a full score.

KABALEVSKY, Dmitri   **COLAS BREUGNON OVERTURE**   Shawnee
Arr. Walter Beeler   4:30

A brilliant virtuoso showpiece for orchestra, superbly transcribed. It opens with a boisterous, energetic introduction (Presto, F, 2/2) leading to a crisp, light staccato tune (2/4) with driving rhythmic underpinning, which is stated several times and expanded using various scoring. A transition leads to a lovely, somewhat melancholy theme in D minor, while the accompanying rhythmic figure continues, worked up to a climactic statement which is suddenly interrupted by a return to the first section. This leads to an extended coda featuring several small groups (clarinets, oboes, horns, trumpets), soloistically treated, gradually building to a stirring climax.

Demands the utmost in technical facility, a fluency of articulation and rhythmic stability and precision from all sections, especially woodwind. The music, both attractive and brilliant, exciting and lyric by turns, is well worth the effort.

LINN, Robert   **PROPAGULA**   C. Fischer

12:00

A highly original, imaginative and exciting work, somewhat like a theme and variations in formal design. It opens with a slow, rather mysterious introduction which presents the basic musical material ("propagula" = "buds", because the ideas are short and motivic), generating all the material which follows) in soloistic fashion (flute, oboe, alto flute – cued in clarinets, trumpet, bass clarinet, etc.) the first variation is rather like a march (Allegro, 4/4), highly rhythmic and also often contrapuntal in texture , with extensive development of several motives. The march gradually subsides, leading to a waltz (Moderato, 3/4) with a gracefully rhythmic melody in solo trumpet followed by a smooth-flowing 8th-note line in woodwinds, succeeded by further statements of the melody and its answer, using several small-group presentations (3 flutes, clarinets, saxes, 2-3 muted trumpets ,3 bassoons, 2 tubas). The next variation is an elegiac, poignant Dirge (Andante, 4/4), featuring a treading motive first stated by baritone duet, later developed and expanded to a rich-textured climax, subsiding into a beautiful statement for 6-part trombone choir. This is succeeded by a brilliant, sparkling scherzo (Allegro scherzando, 6/8) using an intricate rhythmic motivic transformation and complex texture, with important work for percussion ensemble. This is followed by a fanfare (slowly, 4/4) for six trumpets soli, each one of which presents a different motivic configuration, climaxing in a magnificent tutti Chorale (Maestoso with richly-voiced chords. Suddenly a fast, rhythmic Fugue appears (Allegro, 4/4), treating all the motives in fugal or contrapuntal manner, leading to a powerful stretto passage – a series of statements in all different rhythmic configurations – concluding with an intensely climactic, exciting statement in full band (including trumpet and trombone glissandi and ad lib percussion). A magnificent work using contemporary harmonic language and some technically challenging passages, requiring strong players in all section s (some of which are expanded, including 3 oboes and English horn; 3 bassoons and contrabassoon).

LISZT, Franz   **LES PRELUDES**   Hindsley
Arr. Mark Hindsley   15:00

An excellent transcription of a well-known orchestral standard – a tone poem using varying transformations of one main theme to depict the many different aspects of life; doubt, affirmation, serenity, turbulence, relief, triumph, etc. Requires great fluency and facility in woodwinds (especially clarinet) and low-voice instruments, solid soloistic horns, good solo woodwinds, and rich sonority for tutti passages. There is an important harp part, which can be covered by piano, but is more effective on marimba (requiring a very facile player).

MACKEY, John   **REDLINE TANGO**   www.optimusic.com

9:30

A very challenging and interesting work loosely based on the tango dance rhythms. Opening with a flurry of percussion colors with piano punctuations (4/4,multi meters, quarter note =132) the mounting winds add a variety of syncopated interjections. This is further developed with uneven phrases, clever instrumentation and rhythmic drive. Using previous material, a sudden shift appears using the tango dance style patterns beginning with solo euphonium (3/2 half note =56, "Tango, somewhat freely"). Decorated with woodwind and piano ornaments, the dance theme shifts in color (including an alto saxophone cadenza). A quasi recapitulation ensues (quarter note =132, multi meters) but this time it is "redder" with heavier brass, additional cross rhythms and thicker textures. A final burst of tutti texture with rhythmic vitality brings the work to powerful close. Must have an excellent pianist, winds with rhythmic control and independence and an extended and musical percussion section that understands its various roles within the work.

MASLANKA, David   **SYMPHONIES 2,3,4,5,7,8**   Carl Fischer
These symphonies are all epic (29 to 49 minutes) in nature and very worthy of consideration for the most advanced ensembles. Although too massive to comprehensively review all of these symphonies in the present setting, they are singularly substantial additions to the literature. Each contains a specific vocabulary that is both consistent with the composer's palate yet completely distinctive to the work. The use of extreme registers, augmented instrumentation (i.e. harp, pipe organ, piano, contra-bassoon), imaginative combinations of chamber sonorities, and confronting the limits of the dynamic and textural spectrum permeate these works. They are all deeply personal with expressive qualities and demand the highest levels of technique and endurance. Expanded

percussion sections with each member assigned to several instruments is the model. Strongly recommended for ensembles and conductors that possess all the maturity necessary for the musical requirements.

MENDELSSOHN, Felix   **OVERTURE, OP. 24**   Ludwig
Arr. John Boyd   10:00

A fine original, well-adapted for modern instrumentation in this new edition. It opens with a slow, sustained lyric introduction (Andante, C major, 3/4) in transparent scoring emphasizing clarinets, horns, and bassoons. This is followed by a brilliant Allegro Vivace (C major, 4/4) stating two contrasting themes - the first in tutti scoring, using a fanfare-like figure of 8ths and 16ths followed by legato 16ths; the second scored lightly, using some of the same rhythmic figuration, both in the melody and its background. The closing section returns to tutti scorings. The development section takes a dotted 8th-16th rhythm from the introduction and juxtaposes it with a fragment of the 2nd Allegro theme and also uses parts of the first theme, leading to the recapitulation. A brilliant tutti coda using elements of the first theme brings the work to an exhilarating conclusion. Requires fully-developed technical facility (both articulated tonguing and finger fluency) from all players, musical maturity in the lyric introduction, rhythmic solidity and precision in development, and maintenance of tempo throughout Allegro (tends to slow down in tutti passages). This edition is the first based on the rediscovered original manuscript and has excellent critical and interpretative notes. The other published edited versions (Felix Greissle, pub. G. Schirmer; Herbert Fred, pub. Boosey & Hawkes) are not as well-arranged or carefully edited to conform to the original's texture and character.

MOZART, W.A.   **FANTASIA IN F, K. 594**   Shawnee
Arr. William Schaefer   8:00

Though Mozart himself disparaged this work because of the medium (it was commissioned for a clockwork organ), it is a true masterwork with all the hallmarks of the late Mozart style. The opening Adagio section (F minor, 3/4) is poignant and resigned in mood, featuring highly chromatic harmony and transparent scoring. The succeeding Allegro (F major, 4/4) is heroic and rhythmically energetic, with a hint of Handel. At its climax on the dominant, the Adagio suddenly returns with even greater anguish and bittersweet dissonances, ending softly and sorrowfully. This work requires great maturity of musicianship and considerable technical fluency (the 16th-note passages in both upper and lower voices are difficult), but is well worth the effort. Strongly recommended for mature groups.

NELHYBEL, Vaclav   **PRELUDE AND FUGUE**   Frank
         4:50

An exciting and brilliantly crafted work in one continuous movement. It opens with a slow introduction that contains motivic elements of the main themes, followed by an Allegro which states the first theme (a forceful marcato) in brass, then the second theme (a rapid legato line) in clarinets, followed by similar countersubjects and succeeding entries of the theme. A powerful episode follows, using elements of the first theme in both woodwinds and brass, succeeded by a double fugue treating both themes fugally at the same time. A transition leads to a dramatic episode using all the main motives in variation and combination, concluding with an intense, climactic coda using expanded elements of both themes. Requires fluent woodwinds (especially clarinets) for the second theme and subsequent variations and countersubjects using flowing 8ths, which also demands rhythmic precision for alignment of voices. Also requires brass that are rhythmically solid with well-focused pitch, control of attacks, articulative flexibility and precision; and expert, clean, well-defined percussion.

NELHYBEL, Vaclav   **SYMPHONIC MOVEMENT**   Belwin
         8:00

A powerful, dynamic piece, opening with a slow massive unison introduction that reveals the single thematic motive uniting the entire piece. A pyramid sequence then presents the motive as a chord, building to a driving, rhythmic Allegro that presents the theme in various guises, using small motivic units, chordal presentations, rapidly tongued 16th-note figures in brass – increasing in intensity to a climactic chord. This leads to a slower, highly dramatic and suspenseful section using an extended statement of the theme punctuated by rhythmic elements in percussion and brass, with an intricate xylophone solo that plays an ornamental version of the theme. Additional rhythmic elements are called into play, leading to a woodwind ostinato over which a return of the 16th-ntoe tongued brass figures appear. A return of the pyramid idea brings the Allegro to a massive climax, leading to a coda in the slow tempo of the opening – starting with the first note of the theme and gradually adding more notes until all 12 notes are sounded in an intense chord. A rapid flourish using the first segment of the theme brings the work to an emphatic conclusion. Requires very mature brass players with considerable articulative skill and tonal control, rhythmically secure and fluent woodwinds, and technically solid and musically intelligent percussion (especially a xylophone soloist with poise and technique).

NELHYBEL, Vaclav   **TRITTICO**   Belwin
10:30

A highly dramatic work in three movements. (1) Allegro maestoso - vivo marcato – opens with a short, strongly marked rhythmic introduction followed by a sustained marcato theme stated three times (unison trumpets, horns, trombones), leading to a nervous, agitated, driving theme in trumpets punctuated by rhythmic entrances in woodwinds and brass tied together by snare drum. A meno mosso section follows- a variation on the trumpet figure in oboe duet, then clarinets, building to a return of the first theme (in trumpets, saxes, trombones, baritones), punctuated by rhythmic figures in the band. (2) Adagio (3/4 - 4/4) – a series of dramatic recitative and arioso-like passages, beginning with a low woodwind and timpani dialog, then a mournful line in alto and tenor sax answered by a short melodic phrase in woodwinds. The low woodwind recitato figures return along with the sax figure and rhythmic punctuation, building in intensity to a climactic passage featuring horns and saxes decorated with ornamental figuration and trills in woodwinds and piano, climaxing in a trombone glissando. This is iinterrupted by the return of recitatives (alto, tenor, baritone sax) unified by an accompanying rhythm. The movement closes with a final recitative section, beginning with horns, then trumpets (difficult), ending with a tense, dramatic cadence. (3) Allegro marcato (3/4) – fast, well-marked, emphatic – related to the first movement thematically, opening with a modal, chant-like melody in trumpets and cornets, then additional brass and woodwinds. The mode changes to minor with an ostinato in low woodwinds, fragments of the chant, then added rhythmic punctuation, climaxing in an augmented version of the opening trumpet chant in horns (doubled by trumpets). A short transition using a fragment of the chant and rapid scales in woodwinds leads to a return of the 1st movement theme in low brass while woodwinds, trumpets, and horns play the scale figures. A return of the opening section in C major ensues, with woodwinds playing scales against the trumpet theme – extended into a climactic coda using a pyramid in brass and ascending woodwind scales to a 12-note chord which resolves to an octave C. Requires technical facility in all sections, solid, secure brass with upper range (trumpets in 2nd & 3rd movements; horns, trombones) and flexibility; upper woodwinds with fluency in rapid scale passages, solo saxophones and oboes, adept percussion (including 2 timpanists in 2nd movement; precise and rhythmic snare drum, piano and mallets).

NELSON, Ron   **PASSACAGLIA (HOMAGE ON B-A-C-H)**   Ludwig
10:40

A major creative achievement – complex, technically difficult, requiring a large ensemble (including 12 clarinets and 6 trumpets). It consists of twenty-five variations on an 8-bar bass, along with a constant appearance of the 4-note B-A-C-H motive and its transpositions. The variations themselves have many styles of writing – including chorale-like textures, sweeping rapid scales, intricate rhythmic patterns and repeated tongued notes. The final pages are among the most emotionally powerful in the repertory.

NIELSEN, Carl   **MASQUERADE OVERTURE**   G. Schirmer
Arr. John Boyd   4:15

A wonderful work that deserves to be better known. It opens with a brilliant rush of 16th-notes in the woodwinds (Allegro, C major, 6/8) that is developed contrapuntally, along with a folk-like tune in the bass. The middle section (2/4) consists of two contrasting melodic ideas in somewhat humorous vein. The final section features a varied return of the 6/8 opening, followed by a fast, driving coda in 2/4. Quite difficult, especially for flutes, clarinets, and low woodwinds, and will require considerable effort just to master its technical intricacies, let alone the numerous problems of ensemble and precision, but will prove to be worthwhile in every respect. The transcription, remarkable in its fidelity to the original, is exemplary.

NIXON, Roger   **FIESTA DEL PACIFICO**   Boosey & Hawkes
8:00

A very colorful, dynamic and evocative work, with melodies and rhythms that portray the Spanish atmosphere of the festival for which the piece is named. The opening section (Allegro, quarter = 138) is brilliant and energetic, with many solos and transparently scored passages amid the vibrant and exciting tutti passages (solos include: oboe, English horn, E^{b} and B^{b} clarinets, bassoon, alto sax, timpani, castanets, xylophone). The middle section is a languorous but flowing waltz featuring an important celesta par (which can be played on piano) as well as harp. Requires good facility, rhythmically solid and accurate ensemble and conductor (for compound meter passages) and sensitivity to nuance and color.

OFFENBACH, Jacques **LA BELLE HELENE OVERTURE** Kjos
Arr. Lawrence Odom 9:00

A delightful and attractive work, full of wonderful tunes, sparkling rhythms and effective contrasts of tempo, style, texture and dynamics. Requires first-class woodwinds (including two solo clarinets and solo oboe) that are technically facile (particularly in the rapid articulated passages in the finale) and musically sensitive in the lyric Andante and Allegretto waltz; brass that can accompany and play with clean articulation, rhythmically steady and tasteful percussion. The transcription is superb.

ORR, Buxton **A JOHN GAY SUITE** Studio Music Co.
15:00

A challenging and imaginative treatment of tunes from "The Beggar's Opera" in four contrasting movements. The opening INTRADA features a lively tune set with numerous meter changes ($^3/_8$, $^5/_8$, $^7/_8$ etc.) and a variety of scorings. A ROMANZA follows, with slowly flowing legato lines, mostly for woodwinds. Next is INTERMEZZO with rapid 8th-note scale figurations, contrasted with a lilting 12/8 section featuring a piccolo solo. The FINALE weaves together several tunes from earlier movements – full of energy and vitality. Technically and musically challenging.

PERSICHETTI, Vincent **DIVERTIMENTO** Presser
11:00

An appealing yet imaginative contemporary approach to the suite-like form used so often in the 18th-century. In six short, contrasting movements. (1) *PROLOGUE* (Fast, 2/2) – lively and energetic, using a rhythmic motive punctuated with bi-tonal chords. (2) *SONG* (Slowly, 4/4) – a lyric movement with legato melodies over an ostinato 8th-note pattern. (3) *DANCE* (Lightly, 2/4) – using a series of rhythm patterns under a light, somewhat humorous melody. (4) *BURLESQUE* (Heavily; Brightly, 2/4) contrasting a ponderous melody in tuba (with after-beat accompaniment) with a light, flowing line in clarinets delicately accompanied by upper winds. (5) *SOLILOQUY* (Slowly, 4/4), featuring a cornet solo over soft sustained chords. (6) *MARCH* (Spirited, 2/2), a strongly marked rhythmic movement opening with a percussion introduction. Requires solid soloists and section talent (much small-group and choir scoring), with ear and feel for the Persichetti idiom (bi-tonal harmony, crisp rhythmic, light-textured writing).

PERSICHETTI, Vincent **MASQUERADE, OP. 102** Elkan-Vogel
12:00

A complex, intricate and subtly structured theme and variations. After an introduction in fast tempo, the theme is introduced – actually two versions of the same motive (one fast and jocose, the other slow and expressive). *VARIATION 1* – (Andante, 6/8) – an 8th-note legato idea in woodwinds and horns punctuated by a 16th-note figure in trumpets and timpani. *VARIATION 2* – (Allegro, 3/4) – a rhythmic variation of the theme's fast section in both legato and staccato style. *VARIATION 3* – (Presto, 4/4) – fleet, light, staccato, delicate; later more brilliant and aggressive, closing softly and legato. *VARIATION 4* – (Andantino, 4/4) – a lyric melody in oboe (later trumpet, piccolo) punctuated by a graceful rhythmic motive. *VARIATION 5* – (Sostenuto, 3/4; Andante, 6/8) – serene and legato. *VARIATION 7* – (Allegro molto, 6/8) begins in fluent legato, changing to marcato and staccato, concluding with an emphatic, brilliant statement. *VARIATION 8* – (2/4) rhythmic and light textured. *VARIATION 9* – well-marked, accented, vibrant. *VARIATION 10* – complex texture in a robust, energetic setting, followed by a vigorous, dynamic coda. Demands solo talent in all sections, choir and ensemble precision, balance, delicacy and refinement, and awareness of musical construction and direction. Only for advanced groups, but all band musicians should become acquainted with this work.

PERSICHETTI, Vincent **SYMPHONY FOR BAND** Elkan-Vogel
16:00

A major standard work in 4 movements. (1) *ADAGIO* (4/4) – a slow introduction which contains the main compositional material of the movement, with sustained, expressive melodic lines and rhythmically intricate percussion (difficult to put together with precision) – leading to the lively *ALLEGRO* (2/4) which states the Adagio motives in rapid tempo with a wide variety of rhythmic presentations, textures and scorings. (2) *ADAGIO SOSTENUTO* (3/2), a lyric, rich-textured chorale setting, requiring sustained, controlled playing with a strong feeling of line and phrase – featuring solo and choir settings. (3) *ALLEGRETTO* (6/8), presents a lilting 6/8 melody in woodwinds, followed by a contrasting, more rhythmically incisive 2/4 motive, later combining and alternating the two ideas. (4) *VIVACE (2/2)* – fast, fleet, light, brilliant – mostly rhythmic in character, with syncopations and irregular accentuations, using the main themes from the 1st movement at its climax. Requires solid, highly musical soloists, small choirs and full ensemble playing in about equal measure, and percussion that is technically facile and musically sensitive and intelligent. This is a work of considerable subtlety that takes time to get comfortable with, but familiarity will reap rich rewards for players and conductor alike. Highly recommended.

PUCCINI, Giacomo   **TURANDOT**   Bravo Music
Arr. Yo Goto   10:30

A highly effective arrangement of six selections from the opera. The introduction, *Popolo di Pechino*, opens with the familiar thunderous unison statement (half note = 40), Andante sostenuto. This eventually leads to a rhythmically brilliant Allegro section 2/4 (quarter note = 132). A beautiful *Sostenuto* section (largo; quarter note = 58) follows centering on f# minor and cleverly moves to g minor ending the segment on the dominant. *Gira la cote*, the next section, opens mysteriously (Allegro; quarter = 132) with triple figures in percussion, muted brass and woodwinds. This segues into duple figures back in F#. The melody is transferred several times utilizing various colors and tempos until the momentum ends on a satisfying F# minor triad. The beautiful *Nessum Dorma* (quarter note = 54, in G) is ushered in with echoes from the English horn and Oboe. This portion is effective and leads to short but effective renditions of *O', Principi, che a lunge carovane and Diecimila anni nostra Imperatore*! The finale, *Padre augusto*, in D major (quarter = 52), is established by the French Horns and moves quickly to the restatement of the Nessum Dorma theme, now appropriately scored with full instrumentation. Highly recommended for mature ensembles with capable solos, strong brass (including 4 French horns) with endurance and technically secure woodwinds. The harp part is important but doubled in many places with suitable mallet percussion.

REED, Alfred   **ARMENIAN DANCES, PART 1**

                                                                             10:30

An elaborate, large-scale presentation of several contrasting dances. It opens with a broad, sweeping statement leading to a lyrical section with the melodic material in the woodwinds. A new melody in faster tempo follows, succeeded by a rhythmically intricate dance (using 5/8 in both 3+2 and 2+3) which is developed at some length. Next is an expressive section with poignant melodic material. The final dance is fast and brilliant, building to an exciting climax.

REED, H. Owen   **LA FIESTA MEXICANA**   Belwin
                                                                             21:40

A three-movement symphony depicting a religious festival in all its aspects. (1) *PRELUDE AND AZTEC DANCE* – opening with pealing bells and fanfare figures (the opening one for horns is challenging) (Allegro Maestoso, 2/2), developed at some length, leading to a street march episode, featuring an off-stage brass group, followed by a tutti statement leading to the dance (Vivace, 3/4) with driving rhythm in percussion and a well-marked tune with syncopated accompaniment figures, concluding with a brilliant coda. (2) *MASS* – featuring a three-note motive harmonized a number of different ways, and a chant-like phrase in several versions, closing with a statement in off-stage horn. (3) *CARNIVAL* (Allegro con brio, 2/4) – brilliant, colorful, virtuosic, with syncopated rhythmic figures and folk-like tunes leading to an Allegro con spirito (3/4) using a mariachi song and intricate cross-rhythms, gradually adding textural lines and rhythmic figures; succeeded by a return of the Carnival opening, developing the syncopated rhythms to a brilliant and exciting climax. Demands technical facility, rhythmic understanding, precision, ensemble concepts (tonal blend, rhythmic feel, balance, etc.), clarity, and accuracy of articulation. Requires excellent brass (especially horns), good low woodwinds, solid percussion.

RESPIGHI, Ottorino   **HUNTINGTOWER (Ballad for Band)**   Maecenas
                                                                             7:00

This piece, the only original band work by the well-known orchestral tone poet, was commissioned by the American Bandmasters' Association. It is an unjustly neglected piece which has considerable dramatic power and intensity. The opening section, in E^b minor, dark and brooding in character, features low woodwinds and brass, while the second section, a 6/8 Allegro, introduces a galloping rhythm against which fragments of the slow section appear. This leads to a sudden change to parallel major which presents a Scottish reel-melody in trumpets. The tempo and volume gradually subside into an Andante espressivo, featuring a new melody in clarinets which is rhythmically related to the 6/8 tunes, developed and expanded, gathering intensity and building to a sudden return of the opening E^b minor and its brooding music, now anguished and tragic, culminating in a powerful, emphatic conclusion. Only moderately difficult technically, this work requires considerable musical maturity. The opening pages, with the awkward combination of dotted-rhythm and rests, are difficult to bring off without the requisite feeling of "stretch" in the bass lines. The Allegro requires strong rhythmic energy as well as feeling of line and phrase; the Andante demands beauty of tone, long-line legato style; the closing pages require both intensity and control. Well worth the considerable effort needed for successful performance. Highly recommended.

RESPIGHI, Ottorino   **THE PINES OF ROME**   Belwin
Arr. Guy Duker   20:00
A brilliant orchestral standard in a remarkable transcription. Requires technical virtuosity in the opening movement; great control, sensitivity, nuance, color and balance in 2ⁿᵈ movement; well-focused pitch in accompanying brass chords along with an artistic clarinet soloist and mature pianist in 3ʳᵈ movement; and brilliant, yet rich-toned brass, sensitive and musical English horn, rhythmically solid ensemble, and control of upper ranges and volume at the climax in the fourth movement.

REVUELTAS, Silvestre   **SENSEMAYA**   G. Schirmer
Arr. Frank Bencriscutto   6:00
A powerful, explosive, primitive-sounding work by one of Mexico's greatest composers. It is also quite difficult, beginning with the constant use of compound meter (mostly 7/8 with measures in 9/8 and 5/16) and continuing with technically challenging passages (especially in brass) and rhythmically intricate writing throughout. Also requires an extended percussion section (with Latin instruments). Trumpet parts are in C. E^b clarinet, bass clarinet, English horn, and string bass have important parts. Only for advanced ensembles, but highly recommended.

REYNOLDS, Verne   **SCENES**   G. Schirmer
                                                                        17:00
An extremely difficult, complex, highly dissonant and rhythmically involved work, written for large wind ensemble (minus saxophones and bass clarinet). It opens with a dramatic and intense Maestoso (quarter= 56) with many subdivision intricacies and a combination of contrapuntal and parallel motion textures. This is succeeded by a fast, lithe Allegro with brilliant tempos against a 12-note ostinato appearing in a different instrumental group five times. This is followed by a slow chorale-like section in soft cluster-chords leading to a cadenza-like solo English horn passage. The work concludes with a breathtaking virtuoso Presto demanding enormous technical facility, especially for brass.

REZNICEK, Emil von   **DONNA DIANA OVERTURE**   Shawnee
Arr. Carl Meyers   4:45
A sparkling, vivacious work with a winning combination of rhythmic zest, vitality and melodic appeal. Requires advanced technique, great rhythmic precision and fluency, lightness of articulation and wide range of dynamic control. The transcription is faithful to the original. In places it is a bit heavy and thick, but challenges players to work on lightness and brilliance – including the low brass and low woodwinds. Good solo oboe with nice legato tone is needed.

RODRIGO, Joaquin   **ADAGIO FOR WIND ORCHESTRA**   10:30
A beautiful, highly evocative and atmospheric work for the orchestral winds, brass, and percussion. The opening section features a recitative-like melodic line presented by a number of solo instruments (flute, clarinet, oboe) followed by rapid scale flourishes (flute and clarinet) with accompanying 16ᵗʰ-note lines and sustained chords. This is succeeded by a very rhythmic and energetic Allegro Moderato featuring a fanfare-like melody – first in trombone, then trumpets. A contrasting slightly slower section features a dotted-rhythm melody in trumpets and trombones. The adagio then returns followed by the allegro. The work concludes with a varied version of the opening.

ROGERS, Bernard   **THREE JAPANESE DANCES**   Alfred
Ed. By Tim Topolewski   10:40
A highly original, fresh-sounding, colorful work. It opens with a *DANCE WITH PENNONS* (Giocoso, quarter=160), full of delicate traceries of rapid overlapping lines and short motives, eventually working into longer melodic ideas which are definitely oriental in flavor. Highly intricate and texturally complex, requiring considerable effort to work out balances, clarity and precision. This is followed by a *MOURNING DANCE* (Tranquillo), consisting of a slow, unmetered melody in flute, accompanied by sustained notes in harp, celeste, string bass, and percussion. In the middle, an unaccompanied mezzo soprano voice sings a simple chant-like melody

113

(cued in English horn). The finale, *DANCE WITH SWORDS* (Vigoroso e ruvido, half =152) is forceful and well-marked, emphasizing rhythms and short elemental melodic motives, concluding with a burst of color and energy. Technically rather intricate (especially in opening movement) and musically requires mature players with rhythmic precision and control, capacity to play delicately and sensitively, and with clarity and precision of tonguing in finale. Requires five percussion players, each covering a separate battery of instruments. The new edition comes with a full score.

SAINT-SAENS, Camille   **MARCHE HEROIQUE**   Boosey & Hawkes
Arr. Frank Winterbottom   7:00

A wonderful though largely unknown work, originally for orchestra, (Allegro, E^b, 2/2) with a wealth of good melodies, energetic rhythms, effective contrasting material (including a lovely Trio – Andantino, A^b, 3/4) and a brilliant and exciting coda. Technically difficult, especially for bass instruments (rapid tongued 8th-notes) and requires solid brass with good control of dynamics and articulation. Long out of print and should be made available again.

SAINT-SAENS, Camille   **MARCHE MILITAIRE FRANCAISE**   Hindsley
Arr. Mark Hindsley   4:00

A brilliant and exuberant work with lots of rhythmic drive and energy, even in the softer, more delicately scored passages. The transcription is excellent and far more faithful to the original than the Lake version (pub. Carl Fischer). Requires technically facile upper woodwinds and trumpets, and solid, rhythmically secure players throughout the ensemble with fluency of fingers and articulation, refined tone quality with careful attention to blend and balance. It is most important to establish and maintain the correct tempo (indicated in the original as half=132; for some reason Hindsley does not provide this marking). This march is generally played too slowly, and demands the brilliance that the faster tempo can help to provide.

SCHOENBERG, Arnold   **THEME AND VARIATIONS, OP. 43a**   G. Schirmer
14:00

A major work by one of the most important 20th-century composers, consisting of a lengthy theme, seven variations and an elaborate finale. *THEME* (Poco Allegro, 4/4, quarter=84) – in four phrases. The first is flowing in character, yet with rhythmic energy; the second is rhythmically more elaborate but with a harmonic sequence and cadence; the third introduces a new rhythmic element (triplet 16^{ths}); the closing uses rhythmic and motivic elements of the first three. *VARIATION 1* – uses flowing 8th-note triplet against dotted-8th-16th rhythms and legato vs. staccato, all closely paralleling the phrase structure and harmonic shape of the theme. *VARIATION 2* (Allegro molto, quarter=132) – scherzo-like in character and very rhythmic, using the same elements (triplet-8ths; dotted-8th-16^{ths}) – demanding great precision. *VARIATION 3* (Poco Adagio, quarter=60) – slow and lyric in character, contrapuntal in texture, with theme in various instruments (oboe, cornet, clarinets, baritone). *VARIATION 4* (Waltz tempo, dotted-half =60) – a flowing line (theme in solo flute, then various instruments), accompanied by rhythmic details from the theme and its accompanying voices (dotted and triplet rhythms). *VARIATION 5* (Molto Moderato, quarter = 82, 4/4) – rhapsodic in character, with melody in solo clarinet, its canonic inversion in solo baritone, and intricate textural and rhythmic detail which relates to various aspects of the theme. *VARIATION 6* (Allegro, 2/2, half=84) – march-like and militant in style, with the melody (derived from a counterpoint to the theme) in horns and baritone, and use of dotted-8th-16th as a tag. *VARIATION 7* (Moderato, 4/4, quarter=84) – like a song or aria, with a simple legato quarter-note line embroidered by flowing legato 16ths; later the melody is in 8ths with marcato 16ths. *FINALE* (Moderato, 4/4) – using elements of previous variations and elaborated re-statements of the theme, with a short but effective coda. This is a technically demanding work, but the major challenges are musical, requiring careful working out of the many rhythmic, contrapuntal and textural intricacies, along with command of the wide range of styles, moods and characters, even within variations.

SCHULLER, Gunther   **MEDITATION**   Associated
6:00

A reflective, subdued work, often mysterious in mood, written in 12-tone idiom, with considerable rhythmic independence of parts and dense but rich textures. Technically not difficult, but requires good understanding of contemporary idioms (especially aural awareness), good rhythmic control (especially small subdivisions, which is necessary to produce musical continuity), blend of sound, sensitivity to good dynamics and balance, and tonal refinement. Highly recommended.

SCHUMANN, William CIRCUS OVERTURE G. Schirmer
Arr. Don Owen 6:30

A colorful, brilliant, and exciting work, depicting the various acts of a circus, beginning with the ringmaster's "Ladies and Gentlemen" fanfare, progressing through oriental dancers (featuring percussion), the snake charmer (oboe and English horn), animal trainers (brass growls and yelps), acrobats (beginning with unaccompanied baritone followed by a difficult clarinet passage with waltz-rhythm accompaniment), fashion models (graceful woodwind lines), leading to the return of the ringmaster and abbreviated restatements of earlier ideas, concluding with a driving, powerful coda in very fast tempo. Requires advanced technical facility in all sections, including low woodwinds and percussion.

SCHUMAN, William **GEORGE WASHINGTON BRIDGE** G. Schirmer
7:00

A great band classic, full of vitality, energy and melodic ideas. It opens (Maestoso moderato, 4/4) with a massive statement of the first main motive in brass choir, followed by full band. This motive gives rise to a long-lined melodic idea which is given a short expansion. The second section follows (Allegretto, 2/4, quarter= 120), a bouncy, rhythmically intricate idea in the woodwinds which is then given to the brass. This section is brought to an explosive climax, succeeded by a beautiful lyric section (Piu Mosso, 4/4), with a long legato phrase in low brass punctuated by chords in upper instruments. This idea is developed, then subsides into a soft, mysterious brass interlude which leads to the recapitulation of the Allegretto. Its climax leads to the return of the opening section varied, which leads to a powerful coda based on the opening material. Demands strong, solid brass with beauty of tone, range and endurance; brass and woodwinds with clean articulation and rhythmic security, accurate percussion and excellent tubas with upper range and interval accuracy. Most importantly, emphasis should be placed on building an ensemble sonority with brass blending into woodwinds.

SCHWANTNER, Joseph ***AND THE MOUNTAINS RISING NOWHERE*** European-American
11:00

Composed for the Eastman Wind Ensemble, this is a difficult and challenging work, both technically musically, requiring great rhythmic sophistication (with multiple subdivisions, irregular groupings, unusual meters, etc.) intricate rapid passagework for all instruments, unusual performing devices (singing and whistling by players, rubbing glass crystals, bowing vibraphone, etc.) and advanced notational and musical techniques. Scoring calls for four flutes (doubling piccolo), two clarinets, four oboes (two doubled English horns), four bassoons, four trumpets, four horns, four trombones, tuba, piano (amplified - very difficult), five percussion (all doubling various instruments – mallet writing very difficult) and timpani; so that, strictly speaking, this is not a "band" work. It is, however, a true masterpiece of contemporary music, and all serious students of wind literature should be familiar with it.

SHOSTAKOVICH, Dmitri **FESTIVE OVERTURE** MCA
Arr. Donald Hunsberger 6:00

A wonderfully vital, exuberant, exciting work, expertly transcribed. It opens with a vibrant fanfare in moderate tempo, requiring solid and affirmative trumpets and resonant low brass. This leads to a fast, brilliant, animated Presto (A^b, 2/2, half=152), requiring great facility and fluency from woodwinds (especially clarinets) and baritone (difficult); and clean tonguing and precision from brass (soft, delicate double-tonguing in trumpets). Demands solid rhythmic control (especially for many passages of off-beat playing), maintenance of tempo and precision (legato runs and flowing melodies tend to rush, accompaniment figures after rests tend to drag); and beauty and richness of tone, especially climactic moments.

SHOSTAKOVICH, Dmitri **FINALE, SYMPHONY NO. 5** Boosey & Hawkes
Arr. Charles Righter 8:30

A contemporary orchestra classic, generally well-transcribed (except for tongued passages in woodwinds which require more intensity than the instruments can provide, and the trumpet parts in the climactic section, which have not been provided with original high notes or correct voicing – cf. orchestral score). Demands great fluency and facility from woodwinds, power, endurance and tonal richness from brass, technically secure and rhythmically precise percussion. A musically rewarding work which, despite above reservations, provides considerable value for study and performance.

SIBELIUS, Jean SYMPHONY NO. 2, FINALE Aeolus Music
Transc. Joseph Kreines 14:00

This is an extraordinary transcription of a monumental work that is eminently faithful to the original. The heroic and noble opening (3/2, Allegro Moderato, Eb major) presents the three-note motif surrounded by tutti sonorities. The theme is echoed several times in a rondo-like form throughout this movement. The use of consistent syncopation in low winds decorates the motif in its initial form. The variations of rhythm, style and tonal centers provide the catalysis for the reoccurring motif. Huge sweeps of bold brass sonorities with overlapping dynamics are also part of the colors included in the original orchestral version. A logical shift to Eb minor may pose some challenges in terms of key signatures and focus of pitches for woodwinds during a lengthy development section. However, the coda returns to the home key and builds quickly to a very triumphal ending. This provides a unique opportunity for winds to experience the entire finale in this setting. Endurance in brass, range in both brass and woodwinds and tonal/pitch centers (especially in exposed sections) will be the largest challenges. However, it will be an extraordinary musical journey for those ensembles and conductors who can meet the musical and technical demands of this work. Reviewed by RH.

SNOECK, Kenneth SCARAMOUCH (Symphony No. 3 for Winds and Percussion) Shawnee
12:30

A complex, intricate and colorful work in four contrasting movements, requiring a large percussion complement (6 players, many instruments) and considerable technical and musical sophistication from all players. The first movement, in two large sections, features a wide-ranging lyric phrase, stated first in horn, then trumpet, with contrasting accompaniment textures. The second section is a kind of scherzo demanding lightness of articulation and fluency of 16th-note playing. The second movement (entitled *METAL*) is scored entirely for flutes (five parts including alto) and metallic percussion; while the third (*WOOD AND MEMBRANOPHONES*) is for percussion alone, highly intricate rhythmically. The finale returns to full ensemble, similar in style to the scherzo of the first movement, with three contrasting themes which are combined at the end.

SPARKE, Philip CELEBRATION Studio Music Co.
11:00

A very noble and challenging work for advanced ensembles. Beginning with a fanfare in low brass and French horns (4/4, quarter note = 54 in G) the texture condenses quickly with punctuated trumpets and woodwind interjections (very advanced using uneven thirty-second note scales in canonic form). The heroic theme leads to a very virtuosic off stage trumpet solo. Solo bassoon and bass clarinet introduce the new section (Presto, 6/8., dotted half note=88-92). Pyramiding brass lead to flurries of woodwind activity that is accompanied by layering brass fragments. This is developed with contrasting articulations, rhythms and accidentals. A middle section using two meters simultaneously with brass and woodwinds alternating sections. This is developed and varied by rhythm, texture and tonal centers. The material accelerates (super metric conducting recommended) with underlying percussion accompanying the wind alternations into a *Piu mosso* section (2/4, half note = 108, in C). A bold and interrupting horn entrance ensues (moving still faster) which transitions into a final *Prestissimo* consisting of both themes at the same time (2/4, half note = 120, in G). This coda becomes syncopated using unison rhythms into a rather abrupt, yet exciting, ending. Requires very skilled players on all instruments (including separate off stage trumpets) woodwinds with virtuoso capabilities and mature brass with power and endurance. The percussion parts are also challenging requiring 5 players on numerous instruments.

STAMP, Jack DIVERTIMENTO IN F Kjos
15:00

A very imaginative work in five movements that are patterned after noted composers and personal clergy friends of the composer. The first movement, "Fanfare", is dedicated to Fisher Tull and begins with rhythmic brass and percussion colors (multi meters, quarter note =152) using imaginative harmonies, counterpoint and hints of minimalist techniques. A gentle middle section, primarily colored with woodwind choirs, provides a nice contrast to the returning opening style. "Fate" is dedicated to William Schuman and uses polychords as its harmonic structure. Opening with brass choir (multi meters, quarter note= 82, "Somberly, reflectively") and relenting to clarinet choir the movement uses very clever exchanges of colors to convey a Schuman character reminiscent of "When Jesus Wept." "Fury", dedicated to Joan Tower, begins with short-pyramiding brass cross rhythms followed by decorated woodwind runs (2/4 simultaneously with 6/8, pulse =88). A syncopated ostinato-like pattern follows in woodwinds with continued melodic material in the brass. Using quasi-metric modulation, a waltz appears in uneven multi meters. This eventually subsides into a very thin and quiet ending. "Faith", which is dedicated to four clergy friends begins with clarinet choir (4/4, quarter note = 78, Eb major) and relinquishes the hymn to the solo English Horn (cued) and bassoons. Five very well developed variations ensue based on the Scottish hymn tune, "Dundee." The final movement, "Frolic" is lighter in nature (multi meters, quarter note = 152) and dedicated to David Diamond. A woodwind fanfare, using similar rhythms and style from the first movement, provides both energy and color in the opening measures. Brass interjections follow with consistent returns of the opening woodwind color and rhythm. A short canon develops the idea with augmented brass and ostinato-like percussion and woodwind figures. This becomes more syncopated using cross rhythms and multi-meters and leads to a very dramatic and satisfying ending. The percussion writing is extensive and vital to the effectiveness of the work. However, the individual assignments are efficient and require only 5-6 players on multiple shared instruments.

STANHOPE, DAVID   **FOLKSONGS FOR BAND – SUITE NO. 1**   HL Music
16:15

A fascinating, complex and challenging suite of four folk tunes, dedicated to the memory of Percy Grainger and reminiscent of his approach to setting tunes, though the styles and treatment are different. Technically and rhythmically very advanced but well worth exploring. (1) *GOOD MORNING, GOOD MORNING* – a lively, rhythmic setting featuring contrasting choirs and solos. (2) *LOVELY JOAN* – very slow, nostalgic and poignant, with richly contrapuntal texture. (3) *THE BLACKSMITH* – energetic and forceful, with ingenious use of changing meters and accents. (4) *IRISH TUNE* – a beautiful (if somewhat disturbing) setting, with intricate contrapuntal writing, building to a powerful, dissonant climax.

SULLIVAN, Sir Arthur   **IOLANTHE OVERTURE**   C. Fischer
Arr. Erik Leidzen   7:30

A real gem of the operatic repertory that requires the utmost in finesse, beauty of tone, sensitivity to nuance and phrase, and, above all, fluency and control of tonguing and lightness of attack, especially in woodwinds. The opening section is slow, sustained and poetic in character, while the Allegro is light, fleet, delicate – yet also brilliant in the climactic pages. This has been out of print for some time, but is worth searching for and performing by mature, technically facile groups.

SULLIVAN, Sir Arthur   **PINEAPPLE POLL**   Chappell
Arr. Charles Mackerras, Trans. W.J. Duthoit   10:00

A sparkling, charming, and delightful work, cleverly assembled and arranged from many short excerpts of different works (some as short as 2 to 4 measures). In four contrasting movements: (1) *Opening movement* – fast, lithe, and agile. (Allegro vivace, 2/4) requiring great fluency and facility from woodwinds (clarinets especially) and crisp, clean brass. (2) *Jasper's Dance* (Andante espressivo, E^b, 3/4) – a beautiful lyric poem with important solo melodic lines (flute, oboe, E^b clarinet, horn). (3) *Poll's Dance* (Presto vivacissimo, C major, 6/8, dotted-half=80) - fast and brilliant, requiring great facility, especially in woodwinds and bass instruments. (4) *Finale* (Allegro brilliante, E^b, 4/4) in many different styles, ranging from jaunty to crisp to brilliant to heroic – and employing a similar variety of technical writing, especially light-tongued staccato. Builds to a breathtaking, sweeping coda in very fast tempo, providing an exciting and exhilarating conclusion.

TICHELI, Frank   **BLUE SHADES**   Manhattan Beach
10:30

A fresh and innovative work using elements from blues and jazz. Highly rhythmic, this aural portrait communicates energy and liberty while remaining in a traditional and explicit wind band setting. The use of flatted thirds, fifths and sevenths are evident throughout the work beginning with the opening minor third eighth-note motif (With energy, quarter note = 160-168, in 4/4.) Various use of muted brass and percussion mark the accented lines of the woodwind families. These themes become varied in texture, articulation (including flutter tonguing in the flutes) rhythm and meter. Syncopation, both agogic and otherwise, is an important part of the rhythmic content. The energy eventually slows into a "Dark" section, quarter note =60, as introduced by the solo bass clarinet. An extended accelerando ensues revealing a very virtuosic showcase for solo clarinet (quarter note =160-168). As the clarinet solo fades the texture becomes thicker and a triple meter is established. This builds into a tremendous shout-like section ("Wail, Intense") that brings the work to a thrilling and surprise ending. Must have a virtuosic principal clarinet, very strong winds that can negotiate cross rhythms and extreme ranges and dynamics as well as a mature percussion section.

TICHELI, FRANK POSTCARD Manhattan Beach
5:20

A very energetic, rhythmically intricate, fast-paced work, with good variety of texture and color (numerous solo and chamber-like passages contrasted with robust full scoring). Numerous and varied meter changes (5/8, 7/8, 8/8) in addition to syncopated and irregular rhythmic figures, together with a fast tempo marking (= 160-168) and technically tricky passagework, make this a challenge for any band. Very effective and enjoyable in performance.

TULL, Fisher **SKETCHES ON A TUDOR PSALM** Boosey & Hawkes
10:30

A fine original work using a well-known theme by Thomas Tallis as its basis and treating it to a number of contrasting variations. It opens with a short introduction (Andante) using fragments of the theme and harmonic framework containing elements of both major and minor (as does the theme), which makes its appearance in solo alto sax (1st phrase) accompanied by flowing duplet and triplet 8ths. The second half of the phrase is given to horns, then oboes. A short interlude for dissonant muted brass followed by woodwinds leads to the theme in full brass choir with answering phrase in woodwinds. The last phrase appears in tutti - then a short codetta leads to a scherzando variation in woodwinds using dotted-rhythm triplets and 8th-duplets. A subdued extended version of the closing phrase leads to an Allegro which is largely rhythmic in nature, using changing meters (including 5/8, 7/8, 9/8) and asymmetrical phrase-shapes. The clarinets state a version of the closing phrase while trumpets provide a rhythmic ostinato of tongued 16ths. This is developed and expanded at length, including short interludes for percussion alone (7 players required), rhythmic fragments of the theme and expanded and contracted statement of parts of each phrase. This leads to a kind of recapitulation of the theme, stated in low woodwinds and answered by variants, first in brass, then woodwinds; building to a climactic statement of the closing phrase in full band. A coda featuring a return of the scherzando variation provides an energetic, vital conclusion. Technically not too difficult, but requires well-developed rhythmic sense, brass tonguing facility, and solo and choir talent, including oboe and bassoon.

TURINA, Joacquin **LA PROCESSION DU ROCIO** Belwin
Arr. Alfred Reed 7:30

A fine Spanish orchestral classic in two contrasting sections excellently transcribed. The first, *TRIANA EN FETE,* opens with a buoyant, vital Allegro vivo (G major, 3/4 – 6/8) with vigorous energetic rhythms and appealing melodies, including a well-marked one in 3/4 and 6/8; a more lyric one in solo oboe; another more melancholy and subdued in solo muted cornet. The opening 3/4 – 6/8 returns in abbreviated form followed by another variation in 3/4, more legato in style. This leads to a piquant Allegretto 2/4 using staccato-16ths. The Allegro vivo returns with the muted cornet theme extended in treatment, leading to a final statement of the opening material. This flows without pause into the second section, *LA PROCESSION* (Allegretto mosso, 2/4), featuring an expressive, highly ornamented and rhythmically intricate flute melody with drum accompaniment. This is followed by a rather solemn but rich-textured chorale idea, first in trombones, then woodwinds. These two ideas are alternately re-stated and worked over, along with a return of the muted trumpet theme, this time in solo oboe followed by clarinet. After a climactic statement of the chorale, the opening Allegro vivo returns in a final emphatic statement. The procession gradually fades into a subdued tranquil coda, punctuated by a last crescendo to a forceful chord. Requires good solo and section talent, rhythmic precision and clarity of texture, careful balance of accompaniment to lead voices, and overall mature musicianship with a conductor who can negotiate the subtle nuances of tempo, phrase and dynamic shadings. Highly recommended.

VAUGHAN WILLIAMS, Ralph **TOCCATA MARZIALE** Boosey & Hawkes
4:30

A great band classic, highly contrapuntal in texture, with both long, flowing lines and short melodic motives; smooth legato and crisp staccato; soft, delicate passages and massive, powerful statements. It requires great rhythmic precision (for clarity of counterpoint and 16th-note passages in parallel motion), careful working out of balances (highlighting main melodic lines, placing subordinate lines and accompanying figures in proper perspective), definition of varied articulation (for unity of ensemble) and flow of phrase and line for musical continuity. Technically fairly difficult (in both legato and staccato 16th-note passages; and flexibility of range and articulation in tubas), but musically very demanding for both players and conductor; however, well worth the effort required. Highly recommended.

WAGNER, Richard
Arr. William Schaefer

HULDIGUNGSMARSCH

Shawnee
5:00

A wind-band original, splendidly re-scored for contemporary instrumentation. It opens (Moderate march tempo, E♭, 2/2) with a rich textured legato phrase, rather contrapuntal in texture, followed by a soft statement of the main theme's opening motive. This leads to a brass fanfare motive building to an exuberant rhythmic transition featuring dotted 8th-16th rhythms (difficult to keep precise and clean), followed by the first statement of the complete theme in upper woodwinds and 1st cornet accompanied by dotted rhythms. This is repeated, then expanded, with low brass and woodwinds on the theme and counter-melodic material in upper voices. An extension leads to a kind of development in which the first phrase of the theme is juxtaposed with the fanfare figure in sequences. The fanfare is now expanded over a dominant pedal, followed by the dotted rhythm leading to the recapitulation in full band, with the second phrase scored more lightly in soft dynamics. Another sequential buildup leads to an expanded restatement of the main theme with accompanying tongued 8th-note scales in bass instruments, repeated and brought to a resonant, noble climax, with the return of the introduction in full band. A dynamic coda using the first phrase of the theme brings the work to a powerful conclusion with a brilliant trumpet-trombone flourish punctuated by full band chords at the very end. This work is somewhat repetitious and four-square in phrase shape, but represents Wagner's mature harmonic style and rich texture in a noble and eloquent framework. Technically demanding (in terms of staccato articulation, especially), also requires mature musicianship (beauty of tone, rhythmic precision, balance, feeling of long line and phrase, sensitivity to nuance, attention to details of dynamics and textural clarity).

WILLIAMS, Clifton

FANFARE AND ALLEGRO

Summy-Birchard
5:45

A highly dramatic, fresh-sounding work, opening with a brilliant declarative trumpet and percussion statement, which is developed and elaborated, leading to a more flowing and lyrical idea in woodwinds. The Allegro section follows, using a variation of the lyric idea as the basis for a fugato which builds to an exciting climax, leading to a coda based on part of the lyric theme, increasing in speed and energy and hurtling to a brilliant conclusion. Requires excellent trumpets with good command of upper register and flexibility (for accuracy on partials), woodwinds with good tone and blend that can also articulate cleanly and rapidly (in piu mosso section requiring staccato dotted-rhythm tonguing), intelligent and musical percussion, strong baritone with good upper register and flexibility, solid, resonant low brass, and a conductor with good command of tempo and style changes.

WOOD, Haydn

THE SEAFARER

Boosey & Hawkes
9:00

A wonderful, relatively unknown work using several sea-chanteys in contrasting styles and tempos (including *"The Drunken Sailor"*, *"Shenandoah"*, *"Away to Rio"*, etc.) Requires a fully mature group, with excellent woodwinds capable of clean, rapid staccato tonguing and solo melodic style; rich, resonant brass with the same degree of flexibility and control; strong sense of rhythm and precision as well as feeling for line and phrase in lyric sections. Highly recommended.

WOOLFENDEN, Guy

GALLIMAUFRY

Ariel
15:00

An interesting and unusual work in six sections played without pause, based on Shakespeare. (1) *CHURCH AND STATE* (Moderato, E♭, 4/4) – stately and dignified, beginning quietly and building to a noble tutti statement. (2) *INN AND OUT* (Allegro, E♭, 6/8-3/4) – a lively, boisterous and bouncy movement with alternating 6/8 and 3/4 measures. (3) *STARTS AND FITS* – rhythmically energetic 4/4 with elements of the 6/8-3/4 section as contrast, followed by (4) *FATHER AND SON* (G major, 4/4) – a beautifully lyric and flowing movement featuring solo English horn. (5) *ADVANCE AND RETREAT* (Allegro, G major, 4/4) – a march with a lively and energetic tune. (6) *CHURCH AND STATUS QUO* (4/4, E♭), a varied return of the opening dignified music building to a sonorous climax. Though technically not very difficult, there are considerable musical demands made on both solo players (especially oboes and horns) and the ensemble, and the dimensions of the work require a mature, sensitive and intelligent group.

WOOLFENDEN, Guy   **MOCKBEGGAR VARIATIONS**   Ariel

7:00

A challenging and clever work consisting of a short theme and five variations. The Prelude (3/4, Allegro moderato, quarter=120) opens with percussion and solo tuba followed by various instruments in a variety of textures and ornaments. The theme is presented in an eight-measure phrase in C major by fragments of numerous solo woodwind and brass colors. Variation I consists of a syncopated ostinato background for the theme, which is performed by several brass and woodwind sets including mixed meters. Variation II is introduced by the low brass, accompanied by flurries of trills in the woodwinds. The theme is fragmented into rhythmic phrases using chromatic and articulative modifications. Variation III (Andantino con rubato, quarter=60) in 4/4 begins in F major with French horn solo accompanied by woodwinds. Sixteenth-note segments are exchanged through a series of tempo and color contrasts. Variation IV (A^b major, 4/4, quarter=126) is a very imaginative rhythmic alteration using various articulations and percussion colors. Variation V is slow (Lento, quarter=54) and opens with solo woodwind and French horns in 2/4. The eighth-note rhythms become agitated and accelerate into a very short coda in 3/2. The brass and percussion using augmentation state the theme. The work concludes with short fragments of the themes exchanged by soft upper woodwind solos contrasted by a humorous unison tutti C (fff) by the low winds. Must have technically proficient woodwinds, controlled brass in all registers and a musically knowledgeable percussion section of five to seven players. An excellent work for mature ensembles.

• •

ADLER, Samuel · SOUTHWESTERN SKETCHES · Oxford
15:00

An exuberant, energetic work evocative of the American Southwest, with wide-spaced melodic lines, driving rhythms and bi-tonal harmonies. Requires a mature group with good rhythmic sense, technical facility, range flexibility and precision.

ARNOLD, Malcolm · FOUR CORNISH DANCES · G. Schirmer
Arr. Thad Marciniak · 10:00

A fine alternative to Arnold's other dance-sets, with its own unique flavor, coloring and musical ingenuities. Has many technical challenges, particularly the tuba part (many leaps and rapid passages).

BACH, J.S. · INVENTION NO. 8 IN F · Manhattan Beach
Arr. Bob Margolis · 0:50

A brilliant virtuoso arrangement of a keyboard standard. Requires great facility at the recommended tempo from all players. Excellent for developing fluency, evenness, precision of ensemble.

BRUCKNER, Anton · HUNT SCHERZO (Symphony No. 4 - 3rd Movement) · C.F. Peters
Arr. Lee Dytrt · 10:00

A very effective and faithful arrangement of a superb orchestral standard. Technically rather demanding, especially for horns, which play the main material throughout a sizeable portion.

BEETHOVEN, Ludwig van · EGMONT OVERTURE · Hindsley
Arr. Mark Hindsley · 8:00

Though most of Beethoven's output has not been transcribed effectively, this arrangement is generally more successful at conveying the musical and emotional impact of the original.

BENNETT, Robert Russell · SYMPHONIC SONGS · Chappell
12:30

An interesting and unusual work, with a wide variety of styles, moods and musical content. The first movement (*SERENADE*) is particularly noteworthy for its intricate cross-rhythms and textural complexity. The second movement (*SPIRITUAL*) has a lovely melody with rich harmonic accompaniment. The third (*CELEBRATION*) is light and humorous in character, but with intricacy of texture.

BILIK, Jerry · SYMPHONY FOR BAND · Bilik
15:00

A dramatic, intense work in three well-contrasted movements. Requires strong rhythmic control, fluency and facility in all sections, including musically and technically adept percussion.

BORODIN, Alexander · FINALE from SYMPHONY NO. 2 · Shawnee
Arr. William Schaefer · 7:00

A fine orchestral standard, full of drive and energy, sensitively scored. Technically rather demanding, requiring fluent articulation from both woodwinds and brass – and musically demanding, with numerous stylistic contrasts.

CHABRIER, Emanuel · MARCHE JOYEUSE · TRN Publications
Transc. F. Junkin · 4:30

A brilliant, vivacious orchestral standard in an excellent transcription. This is the most effective of current transcriptions. Requires advanced technique, rhythmic precision, and careful working out of innumerable textural and dynamic details.

CHANCE, John Barnes **INCANTATION AND DANCE** Boosey & Hawkes
7:20

A well-written, highly effective piece with strong dynamic contrasts. Requires technical facility throughout ensemble, strong rhythmic sense, precision and maintenance of tempo, and an excellent percussion section.

CHOBANIAN, Loris **ARMENIAN DANCES** Shawnee

An interesting if uneven work which attempts to delineate authentic Armenian rhythmic and metric patterns within a contemporary stylistic framework.

COPLAND, Aaron **THE RED PONY** Boosey & Hawkes
15:00

A fresh-sounding, highly-evocative suite of four contrasting movements in Copland's mature folk-oriented style, scored for band by the composer.

CURNOW, Jim **MUTANZA** Jenson
16:00

A large-scale elaborately conceived work composed of a rich-textured theme and five widely-contrasted variations. Technically rather difficult, with much texturally and rhythmically intricate writing. Require depth of talent in all sections (including 5 percussion, 2 of which require mallet facility).

GOULD, Morton **PRISMS** Chappell
16:30

An unusual, imaginative work in five movements, exploring timbres and textures and using rather advanced harmonic language. Requires strong solo and choir talent, since much of the work is scored transparently (e.g. the opening of the 1st movement, with 4 solo clarinets followed by 3 bass clarinets, 3 cornets and 1 trumpet, contrabass clarinet, alto clarinet, etc., all playing different pitches in staggered entrances). Worth investigating for groups that can cover the required scoring and have the requisite technical resources.

HARTY, Sir Hamilton **A JOHN FIELD SUITE** Boosey & Hawkes
Arr. T. Conway Brown 14:00

A delightful set of three contrasting pieces taken from piano originals, requiring brilliant virtuoso playing, solo talent, rhythmic energy and precision (especially woodwinds).'

HUSA, Karel **AL FRESCO** Associated
12:00

A very dramatic, rhythmically intricate, harmonically dissonant, texturally complex work in two contrasting sections - a slow opening with transparent scoring and a fast, driving Allegro which builds to an intense climax, then gradually slows down, closing in the opening tempo.

HANSON, Howard **LAUDE** C. Fischer

An interesting work in theme and variations format - somewhat lengthy and uneven in quality but with much of musical value.

IVES, Charles **VARIATIONS ON "AMERICA"** Presser
Arr. William Rhoads, from orch. version by William Schuman 7:00

A highly enjoyable, often humorous work, originally for organ. Technically challenging in many places, especially in woodwinds and low brass.

JAGER, Robert **VARIATIONS ON A THEME BY ROBERT SCHUMANN** Volkwien
9:50

An enjoyable and imaginative set of well-contrasted variations, using *The Happy Farmer* as the theme. Requires a number of musically and technically adept soloists (including two tubas!) and good sense of rhythm and precision from ensemble.

KNOX, Thomas   **SEA SONGS**   Ludwig
                                                                     9:00

An evocative work using a number of sea-chanteys as its basis. While in places it seems fragmentary and lacking in continuity and dimension, much of the writing is imaginative and effective.

MARGOLIS, Bob   **FANTASIA NOVA**   Associated
                                                                     14:00

A very interesting and unusual three-movement suite with widely-contrasting styles, moods and characters. Rather light in overall substance but very imaginative in treatment. Worth investigating.

MARGOLIS, Bob   **COLOR | TERPSICHORE**   Manhattan Beach

Two extremely interesting works that should be explored by directors and students. Both selections contain expanded percussion material and offer musically significant challenges for all wind instruments.

NELSON, Ron   **ROCKY POINT HOLIDAY**   Boosey & Hawkes
                                                                     5:30

A brilliant, glittering virtuoso piece in fast tempo throughout, requiring well-developed technical facility, rhythmic precision, maintenance of tempo (sustained melodic line tends to drag).

NELSON, Ron   **SAVANNAH RIVER HOLIDAY**   C. Fischer
                                                                     8:30

A vital, energetic work, beginning and ending in fast tempo with a quiet and reflective slow section in the middle. Technically challenging, especially with regard to rhythmic precision and articulative clarity (for frequent dotted-8th-16th figures in fast tempo).

O'DONNELL, B. Walton   **SONGS OF THE GAEL**   Boosey & Hawkes
                                                                     15:00

A lovely, colorful medley of widely-varied Irish folk-songs and dances. Quite difficult and demanding, especially for woodwinds. Somewhat repetitive in places; some transitions are unconvincing - but its beauties are more compelling. Currently out of print but worth tracking down for advanced groups.

PISTON, Walter   **TUNBRIDGE FAIR**   Boosey & Hawkes
                                                                     5:00

A technically demanding, rhythmically vital piece, requiring upper range playing from clarinets, horns and trumpets, careful working out of interval leaps in trumpets, well-established command of rhythmic subdivisions (especially 16th-8th-16th grouping).

ROSSINI, Giocchino   **SOIREES MUSICALES**   Boosey & Hawkes
Arr. Benjamin Britten, Transc. T. Conway Brown   11:00

A delightful suite of five pieces that are also challenging and technically difficult (especially for woodwinds), with much solo and small-group scoring.

SCHWANTNER, Joseph   **FROM A DARK MILLENIUM**   European-American

A good alternative to *"AND THE MOUNTAINS"* previously listed, in similar style using many of the compositional and coloristic devise. Marginally less difficult (both technically and musically) but still quite challenging for all players.

SMETANA, Bedrich   **THE HIGH CASTLE**   MCA
Arr. Earl Slocum   14:30

A glorious work with epic majesty, lyric tenderness, dramatic sweep and passionate energy. A remarkably good transcription, demanding high-level musicianship and control. Requires harp (the entire opening is for harp unaccompanied).

STARER, Robert **STONE RIDGE SET** MCA

A fresh-sounding, musically intricate and subtle work in four contrasting movements, published separately. Worth looking into – the scherzo (entitled CUMULATIONS) is quite challenging in its use of rapid tempo compound meters.

STRAUSS, Richard **SALOME'S DANCE** Hindsley
Arr. Mark Hindsley 9:00

A sensuous, lush, rich-textured work with a brilliant virtuoso ending, superbly transcribed. Requires solo, small group and tutti playing – all demanding great maturity, finesse and technical control.

STRAVINSKY, Igor **SCHERZO A LA RUSSE** Associated
Arr. Thad Marciniak 4:00

A faithful transcription of an enjoyable work, filled with rhythmic vitality but quite challenging technically, due to difficult keys and intricate staccato passagework in trio section.

THOMAS, Ambroise **RAYMOND OVERTURE** Bravo/Brain Music
Transc. Matsushiro 7:45

An exciting and vibrant opera overture with a number of effective contrasts of mood, style and color. Quite difficulty for clarinets, musically and technically, while other sections are also challenged. Good solo oboe and baritone are also needed. This newer transcription brings the work to its fuller potential in this wind band setting.

TICHELI, Frank **SYMPHONY No. 2** Manhattan Beach
21:00

This substantial work was commissioned by several students and friends of Dr. James Croft in honor of his retirement as Director of Bands at Florida State University. It is a very powerful and imaginative symphony set in three movements. The composer's skilled palate is evident throughout and deserves serious consideration for advanced ensembles.

● ●

CONCERT PROGRAM MATERIAL

NOTE: The lists below are intended to provide a varied selection in each category from the thousands of titles currently available. These pieces are especially suitable for concerts even though many appear on state music lists and can be used for festival evaluation.

WALTZES

ARTIST'S LIFE	J. Strauss / Greissinger	Kalmus	M
BLUE DANUBE	J. Strauss / Leidzen	C. Fischer	M
EMPEROR	J. Strauss / Brown	Boosey & Hawkes	MA
ESPANA	Waldteufel / Brown	Boosey & Hawkes	M
ESTUDIANTINA	Waldteufel / Greissinger	Kalmus	M
ROSES FROM THE SOUTH	J. Strauss / Laurendeau	Kalmus	M
TALES FROM THE VIENNA WOODS	J. Strauss / Laurendeau	C. Fischer	M
WALTZ AND CELEBRATION	Copland / Philip Lang	Boosey & Hawkes	M
WALTZ NO. 2	Shostakovich/Curnow	G. Schirmer	M
WALTZES from "SARI"	Kalman / Morrisey	Marks	ME
WINE, WOMEN AND SONG	J. Strauss / Gready	Kalmus	MA
THE WITCH'S WALTZ	Humperdinck / Davis	Ludwig	M

LIGHTER WALTZES

BELLE OF THE BALL	Leroy Anderson	Belwin	M
THE WALTZING CAT	Leroy Anderson	Belwin	M
WALTZING WINDS	Eric Osterling	Ludwig	ME

LATIN-STYLE

BEGUINE FOR BAND	Glenn Osser	Jenson	ME
BLUE TANGO	Leroy Anderson	Belwin	M
CARIBBEAN RONDO	LaPlante	Daehn	M
CARNAVAL IN SAO PAULO	Barnes	Southern	M
DANZON	Bernstein / Krance	Warner	M
GUARACHA	Morton Gould	Belwin	M
JALOUSIE	Gade / Krance	Warner	MA
JAMAICAN RHUMBA	Benjamin / Lang	Boosey & Hawkes	MA
LOLA FLORES	Tucci / Krance	Marks	M
MALAGUENA	Lecuona / Cacavas	Marks	M
TAMBOO	Cavez / Werle	Belwin	M

MISCELLANEOUS DANCE

BURLESQUE	Grundman	Boosey & Hawkes	M
FAEROE ISLAND DANCE	Grainger	G. Schirmer	M
FOLK DANCES	Shostakovich / Reynolds	C. Fischer	MA
HANEDANS	Nielsen / Moller	G. Schirmer	M
ITALIAN POLKA	Rachmaninoff / Leidzen	Shawnee	M
LITHUANIAN DANCE	Rimsky-Korsakoff / Phillips	Oxford	MA
MAPLE LEAF RAG	Joplin / Frackenpohl	Shawnee	MA
RAGTIME DANCE	Joplin / Elkus	Peer	MA
SUNFLOWER SLOW DRAG	Bourgeois	Wingert-Jones	M
THE WALKING FROG	King / Foster	Barnhouse	M
TROMBONE RAG	Higgins	Hal Leonard	M
TWILIGHT DANCE	Ballenger	Wingert-Jones	M

FAST-TEMPO PIECES

A GALOP TO END ALL GALOPS	Barker	Hal Leonard	M
COMEDIAN'S GALOP	Kabalevsky / Leidzen	MCA	MA
CHIT-CHAT POLKA	J. Strauss / Richardson	Boosey & Hawkes	M
CORKTOWN SATURDAY NIGHT	Arr. William Rhoads	Shawnee	M
DANCE OF THE JESTERS	Tchaikovsky / Cramer	Curnow	MA
DANCING AT STONEHENGE	Suter	Daehn	M
GALLIC GALOP	Hazelman	Boosey & Hawkes	MA
GALOP	Bizet / Schaefer	Shawnee	M
GALOP	Shostakovich / Hunsberger	Boston	MA
THE IRISH WASHERWOMAN	Anderson	Belwin	A
LA DANZA	Rossini / Lang	Belwin	MA
LA TRAGENDA	Puccini / Foster	Wingert-Jones	MA
PAS REDOUBLE	Saint-Saens / Frackenpohl	Shawnee	MA
SCHERZO	Rossini / Schaefer	Belwin	A
TARANTELLA	Reed	Barnhouse	M

SLOW-TEMPO PIECES

ABIDE WITH ME	Arr. Jay Dawson	Arrangers Publishing Co.	
ANDANTE FESTIVO	Sibelius / Beeler	Peer	ME
ARIOSO	J.S. Bach / Leidzen	C. Fischer	ME
BEAUTIFUL SAVIOR (A Chorale Prelude)	Arr. James Swearingen	Barnhouse	ME
CHORALE	Washburn	Oxford	M
DUSK	Bryant	Hal Leonard	M
FIEERLICHER EINZUG	R. Strauss / Spinney	Belwin	M
HARLEM NOCTURNE	Hagen / Pegram	Hal Leonard	M
HYMN FOR THE LOST AND THE LIVING (In Memoriam September 11, 2001)	Ewazen	Southern	M
HYMN SONG FOR SUNDAY	Gillis	Bourne	ME
IN MEMORIAM	Camphouse	TRN	MA
MEDITATION from "THAIS"	Massanet / Harding	Kjos	M
NESSUN DORMA	Puccini/Bocook	Hal Leonard	ME
PACEM	Spittal	Boosey & Hawkes	M
PASTORALE	Clifton Williams	Kalmus	M
PRELUDIO	Osterling	C. Fischer	E
SALVATION IS CREATED	Tchesnokoff / Houseknecht	Kjos	ME
SECONDE PRELUDE	Gershwin / Krance	Warner	M
SERENADE	Pann	Presser	M
SONG OF LIR	Carroll	Maecenas	M
TWO GYMNOPEDIES	Satie /Reed	Belwin	M
WHISPER TO THEIR SOULS	Hazo	Hal Leonard	M

AMERICAN FOLK or FOLK-STYLE PIECES

AMERICAN CIVIL WAR FANTASY	Bilik	Peer	MA
AMERICAN SALUTE	Gould	Belwin	MA
THE BLUE AND THE GRAY	Grundman	Boosey & Hawkes	M
CIVIL WAR SUITE	Walters	Rubank	ME
COWBOY RHAPSODY	Gould / Bennett	Kalmus	MA
DEEP RIVER SUITE	Erickson	Bourne	ME
FANTASY ON AMERICAN SAILING SONGS	Grundman	Boosey & Hawkes	ME
FANTASY ON MOUNTAIN SONGS	Himes	Curnow	M
FIVE AMERICAN FOLK SONGS	Siegmeister	C. Fischer	M
FOLK LEGEND	Hunsberger	Sam Fox	M

FOLK SUITE	Still	Bourne	M
FIVER JORDAN	Whitney	G. Schirmer	M
MOUNTAIN THYME	Hazo	Hal Leonard	M
SALUTE TO AMERICAN JAZZ	Arr. Nestico	Hal Leonard	MA
SECOND AMERICAN FOLK RHAPSODY	Grundman	Boosey & Hawkes	ME
SEE ROCK CITY	Karrick	Alfred	M
SHOUTIN' LIZA TROMBONE	Fillmore / Foster	Carl Fischer	MA
ST. LOUIS BLUES	Arr. Brown	Hal Leonard	MA
TRIBUTE TO STEPHEN FOSTER	Nestico	Kendor	M

MISCELLANEOUS FOLK or FOLK-STYLE MATERIAL

A MOVEMENT FOR ROSA	Camphouse	TRN	MA
A TUNING PIECE SONG	Maslanka	Carl Fischer	M
ARMENIAN FOLK SONG AND DANCE	Khachaturian / McAlister	Masters Music	MA
BALI	Colgrass	Carl Fischer	M
BATUQUE	Fernandez / Wolfson	Belwin	A
BAYOU BREAKDOWN	Karrick	Alfred	M
BELLS	McDougal	Hal Leonard	MA
BLUE AND GREEN MUSIC	Hazo	Hal Leonard	M
COUNCIL OAK	Gillingham	C.Alan / McClaren	MA
CLOUDBURST	Whitacre	Hal Leonard	M
DANZON FINAL from "ESTANCIA"	Ginastera /John	Boosey & Hawkes	A
DRUNKEN SAILOR	Hull	Wynn	ME
ELECRICITY	Bukvich	Wingert-Jones	M
FACES OF KUM BA YA	Zdechlick	Kjos	M
FOLKSONGS FOR BAND	Leidzen	Summy-Birchard	M
FUNICULI, FUNICULA	Denza / Reed	Barnhouse	M
GHOST DANCES	Barret	Alfred	M
GIRL I LEFT BEHIND	Arr. Anderson	Hal Leonard	ME
GREENSLEEVES	Arr. Alfred Reed	Hansen	ME
HAMBONE	Larsen	Hal Leonard	M
IRISH FOLK SONG SUITE	Erickson	Bourne	E
ITALIAN HOLIDAY	Longfield	Barnhouse	ME
ITALIAN POLKA	Rachmaninoff/Rousanova	Alfred	M
JAPANESE SONG	Gershwin / Wagner	Alfred	
JAPANESE SONGS	Akiyama	Marks	ME
JAPANESE TUNE	Konagaya	Hal Leonard	MA
LIBERTY FANFARE	Williams / Bocook	Hal Leonard	M
THE MILLER'S DANCE	Falla / Vinter	Marks	M
THE MINSTREL BOY	Anderson	Belwin	M
MOON BY NIGHT	Newman	Wingert-Jones	M
NGOMA ZA KENYA (JAMBO)	Basler	Carl Fischer LLC	MA
PRELUDE TO REVELRY	Jacob	Novello	MA
QUEBEC FOLK FANTASY	Cable	Chappell	M
RAKES OF MALLOW	Anderson	Kalmus	MA
RHAPSODIC CELEBRATION	Sheldon	Alfred	MA
RITUAL FIRE DANCE	Falla / Morrisey	Marks	M
ROLLO TAKES A WALK	Maslanka	Kjos	ME
RUMBLE ON THE HIGH PLAINS	Sweeney	Hal Leonard	M
SANG	Wilson	Ludwig-Masters	M
SEVENS	Hazo	Ludwig-Masters	MA
SHALOM!	Arr. Sparke	Dehaske	M
SNAKES	Duffy	Ludwig-Masters	M

SONGS OF JOY	Williams	Alfred	M
SOUND THE BELLS	Williams / Lavender	Hal Leonard	MA
THE SPINNER'S WEDDING	Arr. Brisman	Elkan-Vogel	E
THE 8TH CANDLE	Reisteter	Arrangers Publishing Co.	M
THE KINGS GO FORTH	Gregson	Studio Music	A
THREE KLEZMER MINIATURES	Sparke	Dehaske	M
TODAY IS THE GIFT	Hazo	Hal Leonard	ME
VELOCITY	Sheldon	Alfred	M
VOODOO	Bukvich	Wingert-Jones	M
WITH PLEASURE	Sousa / Ed. Foster	Wingert-Jones	M
ZION	Welcher	Presser	A

ADVANCED-STYLE or UNUSUAL PIECES

CONCERT PIECE	Tubb	Presser	A
CAVE	Peck	Galaxy	MA
SOMERSAULT	H. Smith	Frank	M
SPECTRUM	Bielawa	Shawnee	M
STARGAZING	Erb	Presser	M

EASIER LIGHT NUMBERS

DANCE ON THREE LEGS	Hastings	Alfred	ME
ROLLO TAKES A WALK	Maslanka	Kjos	ME
TWO PIECS for MIDDLE SCHOOL BAND	Michaels	Shawnee	E

OVERTURES

AEGEAN FESTIVAL OVERTURE	Makris / Bader	Galaxy	A
CANDIDE OVERTURE	Bernstein / Beeler	G. Schirmer	A
FESTIVAL PRELUDE	Reed	Marks	M
DIE FLEDERMAUS OVERTURE	J. Strauss / Cailliet	Boosey & Hawkes	A
ITALIAN IN ALGIERS	Rossini / Cailliet	Sam Fox	MA
JUBILATION	Ward / Leist	Galaxy	MA
LIGHT CAVALRY	Suppe / Fillmore	C. Fischer	MA
LUSTSPIEL	Keler / Roberts	C. Fischer	M
MADAM FAVART	Offenbach / Barnes	Ludwig	M
MORNING, NOON AND NIGHT	Supper / Fillmore	C. Fischer	MA
OUTDOOR OVERTURE	Copland	Boosey & Hawkes	A
OVERTURE FOR BANDS	Beyer	Volkwein	MA
OVERTURE FOR WINDS	Carter	Bourne	ME
PIQUE DAME	Suppe / Tobani & Kent	C. Fischer	MA
POET AND PESANT	Suppe / Fillmore	C. Fischer	MA
THE RAMPARTS	C. Williams	Marks	MA
STREET CORNER OVERTURE	Rawsthorne / O'Brien	Oxford	A

RHAPSODIES, TONE POEMS, MEDLEYS

ARMENIAN DANCES (PART 1)	Reed	Sam Fox	A
BEAR DANCE	Bartok / Leidzen	Associated	M
BRITANNIA	Edmunds	C. Fischer	ME
EVENING IN THE VILLAGE	Bartok / Leidzen	Associated	M
FINLANDIA	Sibelius / Cailliet	C. Fischer	MA
	Sibelius / Winterbottom	Boosey & Hawkes	MA
GARDENS OF GRANADA	Torroba / Beeler	Marks	M
INTERMEZZO from "VANESSA"	Barber / Beeler	G. Schirmer	MA
INTRODUCTION AND WEDDING MARCH	Rimsky-Korsakov / Harding	Kjos	A

PRAELUDIUM	Jarnefelt / Slocum	Shawnee	M
SYMPHONIC DANCE #3, "Fiesta"	C. Williams	Sam Fox	MA
TRIBUTE TO STEPHEN FOSTER	Nestico	Kendor	MA
THE TSAR'S FAREWELL	Rimsky-Korsakov / Reed	Southern	M

SUITES

AT THE FAIR	D. Waxman / Schaefer	Galaxy	E
CAKEWALK SUITE	H. Kay / Chaloner	Boosey & Hawkes	MA
CARMEN SUITE	Bizet / Bullock	Alfred	M
CONCERTINO	Morrisey	Marks	M
FIRST SUITE FOR BAND	Reed	Belwin	MA
FOUR PRELUDES	R.R. Bennett	Belwin	MA
HARLEQUINADE	Agay	Sam Fox	M
OLD HOME DAYS	Ives / Elkus	Peer	M
ST. LAWRENCE SUITE	Gould	Chappell	MA
SUITE OF EARLY MARCHES	Arr. Erickson	Summit	M
SYMPHONIC SUITE	C. Williams	Summy-Birchard	MA
THIRD SUITE	Jager	Volkein	MA
THREE DANCE EPISODES from "SPARTACUS"	Khachaturian /Hunsberger	MCA	A
THREE DANCES from "GAYNE"	Khachaturian / Leidzen	Kalmus	MA

SHOW MUSIC MEDLEYS

76 TROMBONES	Anderson / Bocook	Hal Leonard	ME
A CHORUS LINE	Hamlisch / Barker	Jenson	M
BRIGADOON	Loewe / Gordon	Sam Fox	M
BROADWAY SHOW STOPPERS	Barker	Hal Leonard	M
BYE BYE BIRDIE	Strouse / Cacavas	Chappell	M
CAMELOT	Loewe / Bennett	Chappell	M
CAN-CAN	Porter / Cacavus	Chappell	M
CAROUSEL	Rodgers / Leidzen	Warner	M
COLE PORTER CLASSICS	Wagner	Alfred	ME
CURTAIN UP	Reed	Hal Leonard	MA
FIDDLER ON THE ROOF	Bock / Tatgenhorst	Columbia	M
FIDDLER ON THE ROOF (Symphonic Dances)	Arr. Hearshen	Hal Leonard	M
FUNNY GIRL	Styne / Bennett	Chappell	M
GIGI	Loewe / Bennett	Chappell	M
GOLDEN AGE OF BROADWAY (THE MUSICALS OF RODGERS AND HAMMERSTEIN II)	Arr. Moss	Hal Leonard	M
HELLO DOLLY	Herman / Cacavus	E. H. Morris	M
KING AND I	Rodgers / Bennett	Chappell	M
LESM ISERABLES (Selections)	Arr. Barker	Hal Leonard	M
MAMBO (from "WEST SIDE STORY")	Bernstein / Arr. Sweeney	Hal Leonard	M
MAN OF LA MANCHA	Arr. Williams	Alfred	M
MARCHING DOWN BROADWAY	Moss	Hal Leonard	ME
THE MUSIC MAN	Willson / Reed	Frank	M
MY FAIR LADY	Loewe / Bennett	Chappell	M
OKLAHOMA!	Rodgers / Leidzen	Chappell	M
OLIVER!	Bart / Leyden	TRO	M
OPENING NIGHT ON BROADWAY	Arr. Brown	Hal Leonard	M
THE PHANTOM OF THE OPERA (MEDLEY)	Lloyd Webber / Vinson	Hal Leonard	M
THE PHANTOM OF THE OPERA (SELECTIONS)	Arr. Barker	Hal Leonard	M
PORGY AND BESS	Arr. Barnes	Alfred	MA
SALUTE TO BROADWAY	Strommen	Alfred	ME

SHOW BOAT	Kern / Bennett	Warner	M
SOUND OF MUSIC	Arr. Buckley	(unpublished)	MA
SOUND OF MUSIC	Rodgers / Bennett	Chappell	M
SOUTH PACIFIC	Rodgers / Leidzen	Chappell	M
SYMPHONIC DANCES (from "WEST SIDE STORY")	Bernstein / Lavender	Boosey & Hawkes	MA
WEST SIDE STORY	Bernstein / Duthoit	G. Schirmer	MA
WIZARD OF OZ	Arr. Barnes	Alfred	M

POPULAR SONG ARRANGEMENTS (Singles and Medleys)

AN ELLINGTON PORTRAIT	Ellington / Werle	Belwin	M
APRIL IN PARIS	Duke / Maltby	Warner	M
AUTUMN IN NEW YORK	Duke / Krance	Warner	M
BEGIN THE BEGUINE	Porter / Krance	Warner	M
CHERISH	Kirkman / DeCamp	Studio / PR	ME
COLE PORTER SYMPHONIC PORTRAIT	Porter / Robinson	Chappell	M
DAYS OF WINE AND ROSES	Mancini / Krance	Warner	M
DEEP PURPLE	De Rose / Beeler	Big 3	M
DUKE ELLINGTON	Custer	Alfred	M
GERSHWIN	Arr. Barker	Hal Leonard	M
IRVING BERLIN SYMPHONIC PORTRAIT	Arr. Ades	Shawnee	M
MANCINI!	Arr. Reed	Hansen	M
MOON RIVER	Mancini	Hansen	M
NIGHT AND DAY	Porter / Krance	Warner	M
STAR WARS TRILOGY	Williams / Hunsberger	Alfred	MA
SYMPHONIC GERSHWIN	Arr. Barker	Alfred	M
YESTERDAY	Arr. Wilkinson	Hansen	ME

● ●

Kreines' Selective List of Marches

Alexander	The Southerner; Colossus of Columbia; Olympia Hippodrome
Alford, H.	Purple Carnival; Law and Order; A Step Ahead
Alford, K.	Army of the Nile; The Mad Major; The Vanished Army; The Thin Red Line; Old Panama; Voice of the Guns; Eagle Squadron; The Standard of St. George
Bagley, E. E.	National Emblem
Barber	Commando March
Bergsma	March with Trumpets
Blankenburg	The Gladiator's Farewell; Flying Eagle
Boccalari	Il Bersagliere; Fiume
Borel-Clerc	La Sorella
Chambers	Boys of the Old Brigade; Hostrauser's March; Chicago Tribune
Chovi	Pepita Greus
Coates	Knightsbridge March
Codina	Zacatecas
Davies	Royal Air Force March Past
Delle Cese	Inglesina
De Smetsky	March of the Spanish Soldiery
Duble	Bravura
Edmondson	New South Wales
Elliot	British Eighth
English	Royal Decree
Erickson	Citadel
Farrar	Bombasto
Fillmore	Americans We; The Crosley; His Honor; The Klaxon; King Karl King; Men of Ohio; Orange Bowl; Rolling Thunder
Fucik	The Florentiner; Entry of the Gladiators
Ganne	Marche Lorraine; Le Pere de la Victoire
Gates	Sol y Sombra
Goldman, E. F.	Chimes of Liberty; On the Mall; Children's March
Goldman, R. F.	The Foundation
Grafulla	Washington Grays
Grainger	Children's March; Lads of Wamphray; Gum suckers' March
Hall	Independentia; New Colonial; S.I.B.A.; Tenth Regiment
Halvorsen	Entry March of the Boyars
Hanssen	Valdres
Heed	In Storm and Sunshine
Holst	Moorside March
Howe	Pentland Hills
Huffine	Them Basses
Hughes	St. Julien
Javaloyes	El Abanico

Jewell	E Pluribus Unum; Quality Plus
Kiefer	Kiefer's Special
King	Barnum & Bailey's Favorite; Bonds of Unity; Cyrus the Great; Trombone King; Hosts of Freedom; The Melody Shop; Purple Pageant; Robinson's Grand Entrée
Klohr	The Billboard
Latham	Brighton Beach
Leemans	Marche des Parachutistes Belges
Lithgow	Invercargill
Lope	Gallito
Maltby	Hail to the Fleet
Nelhybel	March to Nowhere; March in Counterpoint
Panella	On the Square
Pieme	March of the Little Lead Soldiers
Ployhar	The Flickertail; March of the Irish Guards
Prokofieff	Athletic Festival March; March, Op. 99
Radaelli	A Santa Cecilia
Reeves	2nd Regiment Connecticut Guard
Riddle	Beaner's Triumphal
Richards	Emblem of Unity; Crusade for Freedom
Saint-Saens	Marche Militaire Francaise; March Heroique
San Miguel	The Golden Ear
Seitz	Grandioso
Smith, L. B.	The Town Crier
Sousa	Black Horse Troop; El Capitan; Daughters of Texas; Fairest of the Fair; Free Lance; Gallant Seventh; Gladiator; George Washington Bicentennial; Glory of the Yankee Navy; Hands Across the Sea; High School Cadets; Invincible Eagle; King Cotton; Liberty Bell; Manhattan Beach; Minnesota Riders for the Flag; Sabre and Spurs; Semper Fidelis; Solid Men to the Front; Stars and Stripes; The Thunderer; Washington Post
Starke	With Sword and Lance
Strauss Sr., J.	Radestsky
Teike	Old Comrades; The Conqueror
Texidor	Amparito Roca
Turlet	French National Defilé
Vauhan Williams	Sea Songs
Von Blon	Die Wacht Am Rhein; Light Horse; Sounds of Peace
Wagner, J.	Under the Double Eagle
Wagner, R.	Huldigungsmarch
Walton	Crown Imperial
Williams, C.	The Sinfonians
Zehle	Army and Marine
Zimmerman	

● ●

A Selection of Marches for Concert Performance

The above is a selection of over 150 marches that provide a wide variety of titles from which to choose.
Those listed below are some of the best ones, with brief descriptions added to provide a helpful guide.

Alexander, R. – The Southerner
A great classic march which contains attractive melodic and counter-melodic material with interesting harmonic treatment. (The original unedited version is preferable to the Barnum edition which contains numerous scoring changes).

Alford, Harry – The Purple Carnival
A classic with great rhythmic energy and a lovely trio melody. (The original is preferable to the Erickson edition).

Alford, K. – Army of the Nile; The Mad Major; The Vanished Army
Among the finest of all British marches with effective contrasting strains and beautiful trio melodies.

Barber, Samuel – Commando March
Superb writing by a master composer (his only original band work).

Bergsma, W. – March with Trumpets
An exciting, brilliant work in 20th century neo-classic style and a great trio.

Buccalari – Il Bersagliere (the Italian Rifleman)
A classic Italian march with excellent contrasts.

Davies, W – Royal Air Force March Past
A superb British classic – the official march of the R.A.F.

Delle Cese, D. – L'Inglesina
A great march with notable use of contrasting materials and dynamic range in a lengthier format.

Elliot, Z. – British Eighth
An excellent work with effective contrasts between strains and a fine trio brought to a climactic ending.

Fillmore, Henry – Americans We; The Crosley; His Honor; The Klaxon; King Karl King; Rolling Thunder
Six classic American marches with brilliant woodwind obbligatos and great low-brass writing. (Fillmore was a trombonist.)

Fucik, J. – The Florentiner
A great march with rich-textured contrapuntal writing and contrasting material with a beautiful trio. (The original European edition is preferable to the American ones).

Goldman, E.F. – The Chimes of Liberty
One of the best among many by this classic American composer with interesting counter-melodic material (including a brilliant piccolo obbligato).

Hanssen, J. – Valdres
A classic march from Norway with a beautiful opening melody in lyrical style and effective woodwind obbligatos and other interesting contrapuntal details.

Heed, J – In Storm and Sunshine
One of the most technically demanding, brilliant and exciting marches.

Holst, G – Moorside March (transcribed by Gordon Jacob)
Great material well-developed with some of Holst's best writing, originally the third movement of "A Moorside Suite" for brass band.

Howe, J. – Pentland Hills
An excellent potpourri of Scottish songs, effectively put together.

King, K – Barnum & Bailey's Favorite; The Melody Shop; Purple Pageant
Probably the most interesting and challenging of this composer's output of over 400 marches.

Latham – Brighton Beach
An American march with material in the British style, using modal harmony and a broadly noble trio.

Leemans – Marche Des Parachutistes Belges
A continental classic with attractive melodies and contrasting strains N.B. – The Wiley version, while appealing, differs in many ways from the original version, most closely approached by the Bourgeois edition.

Lope, S. – Gallito
Perhaps the best of the Spanish march repertory, with idiomatic rhythms and excellent contrasts of material and mood.

Prokofieff, S. – March, Op. 99
A brilliant and exciting march in fast tempo with woodwind obbligatos, vibrant trumpet calls and rich low-brass writing.

Saint-Saens, C. – Marche Militaire Francaise
Originally for orchestra, this has become a band classic – spiritual and vital in character. (The Hindsley version is preferred).

Sousa, J.P. – Black Horse Troop; El Capitan; The Free Lance; The Gladiator; George Washington Bicentennial; The Glory of the Yankee Navy; Hands Across the Sea; Manhattan Beach; Nobles of the Mystic Shrine; Riders for the Flag; Sabre and Spurs; Solid Men to the Front
These titles were selected from Sousa's huge output (136 marches) to provide a wide range of styles, moods and idioms.

Teike, C. – Old Comrades
Perhaps the best-known of all classic German marches, with attractive material and good contrasts between strains.

Texidor, J. – Amparito Roca
A brilliant, lively Spanish march with typical melodic and rhythmic idioms.

Vaughan Williams, R. – Sea Songs
An excellent potpourri of British sea chanteys in the composer's style.

Von Blon – Light Horse; Die Wacht Am Rhein
Two attractive German marches with good musical materials and imaginative details.

Wagner, J.P. – Under the Double Eagle
Another classic German march with effective contrasting sections and a nice trio melody.

Wagner, Richard – Huldigungsmarsch
A beautiful ceremonial march, somewhat lengthy and repetitious but with many great Wagner moments.

Walton, W. – Crown Imperial
One of the best ceremonial marches, this is in fast tempo with many of the composer's stylistic traits and a magnificent trio melody brought to a powerful climax.

Williams, C. – The Sinfonians
Another excellent ceremonial march, using the music fraternity's hymn as a melodic element.

● ●

INDEX BY TITLE

INDEX BY TITLE

INDEX BY TITLE

INDEX BY TITLE

INDEX BY TITLE

INDEX BY TITLE

INDEX BY TITLE

INDEX BY TITLE

INDEX BY TITLE

INDEX BY TITLE

INDEX BY TITLE

INDEX BY TITLE

INDEX BY TITLE

INDEX BY TITLE

• •

INDEX BY COMPOSER

INDEX BY COMPOSER

INDEX BY COMPOSER

INDEX BY COMPOSER

INDEX BY COMPOSER

INDEX BY COMPOSER

INDEX BY COMPOSER

INDEX BY COMPOSER

INDEX BY COMPOSER

INDEX BY COMPOSER

INDEX BY COMPOSER

INDEX BY COMPOSER

INDEX BY COMPOSER

INDEX BY COMPOSER

INDEX BY COMPOSER

• •